197
'7

PORNOGRAPHY

PORNOGRAPHY
The Other Side

F. M. Christensen

New York
Westport, Connecticut
London

Library of Congress Cataloging-in-Publication Data

Christensen, F. M.
　　Pornography : the other side / F. M. Christensen.
　　　　p.　　cm.
　　Includes bibliographical references.
　　ISBN 0–275–93537–X (alk. paper)
　　1. Pornography—Social aspects.　I. Title.
HQ471.C47　1990
363.4′7—dc20　　　　89–26543

Library of Congress Catalog Card Number: 89–26543
ISBN: 0–275–93537–X

First published in 1990

Praeger Publishers, One Madison Avenue, New York, NY 10010
An imprint of Greenwood Publishing Group, Inc.

Printed in the United States of America

The paper used in this book complies with the
Permanent Paper Standard issued by the National
Information Standards Organization (Z39.48–1984).

10 9 8 7 6 5 4 3 2 1

Contents

Preface

In the continuing clamor over pornography, the claims most often heard are these: (1) it is evil so it should be banned, and (2) it is evil but censorship is a greater evil. The other side—that pornography is not in itself morally bad—is rarely defended. The purpose of this book is to present some of the evidence for that other side. In fact, it will be argued that the current antipornography campaign is in many ways itself morally evil. This will be a startling claim to many, but that is largely because they have been given so little opportunity to see the whole picture. Actually, pornography itself is not the fundamental issue; opposition to it is only a symptom of more general beliefs that are tragically mistaken. What this book is really about, at bottom, is sex—and the evil effects on the lives of all of us that irrational attitudes toward that subject continue to have.

This book is designed to reply to all the standard objections to pornography, to claims that are seen and heard frequently in the media and in conversation. That task is not worth doing, in my view, unless it is carried out with a fair amount of intellectual rigor. After all, sloppy thinking in those objections is a large part of what makes it necessary to reply in the first place. So the book is directed to readers who are intelligent and educated enough to be careful and analytical in their thinking. At the same time, it is meant to be practical: to make the treatment of each charge or argument short enough to be comprehended readily and used by the reader in later discussion. It is not easy to be both brief and convincing, and the reader will have to decide how well I have succeeded.

As a consequence of that design and those constraints, *Pornography: The Other Side* is not directed to scholars or scientists already knowledgeable in various aspects of the subject; that would require specialized articles or a book of a quite different sort. Nor does it attempt to analyze the detailed claims of any individual writers, for the same reason. Instead it cites various sources of information and argumentation on each topic discussed, in the hope that readers will pursue the subjects on their own; some of the more comprehensive ones are mentioned parenthetically in the text. But notes are kept to a minimum, used for referencing only those claims that are both crucial to my case and also not well known within the literature on human sexuality. Certain more specialized points are also discussed briefly in footnotes.

Because my concern is much more for ideas than for their sources, I have made no attempt to cite the origins of particular arguments (for example, the philosopher Immanuel Kant as the primal author of the objectification charges). Moreover, I do not *claim* any of the arguments I use to be original—though I *think* many of them are. I perceive the value of my contribution as lying in putting all together, in a compact and handy form, facts and reasoning to which most people are never exposed. (And I see my education in science, methodology of science, and social ethics, together with considerable academic research on sexuality, as having prepared me to deal with the very broad range of issues that the topic involves.) But I must acknowledge, among all those from whom I have gained valuable insights, the following individuals, who have given me special help and encouragement: Gus Brannigan, Mickey Diamond, Ted McIlvenna, Polly Mitchell, John Money, Mike Ritter, and Layne Winklebleck. To you, and to all people who are both caring and clear-eyed, I dedicate this book.

Post scriptum: I would like to hear from readers who share my concerns about humane sexual attitudes and gender equality (at the Department of Philosophy, University of Alberta, Edmonton, Alberta, Canada T6G 2E5). The struggle to achieve them in this society will require our shared insights and concerted efforts.

PORNOGRAPHY

1

Background: Sexual Desire and Fantasy

To avoid some of the misunderstanding that has attended so much discussion on this subject, let us begin by stating how the term "pornographic" will be understood here. It will be used in the traditional and still most common way, denoting sexual content whose purpose is to arouse or satisfy sexual feelings.[1] This definition is rather vague, of course. Usually the term is applied only when the degree of sexual content or explicitness exceeds a certain ill-defined level. But that vagueness does not matter in this book, since most of what will be said here applies to sexual depictions and presentations in general. Many people confuse the word "pornographic" with the term "obscene." The latter refers to extreme offensiveness in general and need not involve sex. (For example, "obscenely rich." Indeed, early obscenity law was concerned with blasphemy and sedition rather than with sex, notably the landmark *Hicklin* decision.) While many consider pornography extremely offensive, this is evidently not true *by definition;* it is not part of the literal meaning of the word as opposed to its associations. The same is true for the term "erotic": many confuse it with "sensuous," or even with "aesthetic." Traditionally, "erotic" refers to anything relating to or tending to cause sexual arousal, and here it too will be used in the standard way.

Definitions of "pornography" that include more than just the sex have been adopted by some people. These are arbitrary additions to the historical English meaning, however, and none of them has been widely accepted. In some circles—mostly those influenced by feminism—it has become the practice to use this word to mean something like "*a bad sort* of sexual portrayal," the term "erotica" being employed for the kind not considered bad. But among those who talk this way, there is not good

agreement on just what types of things fall into each category. Some have
decreed that the latter term refer to inexplicit sexual scenes, some to artistic
ones, some to affectionate ones, and many to "nondegrading" sexual portrayals—that notion itself being understood in a multitude of ways, as we
shall see. Indeed, people who endorse the dichotomy generally do not even
attempt to spell out the difference, being convinced it is obvious. Because
of this, and because the new usage of terms is so easily conflated with the
standard one, enormous confusion has resulted. Since it is important here
to avoid that problem, and also to have a general term referring to sexual
frankness for the sake of sexual excitement, we will use the word "pornography" in its unaugmented traditional sense.[2] (That, in fact, is what
social scientists tend to do, employing it and "erotica" interchangeably.)
Special *types* of pornography will be discussed where appropriate.

VICARIOUS SEXUAL ENJOYMENT: NATURAL AND UNIVERSAL

To judge from the cross-cultural evidence, the production of pornography is a very common thing for humans to engage in. From all around
the world have come reliable reports of this: sexually explicit pictures and
sculptures, legends and stories, songs and dances. Of course, most human
societies have not had our technology of mass production; but that difference is reflected in everything from phonograph records to silk hats. In
old Tahiti, for example, family entertainment was a performance by the
Arioi society: songs, dances, and a large variety of sexual acts. Elsewhere
in Polynesia there were nude beauty contests. Among the Muria of India,
showing drawings or carvings of sex organs is a socially acceptable way for
a boy to proposition a girl. (In recent years in our society, it would be
called sexual "harassment.") Among the more technologically advanced
nations, the pornography of ancient Persia, Greece, India, and Japan is
well known. In most of these societies, to judge from the ethnographic
reports, the idea that there is something disgusting or degrading about such
materials and performances may not have existed at all.[3]

What is the source of the phenomenon of pornography? For one thing,
it is a manifestation of that special human capacity to get enjoyment vicariously, just by watching others. In this regard it is like theater and
spectator sports. Of course, different kinds of proxy experience appeal to
different kinds of people. Not everyone enjoys watching football or ballet
or soap operas or sex shows, but nearly all find enjoyment in one or another
thing of this general type. Interest in sexual portrayals is also closely tied
to our ability to fantasize. Unlike most if not all other animals, human
beings imagine scenes they find pleasurable or satisfying. In particular, we
fantasize about sex. Surveys show that most people do so during most of

their lives. It is so natural we even do it involuntarily in our sleep, in what is called a "wet dream" because of the lubrication or ejaculation that often accompanies it. So pornography is a simple extension of erotic fantasy used for sexual enjoyment. But "enjoyment" is too weak a word to cover all the uses of erotica. In situations where sexual activity itself is not adequately available, pornography serves as a substitute, particularly in conjunction with masturbation. It is an alternative way of satisfying, albeit quite imperfectly, some very strong needs and desires.

That there are such intimate connections between sexual fantasy and sexual activity is highly significant. It means the debate over sexually explicit materials has consequences far beyond itself—a fact that most people already realize. Comparatively unimportant in isolation, as a symbol of sexuality in general, pornography has a vital significance for all of us, not just those who enjoy or despise it. Objections to pornography are basically just objections to certain types of sexual attitude and behavior; so are defenses of it. So what this book is really about is sex. It is a plea for sane and humane attitudes toward something that, for better or worse, is a central part of human life. This being so, let us begin our discussion with some relevant information about sex itself.

SEX AND THE TWO SEXES

A very significant aspect of sexual desire is that in a majority of males, it is strongly visually cued. It is focused on the female sexual organs, including buttocks and breasts. This fact is consistently reported all over the world, from cultures that in other ways differ drastically from one another. (See, for one source, Clellan Ford and Frank Beach, *Patterns of Sexual Behavior.*) To be sure, there is variation in this, variation created largely by differences in ease of satisfying the visual desire. For example, where sex organs are kept strictly covered, they become even more erotically charged, and adjoining areas of the body become erotic substitutes for them. Not so long ago in this culture, even a knee, a calf, or a "well-turned ankle" could be exciting to males. By way of contrast, among the scantily dressed peoples of the Pacific there was historically little breast attraction, but there was a degree of interest in the vagina that in this culture would be disparagingly labeled "gynecological."

In this respect humans are like the other primates, apes and monkeys. Among them, the sexual arousal by smell that is found in other male mammals has mostly been replaced by visual attraction. For instance, when a female chimpanzee's genital area becomes swollen and pink during her sexually receptive period, the males get extremely excited. In the human species, the females of which are capable of sexual interest at any time of the month, the capacity of female sex organs to arouse males is also continuous. To a large degree, it is the female's calling attention to her sex organs, rather than their mere visibility, that is responsible for the arousal. Either way, it is the primary mode of male erotic arousal in the "higher" species. In fact, this is precisely the reason why covering the sex organs and teaching feelings of shame toward nudity are so common around the world: it is to prevent unwanted sexual arousal. Nature's purposes are not easy to thwart, however.

In contrast, it appears that among human females the primary mode of strong sexual arousal is tactile: more often physical stimulation of the sex organs is required to produce the same level of excitement as mere sight can produce in the male. Or at least, the types of visual scene that are found sexually arousing are very different for most females. Only a tiny percentage of women report arousal from the sight of male genitals. And though a larger minority is attracted by a man's buttocks, it is revealed by surveys and experiments that male nudity by itself has little or no erotic effect on the great majority of women. (For nontechnical discussions of the evidence on this and related matters, see Glenn Wilson's *The Coolidge Effect* or Richard Hagen's *The Bio-Sexual Factor*.) Women are visually attracted to men, but their focus is elsewhere, notably on the face and general build—also important to men, of course—and by itself this attraction does not usually result in the viewer feeling genital sensations. There is evidently no culture on earth where the females as a group show a visual interest in male sex organs, and none where the males fail to show a special interest in those of females.

Lest it should remain a concern that this male-female difference is an artifact of culture rather than natural, there are other lines of evidence. For one thing, the difference holds true for homosexuals of both sexes: "gay" men are comparatively heavy consumers of pornography featuring (male) nudes, while lesbians use little (though perhaps more than women in general). For another, men who have suffered spinal cord damage lose the ability to respond sexually to visual stimulation, whereas women similarly injured experience little or no change in their arousal patterns.[4] Then there are the clinical studies of males and females who during their fetal life have been exposed, respectively, to smaller and larger than normal amounts of the "male" hormone testosterone, or a chemical with similar effects. Females thus "masculinized" in the womb, while the brain and nervous system were developing, on average turn out to have appreciably greater erotic arousal to visual stimuli than other females; the less "masculinized" males have less than other males. Similarly, males whose bodies are less sensitive to the sex hormones they produce have been found to be less susceptible to visual stimulation, more dependent on tactile. Even studies on ordinary populations of men and women reveal that, on average, women who are more "masculine" *in general* are more apt to be sexually aroused by visual stimuli.[5] In summary, the evidence for this biological difference between the sexes is overwhelming.

Interestingly, females tend to have erotic feelings that are complementary to those of males in the present regard. Among primates generally and in some human societies, they display their sexual organs as a way of inviting intercourse. Even in this society, where such actions are highly taboo, the most common single theme in collections of women's sexual fantasies is that of showing their own naked bodies to excite men—often large numbers of men. And some of these women report enjoyably acting on those desires in various ways: sending nude pictures of themselves to erotic magazines, and so on. (Nancy Friday's collections of women's sex fantasies, such as *My Secret Garden,* are a good source of examples of this.) Of course, to be socially acceptable such "sexual signals" are usually much more subtle—those ubiquitous tight jeans, for example. (No, they were not invented by fashion merchandisers.) In one form or another, this sort of female display seems to be universal across cultures. Anthropologist Colin Turnbull tells how pygmy girls decorate their breasts and buttocks to attract the boys, and how one of them danced in a way that called attention to her large breasts. Western women are usually amazed to learn of the efforts women in some cultures have gone to in order to enhance the attractiveness of their genitals.[6]

These complementary tendencies of the two sexes have been summarized as follows: the male focuses on the female's body, whereas the female focuses on the male's interest in her body. As sex and gender researchers John Money and Anke Ehrhardt have noted, this fact is reflected in the different ways men and women tend to enjoy pornography (among those who do enjoy it)—the former by desiring the woman's body, the latter by identifying with the woman thus desired. (See their book *Man and Woman, Boy and Girl.*) Various other consequences of this difference between the sexes will be considered as we continue.

Associated with—indeed, partly because of—this dissimilarity in how sexual arousal is produced is another significant fact: men and women differ, on average, in the strength of their sexual desire. As it was put in the famous Alfred Kinsey study: "Nearly all (but not all) younger males are aroused to the point of erection many times per week, and many of them . . . several times per day. Many females might go days and weeks and months without ever being stimulated unless they have actual physical contact with a sexual partner."[7] To be more precise, a female's sexual feelings tend to be less easily aroused and less autonomous than a male's, more dependent upon deliberate choice and on situational cues of various types. This difference is reflected in reported levels of desire and arousal frequency, including the frequency of erotic dreams. It is also revealed, indirectly, in behavior—especially behavior involving no fear of pregnancy or lack of partner availability—such as fantasy, masturbation, or homosexual activity. In all these things, the male frequency levels are far higher than the female ones.

In spite of the hopes inspired by William Masters and Virginia Johnson's *Human Sexual Response,* the evidence is strong that this second familiar disparity between males and females is also inborn, at least in part. For example, there is the clinical experience with hormone levels. In both sexes, the chemical responsible for sexual desire is testosterone—called a "male" hormone because females normally have less of it. This by itself does not argue that male sexual needs are stronger. But in certain cases studied by doctors, the female body produces, or is injected with, larger than normal amounts of testosterone, and the result is an urgency of sexual feeling that is definitely more typical of males—and which often results in assertive or even "promiscuous" sexual behavior by these women. Normal men, by contrast, already have far more testosterone than they need for this purpose, so even more of it has no such effect on them. (See the books by Hagen and Wilson for compilations of evidence on this topic as well. Perhaps the best single collection of evidence currently available on the nature of male and female sexuality is anthropologist Donald Symons's *The Evolution of Human Sexuality.*)

Actually, it appears that the main biological difference between male and female sexual "drive" is in the degree to which each can be controlled by social and other environmental conditions. For though it is surprising to men, it is not uncommon for women to report that a change in mental attitude toward sex transformed their libidos: they went from having complete lack of interest to strong desire, or the reverse. Furthermore, women's levels of sexual interest vary drastically from one culture or one historical period to another, while men's are evidently fairly constant. For one apparent example, female masturbation rates are dramatically different from one time or culture to another, whereas those of males evidently are not.

Indeed, women's erotic desire can seemingly be as great as men's; in societies where children learn fully positive attitudes toward sex from an early age, it is often reported that they are equally sexually assertive. (Various examples of behavior in "sex-positive" cultures will be cited as we continue.) In less supportive social circumstances, it appears, only the male "drive" remains at a high level. In our own society, with its mixture of positive and negative feelings about sex, the surveys continue to reveal a large gap between the average degrees of male and female desire.[8] This is so even after other female needs such as love and security, to which female sexual desire is linked in this culture, are taken care of. To be sure, the emotions of both sexes can affect their sexuality. But this difference in degree between them is a very large one.

There is a plausible biological explanation for female erotic feelings being less easily aroused or more readily suppressed. Across the animal kingdom, the sex which makes the greatest "parental investment" in offspring is typically more cautious about mating: it is the one that stands to lose the most from a poor choice of partner.[9] Hence among humans, with a long period of gestation and nursing, slower arousal on the part of the female appears to make biological sense. This, in turn, could help to account for women's lesser tendency to be sexually excited by visual cues: being "turned on" that readily would not be conducive to caution in mating. Yet there also seem to be reasons in some biological circumstances for strong female interest in sex. The females of many other primate species are highly sexed and promiscuous, just as human ones are capable of being. (Primatologist Sarah Blaffer Hrdy's *The Woman That Never Evolved* contains a proposed explanation of strong sexual desire in females.) One must, of course, be cautious about theories of prehistoric origins, which cannot be tested directly. Those alluded to here, however, seem to fit the empirical data very well.

Returning to the subject of pornography, these further gender differences also help to explain the sexes' different degrees of interest in such things. It is found in laboratory tests that scenes of sexual activity (not just nudes, again) can be sexually exciting to most women; but the rate of arousal is slow compared to the instantaneous response of most men. Hence women lack the motivation that many men have to seek out such scenes in the first place. Even a chance sight or passing mental image can trigger in him, but not in her, a strong desire for further sexual stimulation. Moreover, the evidence indicates that the capacity for arousal to erotic portrayals is largely a learned response with females. On the whole, those with actual sexual experience find such portrayals much more sexually exciting than those without; whereas with males, previous experience has no such effect.[10] In fact, female sexual desire *in general* is much more dependent on actual experience than that of males. In cultures where females have a high rate of sexual activity at an early age, for example, their "drive" reportedly peaks in the late teens, the same as that of males.

There appear to be yet other differences, on average, between males and females in regard to their sexual desires. These notably include the degree of interest in "casual" sex, without long-term commitment, and in sex with a variety of partners. Both differences are partially a consequence of the one concerning stronger sex "drive": a powerful need cannot wait for a uniquely appropriate long-term partner to come along. But the differences have other important sources as well: these are emotional needs and feelings that can compete with the erotic ones, and further aspects of the latter. These further tendencies, and the corresponding gender differences, are less central to explaining attraction and lack of attraction to pornography. But where salient, their influence on the use of and attitudes toward sexual fantasies and portrayals will also be noted.

NONEROTIC ATTRACTION AND DESIRE

Another type of interest exists between the sexes, one that does not involve genital sensations—though of course it may well be accompanied by them. For both men and women, general physical appearance is important in producing this kind of pleasure or excitement. Among females, certain types of behavior by males are also highly attractive. These include a number of things that have caught the attention of social scientists, notably those that signal competence on the part of the male.[11] In a similar way, in general, females seem to be attracted by economic success and high social status. (See Warren Farrell's *Why Men Are the Way They Are* for a nontechnical discussion of this topic.) Though women's economically dependent state could plausibly account for this reaction, a biological disposition toward it is also a real possibility. In either case, it would help to explain certain other differences between the two genders. For example, a man can be very desirable to the opposite sex for a longer period of his life than a woman can, since high status and success can extend well beyond youth (though *few* men can do so, since status is relative). In addition, women tend to prefer the sight of a well-dressed man to a naked one: it is the look of power and achievement.

Of particular importance, under the heading of things that attract females to males, is a category of behaviors that might loosely be labeled "romantic." These are clearly of much greater importance to females in our society. It is women, not men, who flock to hear a member of the opposite sex sing tender love songs. (Julio Iglesias, who specializes in just that, is said to have sold more phonograph records than anyone else but Bing Crosby and the Beatles—and he is still going strong.) To what extent this difference is natural and to what extent culturally produced is again not clear. To judge from cross-cultural differences, at least part of the difference is due to social influences of some sort. One can also see a plausible biological explanation for a tendency toward such feelings, however. A solicitous and adoring male is more likely to be a good provider later on for her highly dependent offspring, so such attraction might well have been programmed by nature. Whatever the reasons for this difference, there is convincing evidence from other species for the biological origins of affectionate behavior. During courtship, many animal pairs behave toward each other in ways that seem clearly related to the kinds of things they will later need to do to care for the offspring. That is to say, "billing and cooing" are stylized symbols of nurturing the young. The ethologist's explanation is that such behavior is evidence to each of the pair that the other will be a good parent. (Note the biological metaphor; this is not literal. Neither of the pair need have any conscious or unconscious awareness of the connection to childrearing; each is just programmed to like the behavior, and to like a partner who engages in it.)

Closely related to the desire for romantic behavior, of course, is the need to love and be loved—in the romantic sense of the word "love," that is. What we might call human love, a concern for the well-being of others—what used to be called "charity"—should not be confused with this special sort of emotional attachment. Psychologists still know really very little about these emotions, and the brain chemicals responsible for love-attachment and dependency are only now beginning to be discovered. (See *The Chemistry of Love* by Michael Liebowitz.) Evidently "pair-bonding," as the phenomenon is called in biology, evolved in humans for the same reason as it has in various other animals: where offspring need the intensive care that only two parents can provide well, such attachment keeps the pair together for that purpose. Even so, the importance publicly attached to romantic love varies considerably from one culture to another, and the degree to which it is subjectively experienced appears to vary as well. In certain cultures, the sort of male-female attachment that is so glorified in our society is virtually nonexistent.[12] And the idea that love is a moral precondition for sex has seemingly been unknown in history until recent times in the West.

It is again relevant to our purposes to note what seems to be an average difference between the sexes, this time in regard to the felt importance of love. It is not clear how much of the difference is caused by socialization and how much represents biological predispositions. That it is partly biological is argued by the fact that women "masculinized" as fetuses tend to have appreciably less interest in love and marriage than do average women.[13] Females may just naturally have a greater need than males for emotional bonding. Yet a social influence is also evident. In preindustrial societies, in contrast to our own, there is apparently much stronger emotional bonding to the community and the extended family and less to the spouse. Hence it is more difficult in our culture, with its loose ties beyond the nuclear family, for women's (or men's) needs for emotional support to be met outside the marital relationship; perhaps this environmental factor has an unconscious influence on the type of desires they develop. (It may also be that it is not very healthy to be so psychologically dependent on a single other person.) Similarly, the state of socioeconomic dependence in which women have been kept in most technological cultures could contribute to their need for secure attachment to a single provider/protector.

In any case, these male-female differences regarding love, affection, and noneronic attraction are reflected in yet another category of fantasy. It is almost exclusively women and girls who read romance novels and magazines, and mostly they who want to see love stories on television and in movies. The men in their fantasies, rather than naked and randy, tend to be strong, successful, and well-dressed. Now, the parallel between male interest in pornography and female interest in romantic stories is often pointed out. It is reported that 40 percent of all paperback books sold are women's romance novels; this compares pretty well with the numbers of pornographic magazines bought by men. Each of these genres is a means of enhancing real-life experience, or even of substituting fantasy for experiences that, some of the time for all and most of the time for some, are difficult to attain in real life. Yet the dissimilarity between them is also revealing. Although the liberalization in sexual attitudes in recent decades has seen the appearance of sexually frank romances and an interest in nonromantic pornography among some women, the overall differences in male and female needs and feelings that the two types of fantasy reflect are still with us.

All these average differences between the sexes make it difficult for men and women to understand one another. For we cannot see others' minds and needs, as we can their physical behavior; we can only imagine them in greater or less similarity to our own. Hence any time others act differently than we would, we are apt to assume they do so for unimportant reasons, or out of deliberate perverseness or insensitivity. For example, not experiencing the same sexual feelings, most women as well as some men see pornography as a trivial form of entertainment. They do not realize it is—for many younger males, at least—a substitute way of satisfying a powerful need. As we continue, the tragic consequences of this misperception, and of related misunderstandings between the sexes, will become increasingly evident.

2

Background: Sex and Values

Having looked at those aspects of sexuality most relevant to our special subject, we will now consider relevant aspects of the subject of values, that is, of beliefs about what is good or bad in life and what it is right and wrong to do. The treatment will again be brief, but it is essential for an intelligent discussion of the arguments over pornography.

HUMAN NATURE AND THE GOOD

To begin, certain cautionary remarks must be made about the foregoing mention of nature and biology. For one thing, there is wide variation among individuals regarding their needs and characteristics. (Most human traits are distributed according to the familiar "bell curve.") Like other species, the human species has biological mechanisms that promote the existence of large differences among its members. Consequently, what is natural for one person need not be so for another. Some people naturally have little interest in sex, and some are emotionally independent from birth on. It should not be supposed that a given person ought to have a greater or lesser interest in sex or love just because others do. More specifically, there is no reason to think one must be like other members of one's own sex, or different from those of the other one, in these ways. Nor need one be aligned with one's own sex in any other ways; gender roles and expectations may have (or may once have had) some value, but it is clear that rigid ones are harmful to individuals and wasteful for society as a whole. In general, there is more variation regarding a given psychological trait among the members of each sex than between the averages of the two. For the sake of those inclined to turn statistical facts into rigid stereotypes, this point must be stressed.

Furthermore, as has already been emphasized, much of the difference between men and women in this culture is merely the result of social training. More than any other creatures on earth, humans are programmed by their environment; our behavior is the result of an incredibly complex and poorly understood interplay between "nature" and "nurture." In spite of what many suppose, it is not at all clear that most of the familiar gender dissimilarities are just natural, even in part. (At least, by this reviewer's lights, the evidence regarding those that involve eroticism is much more clear than is the case for other nonanatomic traits.) But the opposite assumption is equally unjustified. For some people, the belief that there *could* be no innate psychological differences between the sexes has also assumed the status of dogma—a matter to be settled by ideology rather than by evidence.[1] Part of what motivates this stance is their concern that racists and sexists often claim innate differences that do not really exist in order to justify discrimination. Such a blinkered attitude toward real differences has perils of its own, however. The best solution to invidious discrimination lies not in denying statistical facts but in treating each person as an individual, letting the averages fall where they will.

For our purposes, it will be important to distinguish between those feelings and tendencies that have been learned and those that were planted in individuals or in the whole species by biology. We will continue to make such distinctions, wherever it is possible, in what follows. So many mentions of other cultures have been made here because comparing different human societies is the closest thing we have to an experiment in different ways of living; it supplies evidence concerning which aspects of our own lives are reflective of human nature and which are solely the product of culture. In very many cases, however, we simply do not yet know.

Another point that must be made regarding nature has to do with nature's "purposes": it should not be assumed that they ought to be our own. In fact, the former are not literally purposes or goals at all, at least as understood in science. Talk of such is only a metaphor for the idea that certain inherited traits tended to survive better than others in the original evolutionary environment. Whether it is *good* for any given feature to do so is an independent question, and in fact it is often not good. Nature is ultimately "concerned" only about the survival of our genes, not with our happiness, and the two are often in conflict. The belief that we must not thwart nature's plans—even ignoring the fact that people are usually mistaken about what those "plans" are—has caused much misery throughout history. One instance of this view that most of us have forgotten is the once powerful opposition to vaccination. A tragic example still with us involves birth control, for the dogma that "*the* function" of sex is procreation is even now responsible for vast suffering and starvation in Catholic and Muslim areas of the third world.

The idea that nature's goals are always good is a variation on the wider belief that whatever is natural is good. One has only to reflect on such natural occurrences as earthquakes, epidemics, and drought, and on the fact that every species can survive only through the suffering and death of others, to realize that the latter idea is false. A more restricted claim, that whatever is natural for humans to do is good, is also false. After all, the biological tendencies we are programmed with include such unlovely ones as selfishness, aggression, and spite. Even so, what is natural is most certainly relevant to what is of value. Being natural is evidence for being healthy, and that is a very important kind of good. Nature can definitely be improved upon; but as biologists have long realized, most of the ways in which a given organism's behavior might diverge from the natural are harmful. The belatedly realized harms of our modern diet and low-exercise lifestyle provide a familiar example. Some natural tendencies can be changed or repressed fairly easily; others, only at a heavy cost.[2] Let us adopt the following terminology: a natural need—as opposed to a mere tendency—is any desire whose denial results in suffering, be it physical or psychological.

An even worse error than that of equating the natural with the good is the sweeping belief that whatever is natural is *bad*. Though it is not as commonly held since the rise of anthropology as a science, one still runs across the idea that humans in "the natural state" are amoral if not evil, that we must cling tenaciously to "civilized" ways lest we slip back into "savagery" or "barbarism." Such a view is mostly chauvinism. The main difference between modern Western culture and others in general lies in our accumulation of factual knowledge and technology, not in our basic aesthetic and moral sensitivities. The former have brought much moral progress with them, notably because of the partial elimination of superstition. But if by "savage" one means brutal and cruel, our own culture's history of slavery, colonialism, and war reveals it to have been more savage than many pretechnological cultures. An important manifestation of this chauvinistic mindset is in regard to sexuality. In recent centuries, the cultures with the most positive view of sex have been "primitive" ones, making it easy for us and them to discount their ways as the product of moral ignorance. That situation may be mostly an accident of history, however. The last peoples in the world to be influenced by the sexual beliefs of Christianity and other major religions were the most remote from the centers of civilization and consequently the least technologically advanced. This point will be explained more fully later in this chapter. Meanwhile, it brings us to the question of why our particular society holds the sexual attitudes that it does.

THE PRIMARY CAUSE OF ANTISEXUALISM

The main point of the first chapter of this book is that pornography, together with the desires that underlie it, is natural and healthy. Surely there is something both unnatural and unhealthy about having emotions of fear and disgust and shame toward one's own healthy needs, whether the needs involve food, companionship, self-respect, or sex. Then why does this culture exhibit so much opposition to sexual explicitness and to other manifestations of sexual feelings? The reasons are highly complex but, at least in broad outline, not difficult to explain.

To begin with, opposition to sexual openness is a reflection of our in-grained sense of shame over nudity. In some individuals this reaction is particularly strong; a felt aversion to having sex with the lights on, even with a beloved spouse, is not uncommon to this day. More basically, the opposition to eroticism stems from a general attitude that there is something less than noble about sexual desire. Of all normal human needs and plea-sures, only sexual ones are seen in this society as inherently suspect: such desire is a "baser passion" in need of being "redeemed" by association with legitimate desires. Hence, in particular, sexual explicitness is seen as requiring art or science or romantic love to rescue it from depravity—if it is thought rescuable at all, that is. But it is never said that any one of the latter needs *sex* to redeem *it.* A more moderate version of this attitude does not call sex unclean, but it still insists sex may not be valued for its own sake. It must be used only as a means to some other end, for example, to communicate or to express love or commitment. (That automatically rules out solitary sexual fantasy, masturbation, and use of pornography, even though most people engage in one or more of these activities.) But the idea is still that sex is in a different category from other human needs, requiring one of the others to legitimize it. Most people today would not openly admit to having the harsher attitude. It should become clear as we continue, however, that many do have it, including many who claim to hold the less extreme view.

As we shall see later on, yet other influences motivate the attack on pornography, influences that nevertheless seem to be largely an outgrowth of these attitudes toward nudity and sex. Then what, in turn, is the source of the latter emotions and beliefs? Those who have them generally take them to be natural and obvious—not the sort of thing a rational or moral person could even consider doubting. But they are certainly not natural feelings, even though, as we will also see, certain natural tendencies can help give rise to them. Nor do they represent moral knowledge, as nearly all automatically suppose. Instead, from various lines of evidence, it is perfectly clear that their real origin is mere socialization. Like so many other beliefs and feelings we have, they are produced in us by indoctrination and conditioning from an early age. It will be of worth for us to examine this situation, together with the historical and biological forces that have given rise to it.

The power of socialization should, with a little reflection, be obvious to everyone. It is not a colossal coincidence that the vast majority of, say, Buddhists or Catholics or Communists in the world were raised as Buddhists or Catholics or Communists. So great is that power, in fact, that the human mind is capable of being caused to believe almost anything, no matter how arbitrary or irrational or even cruel it may be. That this is so is clear from the incredible diversity of moral beliefs throughout history and across cultures. Let us note just a few striking examples. In Thailand, it is considered highly offensive to touch another person on the head. (Perhaps Thais regard Westerners, with our promiscuous head-touching, as frequently degrading one another without knowing it.) In many human cultures, numerous strong taboos surround the eating of food. In some, for instance, eating together is the important mark of marital union; hence it, rather than sexual intercourse, is forbidden to those not married. And even for married couples, eating together in public is prohibited in certain societies; conjugal dining is considered strictly a personal, private affair. In a more serious vein, a widow in India used to be convinced it was her moral duty to kill herself on her husband's funeral pyre. For a final example of such variation in moral beliefs, it is only since World War II that our own venerable tradition of racism has come to be widely regarded as evil. It wasn't so long ago that segregation of the races, particularly in regard to sex and marriage, was considered not just morally permissible but morally obligatory.

Turning more specifically to sexual attitudes, we again find some remarkable variations across time and space—good evidence that they are only the product of training, not moral truths obvious to anyone. In the Trobriand Islands, where children are allowed to have unfettered sex from their earliest years in the privacy of the bush, any display of affection *in public* is regarded as disgraceful; open hand-holding among a few of the youth was described by tribal traditionalists as a new immorality, one that was introduced along with Christian ideas. (See Bronislaw Malinowski's anthropological classic *The Sexual Life of Savages* for a discussion of this culture.) During the "sexual revolution" of the 1960s and 1970s in our own culture, a remarkable change in beliefs took place in regard to oral-genital sex. For centuries it had been regarded as a heinous sin and a serious crime. (The laws are still on the books in many places and are sporadically enforced.) It was considered too loathesome even to be described aloud or in print; the laws mostly used euphemisms lest they give ideas to the unchurched. Yet oral-genital sex has come to be practiced by a high percentage of the sexually active. That is a staggeringly large change in attitude to occur in such a short time.

As for bodily shame, nearly everyone is aware of the wide disparity in regard to what degree of nudity elicits such feelings. Some people spend their whole lives naked without distress; in some places women always go topless, and in others, women's arms, legs, and even faces are perpetually covered to avoid the leering gaze of men. In this regard, too, our own society has seen large changes just in the present century. Yet in spite of the clear transiency of such attitudes, each generation treats its own views about where to draw the line between acceptable and unacceptable body exposure as if they were timeless truths of great moral significance. For another way to realize that bodily shame is only an internalized response to societal disapproval, not "just natural," consider a fact such as the following: many a young woman who feels comfortable at a public beach in a bikini would be mortified to find herself there wearing just panties and a bra—even if they cover more skin than the bathing suit does.

The exact way in which sexual aversion is learned in this culture, and how our socialization differs from that of those in which children are raised to view sex more positively, is a complex subject, but a few examples can serve to illustrate the point. Even among those parents who do not overtly punish their children's expressions of eroticism (which many do, physically or psychologically), the message is sent in subtle ways. If a child is playing with its genitals, the hand is pushed away. The sex organs are studiously avoided in conversation, except in connection with the pollution of waste elimination. Of course, there is also the perpetual anxious avoidance of nudity and of sex talk around children. The message is subliminal but clear: there is something sinister about sexuality and certain parts of the body. The unnaturally high degree of sexual privacy in which modern children are raised is another factor in all this. Through the long prehistory of human evolution, the norm was for large families to live together in a single enclosure, where children could observe nudity, sexual activity, and child-birth from their earliest years.[3] That our practice of shielding children from such things is a contributor both to an increased sense of "modesty" and to a heightened male interest in nudity is virtually certain. It is also worth noting that bodily shame is more strongly reinforced in girls than in boys. For example, the practice of requiring boys to shower together while girls shower separately from each other has long been widespread in schools.

So it is clear that people do not have rational reasons for many of their strong feelings and beliefs. They are instead the product of blind sociali-zation, passed from one unsuspecting generation to the next. Even so, it is often claimed, there are also *good* reasons for accepting the attitudes tradition has brought us. After all, it is argued, they have stood the test of time; our forebears must have had grounds for retaining them. There is some truth in this, enough to warn us against too rapidly making big changes in society. But it has not nearly so much validity as traditionalists standardly assume. The ability of human beings to realize the consequences of their social institutions over time is often far outweighed by their capacity for indoctrination, and human ability to survive is great enough to do so in spite of customs that are contrary to everyone's well-being. Consider how long our own civilization lived with such medical atrocities as blood-letting, and such moral ones as witch-burning, religious persecution, and slavery. Those who unthinkingly defend all "traditional values" need to be reminded that racism is a traditional value.

Beyond this is the argument that other societies have, over even longer periods of testing by time, come to such different conclusions. (That being so, perhaps we should adopt some *other* culture's traditions about sex!) Logically, however, the various groups cannot all have been led to the unique right answer. To this it is often replied that each human community is just naturally guided to the best customs for its particular circumstances. Those who make this claim have no real justification for it, however; in fact, the evidence argues otherwise. For one thing, vast differences standardly exist between distinct groups in the same external conditions. More to the point, once again, countless thousands of clearly harmful and downright horrific customs, from footbinding to headhunting, are to be found in the world. There is hardly an evil one can name that has not been a tradition somewhere, sometime. It is certainly not implied here that traditions play no valuable social role, only that they often do not; and even when they do, they frequently could be replaced by better ones.

As for our own Western culture, its beliefs and practices have become progressively less brutal and more compassionate during the last few centuries—always over the protests of the well indoctrinated. This does not prove there are yet more changes to be made, of course. But it does reveal the utter madness of assuming our society's moral standards have already been perfected. The system of beliefs we have inherited is not a seamless web but an eclectic mixture; the error of traditionalism is that it embraces the chaff with the wheat, indiscriminately. Indeed, on the assumption that our progenitors must have learned from experience the value of what they did, it paradoxically bids us to renounce learning from experience ourselves, cutting off the possibility of further progress. What is demanded, clearly, is for us to examine the evidence carefully, to *find out* whether there are (or whether our ancestors had) good reasons for a given belief. With the rise of science and universal education, we are in a better position to do this than any peoples before us in history. Whatever value the tendency toward blind conformity may have had in the course of human evolution, whether tribal harmony and strength, the training of children, *or* avoiding the dangers of the untried, it is not the wise course now. (To be sure, blind *non*conformity is also irrational.) Indeed, science only developed as individuals learned to think critically, to question their own beliefs and demand justification for every knowledge claim. In issues where much is at stake, we must do no less.

ULTIMATE ORIGINS OF ANTISEXUALISM

In the Western tradition, compared with others of the world, attitudes toward sexuality have been extremely negative. Some would trace the negative mindset back to roots in a general belief that the body is corrupt while the mind or spirit is pure, a belief which arose in the Mediterranean area in pre-Christian times. Adopted into Christianity, it was largely responsible for the pervasive asceticism of the early church, including its denigration of sex, bathing, human companionship, and other "worldly pleasures." (See, for example, Vern and Bonnie Bullough, *Sin, Sickness and Sanity*.) In any event, the historical view of the church was that sex was polluting, so that the holy would avoid it altogether. It could be tolerated only to produce children—hence the traditional ban on contraception and nonprocreative sexual practices.[4] Christianity's high moral principles have unfortunately been accompanied by a few tragic errors, which have caused much suffering through the centuries. Most of these have been greatly modified, of course, but parts of that attitude toward sex and the body are still with us. The purpose of mentioning such facts is not to disparage Christians; it is to bring some historical realism to the religious debates over sexuality. Most of those who think they got their sexual values from the Bible or from Christian tradition soon realize, when they examine the situation more closely, that some of those values are not to be found there (e.g., that one purpose of sex is to promote spousal love) and that they themselves find it painful to accept some of what *is* taught there.

For present purposes, what is most important about historical origins is the following fact: It was largely through the spread of Christianity and Islam that most of the world acquired its traditional sexual attitudes. More liberal views evidently prevailed before that time in most places. Those attitudes went along as part of a package deal, rather than being adopted and retained because of any intrinsic superiority that had been independently discovered. As for the spread of those religions themselves, their general, though not total, moral superiority over most of their competitors no doubt played an important role. But purely political influences were also crucial, from Constantine's making Christianity the state religion of imperial Rome, to the long history of Christian and Islamic military conquest and proselytizing that followed. By this stage of history, colonialism and technological superiority have spread Western values over the globe. Because certain moral beliefs about sex are now so widespread, most people suppose they must be true. But a little study of their dissemination over time reveals the real reasons for their unquestioned acceptance.

To be sure, not all the ultimate origins of sexual aversion lie in accidents of history. There is at least one biological root as well. To begin to explain, let us note that humans, unlike some other mammals and many birds, are not biologically monogamous. They exhibit what ethologists call a "mixed reproductive strategy"; that is, they have a strong tendency toward pair-bonding, unlike their closest primate relatives, but also strong tendencies on average to desire more than one sex partner. Though monogamy is the cross-cultural norm, the overwhelming majority of human societies also allow multiple partners, in the form of spouse-sharing, polygamy, and "promiscuity" among the unmarried.[5] The few, and now dominant, cultures that officially insist on strict monogamy must constantly fight or wink at the other behavior. Like those for pair-bonding, the reasons behind the desire for partner variety are explored by students of evolutionary biology.[6] They need not be discussed here, except perhaps to note that "promiscuity" in primate and human groups seems to promote a more diffuse type of emotional bonding among greater numbers of individuals, in contrast to the strength of the pair-bond.

Now, standing in opposition to the desire for multiple sex or love partners is another biological tendency, namely jealousy. The desire for a mate not to have other partners is also biologically programmed into human and animal nature—to varying degrees, that is. Some species or individuals are highly monogamous, some are "promiscuous," and many exhibit a "double standard." Biologists have also discussed the apparent evolutionary reasons for jealousy, also called "mate-guarding." However, this emotion is heavily influenced by culture as well as by nature. Jealousy would seem to be particularly strong in societies that place a high value on private property rather than on sharing, hence on sole possession of one's spouse. Moreover, those in which property or social standing is inherited make it much more important to a man to be sure he is the father of his wife's children, causing mate faithfulness to be more highly valued. Finally, as already noted, accidental historical forces have a powerful influence on the social norms that develop. One of the apparent effects of Graeco-Roman domination was that their official monogamy, rather than Judaism's polygamy, became the standard for Christianity and later Christendom.

What is significant about this topic for our purposes is the following fact: sexual jealousy tends to promote sexual repression. With its attendant desire to control the sexuality of others, including partners, potential rivals, and even offspring, it seems to have been unconsciously at work in producing much of the sexual restrictiveness in the world. Indeed, jealousy and sexual repression form a vicious circle: the more difficult it is for males to get sexual needs satisfied, the more jealously they guard what opportunities they have—and conversely. (Similar things may be said about love, of course.) It is especially relevant to our subject to notice one apparent result of that tendency. Prohibitions on public sexual behavior, and also on openly inviting sex by calling attention to or gazing at sexual organs, are widespread in human societies. This is generally the case only for everyday public situations, however, where the occasioning of sexual jealousy could be highly disruptive. Such prohibitions are not often given the absolute status they have in the minds of many individuals in our culture, that of being inherently evil.

It has been suggested by certain scientists that humans have an innate tendency to feel anxiety when their own sexual behavior is observed by others—*nature*'s way of avoiding jealousy and vulnerability. Some also opine that children naturally experience distress on seeing sexual or even just affectionate activity. On the basis of current information, these possibilities cannot be ruled out. Yet this much can be said: if such tendencies exist, they are mild compared to the antisexual feelings our society has built on top of them. Sexual sights do not possess the highly negative emotional impact in most cultures that they have in this one. In many cultures, for example, one who encounters or occupies the same shelter as a copulating couple is expected to avert his or her eyes and ignore them; but the experience is hardly traumatic for anyone involved. Moreover, there is certainly no natural tendency to have feelings of shame or disgust over mere nudity or over one's own sexual behavior per se.

A final major source of negative attitudes about sex, of course, lies in the dangers of venereal disease and of pregnancies in which conditions for adequate childcare are absent. Although the moral significance of these matters is very great, it will not be discussed at length in this book, since the subject here is sexual fantasy, not sexual behavior. (Later on, however, we will be looking at the claim that pornographic fantasies incite such actual behavior as premarital sex and infidelity.) Like jealousy, these two sources of social trauma are likely to have contributed to this culture's sexual aversions in an indirect fashion. For our purposes, what is most important to point out is that the legitimate fears involved with venereal disease and unprepared pregnancy are not adequate to justify or even to explain the common feelings of revulsion and shame in regard to sex. A simple analogy may help to illustrate this fact. Many people consider activities like hang-gliding and mountain-climbing highly dangerous and hence would not dream of engaging in them. They might even regard it as immoral for someone with a dependent family to take those chances or for anyone to try to recruit others into sharing the experience. But it would never occur to them to describe such things merely on account of the grave danger to self or others, as disgusting or degrading. Similarly, this culture's traditional aversion to sexuality is not adequately accounted for by real threats to well-being; there is something profoundly irrational about it.

REAL MORALITY, SEXUAL AND OTHERWISE

A major point of the foregoing discussion of attitude origins is to reveal our obligation to critically examine all our moral beliefs. Also revealed by the discussion, however, is the fallibility of moral gut reactions. From this

fallibility, some have drawn the pessimistic conclusion that moral knowledge is not possible. But that does not follow. One can understand the
psychological influences that distort perception of good and evil without
granting that there is nothing to be perceived. What it does make clear is
that we need to have a way to distinguish true moral standards from false
ones, rather than being at the mercy of nonrational sources of belief. And
we do have such a way, a simple set of basic ethical principles. Though
often buried under superstition and tradition, these fundamental moral
concepts appear to be universally recognized to one degree or another. In
recent centuries, with the rise of self-critical thought, they have finally
become the dominant force in our moral reasoning.

In a word, the central principle is that values must be based on needs—
on what makes for suffering or happiness in life.[7] Rather than *a priori*
values telling us what our needs ought to be, it is the latter that determine
what is or is not to be valued. Food and friendship and personal dignity
are important because we need them; if we did not need them, they would
not be important. To paraphrase the similar point made by Jesus, people
were not made for rules, rules were made for people. As a corollary, what
is valuable for one person may be very different from what is valuable for
another, owing to their *different* needs. Historically, much of what has
been regarded as bad does not intrinsically tend to harm anyone, and much
considered good does not have any tendency to produce happiness. But
in the modern world, this need-principle is widely recognized, at least
implicitly. As a consequence, most modern attempts to defend antisexual
attitudes do so in one or both of two ways: by denying that sexual desire
or some aspect of it is a strong need for anyone, or else by claiming it
violates the needs of others in some manner. We shall be examining many
such attempts in detail.

A second major principle determining what is good and bad in the world
is that of equality, that each individual's well-being counts just as much as
any other's. (Indeed, it perhaps follows from the first one, which makes
no reference to the needs of any particular persons.) Every person has the
same right as any other to have what she or he needs, or the opportunity
to get it. Unfortunately, human nature contains a strong tendency toward
selfishness, an inclination to place one's own welfare above that of others.
It also contains feelings of empathy and concern for our fellow creatures,
which act to offset the selfish impulses. But these are felt more strongly
toward those who are close to us or similar to ourselves. Though certain
ideals of justice and moral right have perhaps been universally recognized
in human cultures, they have historically been applied mostly to one's "own
kind," not to "the tribe over the hill." It is only with great difficulty that
the principle of equality has come to be seen as encompassing all of humanity, including those who are far away or very different from ourselves.
Like socialization, then, selfishness is a serious impediment to recognizing

what is genuinely good and bad in human life. In fact, the writer of this book would say they are the two major problems in that regard and will be illustrating them both with respect to issues of sexuality.

The third basic element in determining what is to be valued or disvalued, one that is crucially relevant to *moral* good and bad, is that of agency, that is, the principle that one is responsible for the choices one freely makes. What it is good or bad to do depends, among other things, upon how one's actions may affect oneself or others. And what is moral or immoral, as opposed to merely prudent or unwise, depends more specifically on its probable effect on others. What makes an act morally right or wrong is, very roughly, that the one performing it knows the act is likely to help or harm someone else—to give to or take from that person something that is needed to have happiness or avoid suffering.[8] In contrast, things which are not in one's power to control are not morally creditable or blameworthy. For example, part of what is evil about racism is that it condemns people for something they cannot help, such as the color of their skin. Another part is that it condemns for something that is not bad, because not harmful.

The point about things one is *not* responsible for is also significant for our purposes, since we do not have ultimate control over our most basic capacities and needs. Unreflective people usually assume that we choose our needs, just as we do our actions; hence they give themselves and others credit or blame for having them. A little thought reveals that it is not so, however. You did not at some early age say to yourself, "Shall I or shall I not be a creature that feels hunger and thirst?" and then flip a coin to decide; you simply discovered those sensations in yourself. Through conscious repression and the power of suggestion, we can modify some of the emotions and sensations with which we were programmed, but only to a limited extent.[9] (Even at that, people are endowed with different degrees of suggestibility and of intensity in various desires, so that some can do so more successfully than others in each case.) If you do not believe this, try an experiment: find an ugly old rock and simply *will* yourself to feel from its mere presence whatever satisfaction you now get from food, or from love or friendship, or from breathtaking scenery. It is safe to say that if you could do that, you would have solved all the problems in your life long ago. On the other hand, we certainly do have control over the beliefs that direct so many of our feelings. If, for example, we discover certain attitudinal emotions were the result of false beliefs or selfishness, we can change them—as when this society as a whole finally realized the evil of its racist attitudes.

Of course, the foregoing value-principles are highly general and require much further elaboration. Though they are simple in themselves, their consequences are far from being always clear, especially in a complex and uncertain world. The subject of ethical values cannot be pursued here in its own right. The purpose of discussing it to this degree is just to make the following appeal: that we overcome certain prejudices and apply to the issues of sexuality the same basic precepts we already employ in most other areas of moral concern. On these grounds, it is here submitted that sexual feelings are neither more nor less noble, intrinsically, than any other basic needs. The desire to share sex with another person is no more degrading to that person than is the desire, for example, to share companionship. And presentations that arouse or vicariously satisfy sexual desires are no more to be despised than those that arouse or satisfy the desire for friendship, love, or self-respect. They all involve important human needs, and all involve the principles of equality and agency in the same way. In the next few chapters, that claim will be defended against a multitude of standard charges to the contrary.

"But don't these precepts give us obvious grounds to object to pornography?" it might be asked. "After all, many people are caused to feel emotional pain by it—even if that feeling is only a conditioned response." The answer to this question can perhaps be made most clear with an analogy. Consider the reaction one socialized in a racist society might have at the sight of a mixed-race couple on the street: "There's one of my own kind, degrading herself!" The racist, identifying with that member of his or her group, feels emotional pain, and the feelings are real. (Real enough to have often led in the past to acts of violence, both outside of and by means of the law.) But they are not morally justified. Indeed, it seems wrong even to say that the couple's presence is the cause of the racist's distress. Rather, it is the latter's social training that is responsible; people can be socialized to have such aversive feelings toward anything. In any case, the mixed-race couple's being together is not harmful by its own nature (and by human nature), independently of moral prejudgment. Hence it is not wrong. On the contrary, it is the racist's response that is morally evil—evil because of its potential for bringing psychological or even physical harm to those who are innocent of any harm to others. This simile should be clear. At least as regards the claim of directly causing psychological hurt, pornography and the fantasies it expresses are not evil. Instead, ironically, the intolerance traditionally heaped upon those who feel a need for such fantasies is itself morally wrong.

This last point needs to be stressed. Irrational attitudes toward sexuality have caused, and continue to cause, vast amounts of human sorrow. The reader may already have firsthand knowledge of this kind of pain, but a particularly revealing example can be cited from the not-too-distant past. Largely because of the belief that only the possibility of childbirth can redeem sexual activity from being evil, masturbation was long regarded with horror. Although by all the evidence it is a perfectly natural and healthy activity for children to engage in, strenuous efforts have been made to prevent it. During the Victorian era, many parents resorted to such deterrents as mittens and straps, chastity belts and devices to cause pain if an erection occurred—even painful types of circumcision and cutting out or cauterizing the clitoris were used. Loving parents were willing to inflict pain, humiliation, and mutilation on their children to prevent the supposed evil. Such is the power of superstitious fear. So the subject of this book is hardly a trivial one; its ultimate concern is human happiness. And though we cannot here discuss the entire issue of sexual morality, it will be further developed in regard to our restricted subject.

3

Common Charges Against Sexual Explicitness

In the next few chapters we will look at some of the reasons commonly given in making the claim that pornography is bad in itself, intrinsically, or else bad because awareness of it creates emotional distress. The question of whether it causes harmful mental states or behavior in those who use it will be delayed until the second half of this book.

Let us begin by making the following observation: Where beliefs are produced by nonrational influences such as wishful thinking or indoctrination, the mind typically attempts to create a rational basis for them, after the fact. A large arsenal of such rationalizations has been employed in the attempt to justify this society's traditional attitudes about sexuality, including pornography. In general, one thing that exposes an argument as a mere rationalization is the fact that it is so clearly fallacious once it is actually examined. Often, for instance, those who employ a particular argument would not think of making the same claim in relevantly similar situations. In other cases, the reasoning requires a distortion of the facts in order to be convincing. Indeed, some such claims are virtually empty of factual content; they are mere shibboleths one has learned to recite on cue but which describe nothing in reality. This is exactly the situation, we shall see, in regard to the standard moral objections against pornography. They all reveal an any-stick-will-do abandonment of critical judgment.

DEBASEMENT CLAIMS

First consider an obvious example of rationalization. Certain human cultures have a tradition of disfiguring the teeth: blackening them, filing them down, even knocking them out. When the people of one such group were asked why that should be a desirable thing to do, they replied that having natural-looking teeth would make them "like *animals*." This should sound familiar; a common charge against pornography is that it is by nature "animalistic" or "dehumanizing." On the contrary, as has already been pointed out, nothing is any more human than sexual fantasies and feelings, along with their representation and vicarious enjoyment in various media of expression. If anyone is trying to dehumanize us in this regard, it is those who would denigrate our sexuality and its celebration, for they are denying a significant part of our humanity.

This sort of argument is based on the assumption that anything uniquely or specially human is good, or that whatever is typical of animals is inferior. And it is plainly false. That dogs are affectionate, and caring toward their young, does not make it degrading for humans to be so. Nor does the fact that the capacity to destroy all life is uniquely human mean it would be a good thing to do. Alas, arrogance and cruelty are as human as generosity and compassion. It may be that we have a greater capacity than other animals for emotions such as the latter, but the same is true of the former. As a matter of fact, those who employ such rhetoric usually know little about human *or* animal nature. They typically assume that things like love, sex with love, monogamy, or long-term bonding are peculiarly human; but as has already been brought out here, they are wrong on every count. Or else they talk as if sexual nonexclusivity, unbonded sex, visually caused erotic excitement, and so on, were somehow unnatural for humans. Even they know better than that.

Their reasoning is often based on an erroneous view that animals and humans are utterly different in their natures, the one moved by blind instinct, the other by emotion and reason. In truth, all the dissimilarities are differences in degree, not in kind—mostly just degree of intelligence. Even conscience (guilt, sympathy, and so on) is found in many other animals, as any dog owner should know. Even if some traits are uniquely human (or uniquely nonhuman), that does not mean they are good (or bad); they must be evaluated on their own merits. A second mistaken belief sometimes underlying this assumption is a misunderstanding of evolution, the idea that it is a benevolent force whose goal is to produce ever more noble characteristics. But this is contrary to all of our scientific understanding. For example, it is said on these grounds that lust, in contrast to love-bonding, is "primitive" and hence morally inferior. Yet as we have seen, love-attachment is not an emotion that nature values for its own sake; its ultimate "purpose" is the same as that of lust, to help propagate the species or the genes. And both needs are very primitive indeed. Also once again, none of this implies there is no good or bad in nature—only that it is not to be identified through misunderstandings of nature like these.

Actually, many who do the "animalistic" and "dehumanizing" labeling are not even concerned about what their rhetoric literally means, only with its emotional impact. For them it is just a way of degrading other people whose sexual beliefs or proclivities differ from their own. Yet surely one who says "You're different from me, so you're just an animal" in matters of sexual needs and feelings is no less a bigot than one who reacts similarly in matters of race. These words are no less vicious than the charge that those with more body hair or darker skins ("more like animals") are lesser human beings. There is indeed degradation involved in differences over sexuality, but the shoe is precisely on the other foot. To add further irony, we might reflect on the fact that sexual aversion is produced in the first place by blind conditioning—a capacity humans share with the lowest sea slug. Humans have the ability to transcend such gut reactions by critical thinking, however; so if anyone is acting like a mere animal in this regard, it is those who fail to question their preprogrammed responses.

Another standard accusation against sexually explicit materials is that the persons portrayed in them are thereby treated "like objects." Now, what this is supposed to mean—or even whether it means anything at all— is not at all clear. The objectification charge has come to be repeated so ritualistically, without explanation, that it appears to have no more descriptive content than "son of a bitch": it expresses the speaker's anger or contempt but nothing more. After all, "sex object" sounds like a contradiction in terms: objects do not have sexuality, but people do. Of course, to charge angrily that pornography treats people as sexual *beings* would have no negative impact, so that is not said. Notice in this connection how seductively easy name-calling is. Anything can be made to sound awful by an appropriate choice of epithets. One might charge, for example, that in a love relationship, or a movie about one, human beings are treated as "emotional security blankets"—that to be loved is to be regarded as a "love object," no better than a child's teddy bear. Or it might be said that to expect sexual exclusivity from a mate is to treat him or her like private property, that is, like an object one possesses. Such claims would be no more mindless than the familiar rhetoric under discussion here.

Nevertheless, various things might be meant by the objectification charge; let us examine them to see if any are at all cogent. Sometimes what is intended is fetched pretty far. For example, there is the claim that since pornographic pictures (still photos, movies, etc.) are themselves objects, the persons portrayed in them are *ipso facto* regarded as objects by the viewer. Those who talk this way do not seem to consider that the same charge would apply equally well to pictures or even written descriptions of any *other* kind, including love stories: the latter too are only objects, not real human beings. It is also claimed that using such erotic items for one's own purposes is akin to treating the people portrayed in them as mere objects. With similar lack of reasoning, it might be alleged that a little girl's doll represents real people as passive objects to be used and manipulated. The same would be true of all those posters of pop stars that women pin up, or even photographs of loved ones, if there were any value at all in this argument.

At other times, what the object charge alludes to is that the reader or viewer does not personally know those depicted in sexual materials, or else that the sex portrayed is itself between strangers. Now, sex with a stranger is an extremely common fantasy of both men and women, and whirlwind romance with a stranger is *the* major love-story theme. Moreover, the models and actors of pornography are about as well known to the viewers as are the models and actors of nonerotic films and publications—there are even fan magazines for aficionados of X-rated movies. In any case, the claim here is that sex, even fantasy sex, with someone one does not already know intimately is "impersonal" or "depersonalized" and hence treats the other as an object rather than a person. That non sequitur evidently rests on an equivocation between the words "person" and "personal": the latter refers either to what is unique or to what is not publicly shared about an individual, the former to one's status as a human being. In this confused thinking, then, if one is not treated as a uniquely special person one is not treated as a person at all. The absurdity of the argument is also evident from the fact that it would render objectionable most *non*sexual interactions with other people, along with all other media presentations. Consider how bizarre it would be, for instance, to say that giving compassionate help to someone is depersonalizing, or that so doing treats the person as an object, if she or he is a stranger. If pornography *or* "casual" sex is to be condemned, it will have to be on more rational grounds than these.

At least part of the motive for all the talk about objects is the fact that the human body is involved, for it is, among other things, a physical object. And the portrayal of the body, hinting at or engaged in the physical activity of sex, is a central characteristic of pornography, while the arousal or satisfaction of desires toward the body is its raison d'etre. Hence, it seems pretty obvious that our long tradition of devaluing the physical body, and physical sex in particular, underlies this charge. But it is a serious and destructive error. Having a body is just as much a part of being a person as is having intelligence or emotions. Consequently, attraction to the former no more treats someone as a nonperson than does attraction to one of the latter. Since real objects have no sexuality, regarding a person as being *without* a sexual nature would come closer to treating him or her as a mere object. Once again, moreover, *being* attracted to the body is as completely human as being attracted in any other way. Some of those who use the "object" rhetoric sound as if they have been alienated from their own bodies, from an essential part of their nature as human beings.

In at least a mild way, disparagement of attraction to physical attributes is common in this society. We should be interested only in the personality of another individual, it is often averred, not in something as trivial as beauty. Those of us who have received much pleasure over the years in getting "looks" from the opposite sex see this as an attempt to deny one of the joys of life for both sexes. More frequently, it is merely said that physical attributes ought to be much less important to a person than the others. However, it is revealing to notice what the consequences would be if personality traits *were* the only strong source of attraction between individuals, say, things like intelligence, affectionateness, and sense of humor. Since both sexes display such qualities, there would be no reason to be attracted, erotically or otherwise, to one sex more than to the other. In other words, we would all be either asexual or bisexual! While there is nothing intrinsically wrong with being either one, the conclusion that being heterosexual is bad reveals the absurdities to which unthinking dogma often leads.

The crucial point is that how trivial or important something is cannot be settled by decree but depends on one's antecedently given needs. Of course, some of those needs are not always immediately apparent; *that* is why we must often be reminded of the real value of the less glamorous ones. But it is equally erroneous to deprecate the others. One common attempt to defend the anti-body claim points out that personality traits can last much longer than physical ones. This does not gainsay the value of the latter while they last, however, or the warm memories they can leave behind. (Being a ballerina or an Olympic star is seldom denigrated for existing only as long as youth does.) Sometimes the argument is given that we can change our personalities more than our appearances, making it unfair to the less attractive to value the latter. It is not at all clear that this is true, especially in an age of cosmetics and plastic surgery. The basic mistake of this point of view, however, is its assumption that one can freely pick and choose what kinds of things will attract one. We certainly have no more control over them than we do over how we look—unfortunate though either fact may be.

Actually, most of our ancient negative tradition about the body is dead and buried in the contemporary period, with its emphasis on beauty and bodily health; only the aversions toward sex linger on. The result is a glaring inconsistency of attitude, one that is revealed by the claim of objectification. For pictures of clothed people are no less pictures of bodies— the clothes themselves are mere inanimate objects. And video movies of, say, exercise classes (a bunch of "anonymous panting playthings"?) are just as much a focus on the physical body and its activities as is one involving sexual activity. But charges of treating people as objects are never raised against them. Though attraction to the body is considered less good than other sorts of interest, it usually is not seen as positively bad, much less as downright degrading, unless erotic excitement is involved. To realize how contradictory common thinking is on this matter, one has only to consider the general importance of warm physical contact in human life:

deprecatory remarks about the body are never made when the subject is the value of being held close. In a similar vein, a lover of things like painting and ballet would never grant that their purely physical nature makes them an unfitting source of gratification.

As for the gratification itself, a common belief about pleasure or satisfaction runs parallel to the attitude about the two types of things that produce them. Feelings and desires are likewise traditionally divided into two categories, those that are "merely physical" (e.g., sexual ones) and those that are emotional—the latter being claimed to be morally superior. This is also a confusion. One has only to reflect carefully on some of these other experiences to realize that they too are physical sensations; they are merely felt in a different part of the body, notably the face and chest. As was hinted earlier, moreover, *all* of our feelings are mediated by chemicals in the brain. There are ways to distinguish emotional feelings from others, but they are no less physical. Love and lust belong equally to the body and the soul. More to the point here, there is no reason to suppose the emotions are necessarily superior; on the contrary, things like hatred and envy are in the category of emotions. Along with the sharp dichotomy between humans and animals, the old myth of a noble soul trying to control a rebellious body is obsolete and obstructive of moral vision.

One particular type of emotional feelings, namely moral ones—those that reflect concern for the welfare of others—*are* in an important sense superior. They are superior to all the others, both "physical" and "nonphysical." But it does not follow that any of the other emotions or sensations are *bad*. Indeed, without those other feelings, the moral ones would not exist, for there would be nothing to feel concern *about*. On a closely related point, consider the familiar idea that the mind ought to control the desires of the body and also the emotions. The implication is that certain basic needs and feelings are more rational to have than others and hence are superior in that sense. But intellect by itself has no preferences about how to behave; unless there are desires or needs already given, it has no grounds for making any choices whatever about what is good and bad in life. Once again, real values are determined by how we are made. The legitimate intent of this mind-over-passions sentiment is that one should not just act on the needs and desires of the moment but should take account of others as well, over the long term. When all the confusions are cleared away, the arguments that desires in or toward the body are morally objectionable are found to be bankrupt.

Sometimes the objection raised is not to bodily attraction per se but to the visual focus on special areas of it. It is said, for example, that pornography reduces its subjects to a "collection of body parts." This is fatuous rhetoric. Interestingly, however, something like that description might apply to various things in the media.[1] Look through any of a great number of *non*erotic magazines, and you will find ads and articles featuring pictures of hair, ears, feet, hands, all by themselves. (They may be selling anklets or fungicide, or discussing the cause of lower back pain.) Yet they are rarely condemned for reducing people to their organs. Moreover, it is certainly not the case that displaying sex organs all by themselves is the point of pornography. Most males and a small minority of females are biologically primed to focus especially on them, but only as part of the wider bodily *gestalt*. The face is another body part, it should be noticed, and special attraction to it is universal.

The real reason for attacking the showing of sex organs seems clear, namely, that they alone among body parts are considered shameful. Ironically, in fact, it is the traditional aversion to nudity that comes closest to fitting the derogatory description under discussion. By decreeing that only certain body parts may be shown or appreciated, it divides them off from the rest; it prevents us from enjoying our whole selves. In any case, the point remains that the biologically healthy attraction to certain areas of the body is not degrading to anyone. Another analogy should be helpful here. All of us find certain things about a given individual's character or personality more interesting or exciting than others, say, the person's wit or flair or intelligence or charm. No one would charge that the latter type of focused attention carves a person into pieces.

This leads us to another way of interpreting the "object" charge, one that clearly is intended by some who make it. It is not the fact that pornography displays or describes bodies and bodily activities, but that they are *all* it presents, that is supposed to "objectify" those involved. Pornography treats people as if they were *"nothing but* sexual objects," the claim is often worded. Similar charges abound. Pornography presents a "one-dimensional view of life," it is said; it "reduces its subjects to their bodies and their physical appetites rather than treating them as whole human beings," or else it "carries the tacit message that sex is all they're good for." Now it is quite true that most pornography has a very limited scope; it contains little else besides sex. (To some, in fact, that is a defining characteristic of it.) This is partly because overt sexuality has traditionally been excluded from socially respectable portrayals of human experience; it has been driven out into a realm by itself. In any event, it does not follow from its limited content that pornography treats its subjects as if they were nothing but sexual entities.

The illegitimacy of this new charge is once again revealed by the fact that no similar claim is or can be made in analogous cases. All of our media presentations to a greater or lesser degree are specialized in their content. From sporting events to symphonies, they portray a "one-dimensional view of life" indeed—and many people spend an awful lot of their time enjoying such things. Yet is there anything wrong with that? Among the periodicals are magazines specializing in sports, food, romance, en-

tertainment, hobbies, fashion. Shall we say such publications do not portray
people as whole human beings? Do fashion magazines, to mimic some of
the purpler prose we hear denouncing pornography, turn their models into
human mannequins or a bunch of clothing racks? For that matter, do
traditional movies and novels, which scrupulously avoid frank eroticism,
deny our completeness by ignoring *that* important aspect of us? Human
wholeness in no way precludes focusing on one aspect of ourselves at a
time. If there is some *special* reason why sex should only be portrayed in
combination with other things, moreover, this argument again fails to give
it. Fallacious arguments about personhood aside, these parallel cases also
reveal that many who complain pornography portrays nothing but sex
would find its explicitness offensive regardless of the rest of the content;
for some that objection is only a pretext.

Underlying this last charge against pornography, very often, is the wider
one that sexual desire toward another person, or even mutually between
persons, is "objectifying" unless certain other sorts of feeling are present
as well. The status of this claim as a rationalization is also clear. We never
hear the converse claim that desiring another's companionship but not his
or her sexuality treats that individual as less than a whole person, even
though the interest is no less partial. More generally, that certain aspects
of an individual should be of special or sole interest to someone does not
mean that person has no other human worth. Shall we say that students
treat a professor as a mere intellect object, devoid of other human attributes, because their only reason for coming to her or him is to learn about,
say, history or logic? Does their limited interest mean they think he or she
is good for only that? Only ideologically induced blindness leads people
to say such things in a sexual context.

It is instructive to consider one specific example of the "whole person"
charge. (From Beatrice Faust's *Women, Sex and Pornography*. Overall,
Faust's treatment of the subject is unusually level headed and well informed.) Contrasting the similar scenes of men watching a stripper and
young women getting excited over a rock music star, the writer says, "Men
react impersonally to the stripper's body and sexual aura; girls react to the
pop star as a person, not as a sexy body." Aside from its standard confusion
of being personal with being a person, even the distinction this statement
makes regarding the former is spurious. Male celebrities commonly report
that before they achieved that status they got no special attention from
women, yet they haven't changed *as persons*. Nor is there anything particularly personal about the star's highly contrived aura or stage persona;
the young women are excited by the artificial image and high status of an
individual they have never even met. In fact, one's body is clearly more
unique and intrinsic to one's self than status and fame; it is *more* personal.
The important point here, however, is that there is nothing disrespectful

about the reaction to the star *or* to the stripper. Neither in any intelligent sense treats him or her as other than a complete human being.

CLAIMS OF CALLOUSNESS AND EXPLOITATION

One more thing could be meant, and manifestly is often meant, by the claim that pornography treats people as objects. It is that those who enjoy such presentations do not care about the welfare of the subjects portrayed, about the fact that they are beings with feelings, not just objects. Only one thing is to be said in response to this charge: it is a vicious libel. Sometimes the allegation involves a deceitful conflation of "the interest is in the body" with "the person is seen as being *only* a body, an unfeeling thing." In any case, the conclusion is grotesque. Sexual desire, including its expressions involving pornography, represents a need, not an attitude; and there is nothing intrinsically uncaring about a need—though of course, any desire can be accompanied by callous attitudes or pursued in a callous way. Part of what animates the opposition to "uncommitted" sex, hence to pornography, is the idea that it is necessarily devoid of warmth and friendliness. Now, *any* sort of human interaction fitting this latter description is certainly bad. But it does not correctly describe that kind of sex in general, not in reality and not in fantasy. The extent to which it does, moreover, is largely the result of the shame and furtiveness born out of this culture's antisexualism.

On the part of some, the error in this attitude seems to lie in confusing romantic love with human love; they pretend that feeling sexual desire without the former sort of emotional involvement simply *is* being cold and uncaring. (Interestingly, repeated surveys have revealed that a majority of married people no longer feel they love their spouses. That means an awful lot of socially legitimate sex is loveless.) Now, human love is the essence of morality, whereas romantic attachment is only one need or desire among many. For a person who feels the latter yearning, it is important that the need be met. Nevertheless, it is no more inherently noble than any other interpersonal need. The truth in this matter is, in fact, just the reverse of what has been charged. It is those who despise the sexual and emotional makeup of others—their greater need for sex, greater emotional independence, or both—who reveal a lack of caring and human concern. The hateful charge that a person regards others as objects treats him as if he had no feelings—as if he were nothing but an object.

If one does not care about the feelings of others, of course, one is apt to take what one wants from them. This leads us to an accusation that often accompanies that of callousness. Sexual presentations, it is said, "exploit" their subjects; the latter are simply "used" for the gratification of one's own selfish desires. Once again, the underlying attitudes here transcend the specific issue of pornography. Of all the things that people desire for themselves, and all the ways in which they wish to satisfy needs through or get pleasure from others, it is uniquely the sexual ones that are regarded in this culture as selfish and exploitive. This has become such a kneejerk response, in fact, that people do not even stop to ask whether or not the charge is appropriate. Let us therefore remind ourselves of the meanings of these words. In its most basic sense, to use or exploit something is simply to make it a means to a desired end, for example, to exploit natural resources for human benefit. In this sense, people in any sort of relationship use each other: I use a sales clerk to get goods and he or she uses me to obtain money; two friends use each other to get the pleasure of another's company. Under this meaning, pornography exploits the people it portrays, or sex itself, no differently than a television program such as *The Waltons* exploits families or family life.

But to use/exploit someone in the negative sense must involve more than this; it means getting something from him or her in a way that is knowingly hurtful or unfair. Whatever else may be good or bad about the situation, if it is consensual and equally beneficial, it is not exploitive. Similar remarks may be made about the much misused word "selfish." *All* the things that attract one person to another, after all, are things that give one pleasure or satisfy one's own needs. In other words, what one values in another person is that which will do something for the *self*. (Nor would the other party have it any other way; no healthy person wants to be the recipient of mere charity.) This fact alone does not make those desires bad, however. To be selfish is to feel or act out of concern *only* for oneself, not others. While there is nothing morally noble about wanting to satisfy one's own needs or desires (be they for sex, love, friendship, or anything else), there is nothing inherently *ig*noble about it either. It often happens, of course, that two people's needs are not well matched, so that they cannot both get what they want from the other. But this unfortunate situation is not the fault of either, and it does not by itself make the wants of either one of them selfish.

To illustrate the inconsistency of common attitudes in this regard, consider something one observes not infrequently: a woman's eyes lighting up at the sight of a cute baby in a magazine or on TV. "Oh, what a darling little thing!" she may say, focusing intently. She is getting pleasure for herself from the visual experience, and perhaps fantasizing getting pleasure from a real child. Is this being selfish or exploitive? Does it mean she regards babies as mere objects for her gratification? Of course not. Indeed, her desires include *sharing* pleasure with the infant of her fantasy. Yet it is no different from this, for normal persons, in the sexual enjoyment of others—whether in fantasy or in real life. Sexual desire is fundamentally a desire for mutual pleasure; nothing is any more gratifying, or more sexually exciting, than to have one's erotic interest returned. It is therefore hardly surprising that the commonest theme of male-oriented erotic movies is that of women who are uninhibited in seeking sex. She wants him the same way he wants her! Its appeal rests precisely on the fact that it makes the need and pleasure equal and mutual.

To be sure, attempts to satisfy sexual needs can and often do employ exploitive means. (This seems to be less common in sex-positive cultures, where satisfying such needs is much less difficult. To a degree, at least, the attitude that sex is exploitive is a self-fulfilling prophecy.) People with unmet needs will often settle for less than the mutual ideal, but this is true of all other strong desires as well, including romantic love—as is made plain by the scheming manipulations so often engaged in by jealous or insecure spouses and lovers.[2] If any emotion deserved to be called *inherently* selfish, it would be jealousy, with its distress at the thought of the other person sharing pleasure with someone else. Yet it too is a legitimate emotional need; it is merely exaggerated to an unhealthy degree in this society. In fact, it is germane to point out here that false moral charges are themselves used in the selfish manipulation of other persons. If some can convince others that the latter's desires are ignoble, they can more easily get what they want instead. This motive seems to underlie a lot of negative attitudes involving sexuality; the reader should keep it in mind as we continue.

In the case of pornography, certain special exploitation arguments are commonly employed. Sometimes sexually frank performances and materials are called exploitive even if all those directly involved enjoy their experience. The grounds are that being inadvertently exposed to such things or even just knowing they exist offends the deep feelings of others; evidently it is these other people, or people in general, who are thought of as being exploited this time. "Sex is sacred and personal," it is often said; "its privacy should not be violated." A case for not exposing the unwilling can certainly be made, but as the mixed-race-couple analogy employed earlier reveals, these third-party arguments are often tinged with hypocrisy. It is the censors who want to invade the personal lives of others, to tell them what they may participate in making or what they may use even in private.

More to the point, it is difficult to see why we should not apply the same reasoning to many other things. Does *The Waltons* invade family privacy? (What could be more sacred or personal than that?) Such comparisons make it clear that sex and nudity are covered up because they are considered shameful, not because they are perceived as sacred.[3] Feelings of shame are the reason sex is regarded as private and personal, not the other way around. Moreover, those conditioned feelings have no more ultimate claim on our moral values than any other taboos we have inherited. Even with these emotions as they now are, however, the argument is fallacious. Both drama and psychology texts lay bare the most personal of human affairs;

but what they expose can be highly rewarding for everyone involved. What *is* apt to be bad is invading the privacy of individuals in real life, in contrast to consenting staged portrayals. Consider the television cameras staring brazenly at a grief-stricken couple as they watch their daughter die in the explosion of *Challenger: that* is obscene.

The notion of exploitation also appears in a different sort of claim, one involving the commercial aspect of most pornography. The idea that making money by portraying sex is illegitimate has become so common that the term "sexploitation movie" is recognized by everyone. We hear nothing about commercial exploitation of the family, however, even though programs like *The Cosby Show* make a lot of money. "Porn makes profit from women's bodies!" shouts one slogan. And the construction industry makes money from the bodies of men—what does *that* tell us? Actors and models of every other type perform their services for pay, and create profits for their employers, to almost no one's dismay. No reason why sex should be so different in this regard is ever given. In a similar vein, the buying of sexual materials is often equated with the buying of sex itself. Selling such things, it is charged, turns an intimate act into a mere commodity, and the persons portrayed, into objects of purchase. Yet we never hear it said that spending money to read or watch love stories, with the vicarious emotional experience they provide, makes a commodity of love, or that buying *non*-sexual depictions is tantamount to buying the people in them.

Sex is said to be likewise besmirched when erotic portrayals appear in periodicals that are full of advertising for consumer goods. This ignores the fact that magazines on any other subject are also loaded with such ads. In sponsoring programs like *The Cosby Show,* big business is using the family as a means for the selling of goods, and yet no one complains. Something that, arguably, *is* objectionable is the attempt to sell things by associating them directly in people's minds with sex—or with love, friendship, or anything else people find desirable. This tactic of mental association is standard in advertising these days, but it is rather far removed from our central concern. Since it is by no means used only with sex, it will not be pursued here. Notice one thing well, however: adorning some product with a handsome, high-status, or high-competence male is "using sex to sell" no less than is doing so with a voluptuous, scantily clad female.

One last charge of exploitation specifically involves those who are paid to appear in pornographic portrayals. The claim this time is that they are often forced by their economic circumstances into doing so, and that this amounts to their being taken unfair advantage of. By analogy, a law that allowed the sale of body organs from living donors might be said to exploit the desperation of the poor. An argument of this kind has value only if it has already been established that the activity in question is painful or harmful to the participants. Otherwise, offering *any* job to an unemployed person would have to be considered exploitive. But that has not been done;

indeed, it has been argued here that any distress felt by those consensually making pornography is the product of prior antisexual attitudes, not of some sort of vileness innate to the activity. As a matter of fact, however, most of the participants do not find the work distressing. In a world where most people toil at back-breaking or mind-numbing jobs that they hate, many in the "sex industry" find theirs rewarding and enjoyable. Ironically, many more would consider such employment attractive were it not for antisexual attitudes fostered by the very people who lay charges like this one, which is evidently part of what the latter are afraid of.

The rhetoric about individuals being economically "forced" into such work is also ironic. (Those who produce the portrayals are never allowed the excuse that poverty made them do it.) For the people who employ the argument are out to eliminate porn, thereby denying those who want that kind of work any choice in the matter—and "forcing" them, by its own premises, to accept lower wages or unemployment instead. At the very most, this often heard objection is an argument against poverty, not one against pornography. Let us give aid and support to the poor and allow them to make their own choices. The reader should be aware that similar responses can be given to standard charges against prostitution, though that is another complex subject. Notice also that the last three objections to pornography are not directed at sexual explicitness per se. They belong to a category of charges that involve particular types of sexual portrayal, or of conditions surrounding it, which are or are alleged to be fairly common. We will be seeing much more of that sort of claim from this point on.

NONMORAL OBJECTIONS

In addition to claims that it is immoral, pornography is frequently accused of being inherently bad in other ways. For instance, it is said that explicit sex is "ugly" or "not really erotic." Beyond the failure to realize how fully mere conditioning is responsible for their aesthetic reactions, what these speakers reveal is their ego-centeredness.[4] "My tastes, the tastes of my group, are true and beautiful; what turns me on is genuinely erotic. But as for you . . . " To be sure, much of the content of explicitly sexual literature and movies traditionally produced would seem inferior to the tastes of nearly everyone; they are very cheaply made. Clearly, though, this is an artifact of the low level of social acceptability of really explicit pornography. If it were even as "respectable" as media violence has always been (consider the high levels of both artistic excellence and brutality in, say, *Hill Street Blues*), much more of it would be produced by those who make quality films and magazines, as is already the case for mildly and implicitly sexual productions.

Many detractors of pornography deplore its inferiority to real sex. (What else is new?) For example, they decry the sad tawdriness of the peep-show parlors. In this they are partly right, though perhaps not in the way they think. There you will often find men who are painfully shy or sexually inhibited, men whom women regard as unattractive or as losers, military men cut off from other sources of female companionship, men who are physically or psychologically impaired, old and middle-aged men whose biological cravings defy social dogma by yearning for young women, young men whose female acquaintances do not want sex, and so on. The things they all have in common are a powerful need and an inability, temporary or long term, to get "the real thing." So they accept a poor substitute, a commercial fantasy. (And it is said that *they* are exploiters—exploiters of the women who make money from their plight!) Sad and tawdry indeed. What is amazing is not the indifference foes of pornography show to that suffering, for "Let them eat cake" is often the attitude of those not in need toward those who are. Nor is it their failure to grant that a poor substitute is better than nothing at all. It is the tacit or explicit message that somehow pornography is the cause of the sad situation. Like many another social epiphenomenon, it gets the blame for problems whose real source lies in nature or in the structure of society.

Another familiar objection to pornography in general is that it is not true to life; it does not present people's sexual behavior as it actually is. This claim is largely correct, at least as regards usual behavior in our own culture. But some of the reasons for that lack of realism lie in the social conditions under which it has had to be produced. These include such things as the poor writing and acting that characterize low-budget productions and the fact that, once again, much porn has been made by people on the fringes of society, many of whom are themselves rather ignorant about human sexuality. Even so, lack of realism also characterizes most other fiction, from adventure stories to romance novels. Just consider all those happy endings, for example, where justice always triumphs and true love lasts forever. To one degree or another, fiction is always idealized. Moreover, it can hardly be said that typical pornography is less realistic than other genres. Just how true to life are all those traditional books and movies that never portray sex at all, in spite of its importance in real life? How realistic is, say, the charming but sexless and raceless world of *Mayberry, R.F.D.?*

In fact, a major reason why people enjoy fantasy in the first place is precisely that it is different from, and an improvement upon, real life. It represents life as they wish it were. This leads us to another antipornography charge, that it is "propaganda," a claim about how everyone should behave sexually. In truth, it is the antipornography ideologues who want to lay down such rules for everyone. Most sexually frank productions merely reflect their creators' own preferences or else what they, perhaps quite mistakenly, regard as the tastes of certain others. To the extent that such depictions do attempt to influence preferences, they are again no different from many other media portrayals. The selective attention involved in yet another standard argument against pornography reveals yet again that its motivation is not what it pretends to be.

The supply of arguments for the badness of sexual explicitness goes on and on, but the foregoing are common and representative.[5] And they are all worthless. The fact is that all the standard arguments against pornography in itself are logical fallacies of one kind or another. That such patent rationalizations have been convincing to so many is a testament to the power of socialization, once again. It is very, very difficult even to recognize the real sources of, much less to consciously overcome, the beliefs one has been indoctrinated with and the feelings one has been conditioned to have; they seem so natural, so obviously right. But the price humanity has always had to pay for such blindness is a terrible one. Summoning the will to be honest in this regard is not only the moral thing but the only intelligent thing to do, for the sake of the welfare of all—as we shall continue to see.

4

Pornography and Women

A very important aspect of the charges against pornography has so far gone unmentioned. Sexual portrayals are often said, not just to be degrading to their subjects (and consumers), but more specifically to degrade women, to "objectify" and "exploit" females. This attitude too is part of a traditional belief, one that sees openness about sexuality in general as degrading to women; it is the "Please—there are ladies present!" mentality. Women were supposed to be too pure and noble to be subjected to anything so crass and ugly as sex. To some extent, this view was buried during the "sexual revolution." It was never buried very deep, however, and concerted efforts are being made to bring it back. Here again the multitude of voices makes a full analysis impossible, but we can at least survey the salient issues.

FEMINIST OPPOSITION

Of course, the resurgent religious fundamentalists and other traditionalists are pushing in this direction. However, here they have what otherwise might seem an unlikely ally, namely feminism. For one familiar example of the influence of the latter movement, the term "sexist" is often virtually synonymous with "sexually oriented"; it includes even appreciative remarks about someone's physical attractiveness. As for the specific matter of pornography, certain branches of feminism have come to see fighting it as one of their major concerns. It has been argued here that there is nothing in the least degrading about any degree of sexual explicitness, to women or to anyone else. But the ongoing campaign to associate it with the genuine evils women have traditionally suffered is an ideological distortion of the first magnitude. The battle for equal rights and equal dignity for the sexes, which all moral individuals must support, does not in any way justify this degradation-of-women claim against pornography.

It seems quite clear that the most fundamental source of feminist views about pornography and women is the sex-negative conditioning we all have received, but which females receive in greater degrees. This is evident partly from the statements of those who hold them, statements which often reveal the inability to imagine that any normal human being could fail to feel disgust and shame at sexual explicitness. But as feminists themselves stress in the context of discussing our conditioned gender roles, we should not allow entrained emotions to blind us to what is genuinely moral and immoral. Furthermore, by no means have all women succumbed to anti-sexual socialization. Indeed, not all feminists have done so. Certain of the latter label themselves "pro-sex" feminists and have vigorously opposed the others' retention of traditional sexual attitudes, including those involving pornography. Some of the most effective opposition to recent efforts at censorship in the United States has come from such women, notably from the scholars and scientists of the Feminist Anti-Censorship Taskforce.

So the presumptuous claim that women in general feel degraded by pornography is just not true. Not only that, but as has been mentioned before, many women enjoy sexually explicit presentations themselves. Video dealers have consistently reported that most of those renting X-rated movies are women and couples.[1] Evidently it is the new opportunity to view porn videos in the comfort and anonymity of their own homes, without fear of censure, that has finally disinhibited many women regarding them. Although most women prefer materials that are more romantic and less explicit, some pornography designed by and for women is very similar to that made for men (for example, magazines like *Eidos* and the whimsical lesbian periodical *On Our Backs*). On the other hand, the persistent charge that "real women hate pornography" could become a self-fulfilling prophecy if it promotes this society's slide back to the even greater sexual shame of the past.

A second factor that seemingly influences the attitudes of some feminist and non-feminist women toward pornography lies in the fear most women feel about sexual assault, especially those who have been assaulted. This can make anything that is sexual anxiety-promoting. To those who experience such broad anxieties, only sex surrounded by the greatest warmth and security is reassuring; the brassiness and casualness of the sex in most pornography can thus have a most unsettling effect on them, even if it contains no elements of coercion at all. The response that follows must not be understood as in any way belittling women's fears, which have been ignored much too often in the past. Nevertheless, to allow such emotions to influence beliefs about pornography is the wrong thing to do, for the existence of violent sex in no way impugns nonviolent sex or its portrayal.

Consider an analogy. A person who is attacked by a member of a different racial group is likely to have aversive feelings around other members of that group later on. If the victim is wise, however, he or she will respond intellectually in this manner: "It is natural for me to feel this emotion, but it does not represent knowledge that these other people are evil. They are not to blame for the actions of someone else." The alleged evidence that nonviolent pornography somehow incites sexual assault will be discussed later; the reaction described here has nothing to do with evidence. It is merely a case of psychological conditioning, which will be recognized as such by honest men and women. Those who are not honest often play on women's fear of sexual assault, thereby increasing their trauma, in order to promote an ideological position regarding sexuality, including pornography. Such persons are contemptible. As will be discussed in the next chapter, they have been working hard to associate sexual portrayals with violence in the minds of the general public. Much of the anxiety triggered in some women by sexual frankness must be blamed on these efforts.

Of course, there are special sources of the feminist opposition to sexual explicitness, amplifying the original one or two. One of these finds expression in the charge that pornography treats women as "nothing but sex objects." What the claim seems to reflect in this context is anger over the fact that women have been highly restricted in their social position and life opportunities. In the past females were largely limited to the roles of sex partner and mother. Hence women were not valued as much as men, by the society or by themselves, for their intelligence, emotional strength, creativity, or other virtues not closely tied to these two callings. Only for such attributes as beauty and nurturance have they been highly acclaimed. What has seemingly happened, then, is this: the roles that have been allowed to women in the past have been aversively associated in the minds of many with those they have been denied; the former have become symbols of the latter. Consequently, emphasis on female sexual desirability to males has come to be seen as something bad in itself. (Similarly for nurturance: "breeding machine" is the rhetorical counterpart of "sex object" vis-à-vis the motherhood role. But the antichildbirth feminist talk of earlier years has disappeared, as it has come to be realized how many women really want children.)

Now, this sort of guilt by association is a familiar part of human thinking, something to which anyone might succumb. The fact remains, however, that it is utterly fallacious; indeed, such reasoning is potentially very harmful. Like wishful thinking and conclusion-jumping, it is something we must constantly resist. To the point here, the only intelligent way for women to cease being regarded as nothing but sexual beings is to be seen as other things *as well*. It would accomplish nothing for them to be seen as not *even* being sexual creatures—as not being anything at all! Women *are* sexual beings, after all; hence it is not misrepresenting so to portray them. And the oft-hinted charge that only women are singled out as sexual beings by pornography is simply false. Men are portrayed as sexual no less than women; it could hardly be otherwise, given that eroticism normally involves two sexes. Though, even if the charge were true, it would constitute sexism against women only if sex is something bad; if sex is good, it would be discriminatory against men.

What about the objection that in portraying little else but sexual attractiveness and behavior, pornographic magazines and movies convey the message that that is all women are good for? As answered in the preceding chapter, there is no such message. It would be foolish to suggest that the media try to depict anyone as being all things at once, say, to insist that a magazine about knitting show women doing all sorts of other things as well. Moreover, its very lack of nonsexual content means that pornography tends to portray neither sex as more important in all the other aspects of life. Yet there is a serious problem in the media in general, which even today sometimes portray women as one-dimensional creatures. For example, in the "chaste" but violent movie *Indiana Jones and the Temple of Doom,* the female lead is an empty-headed adornment whose only purpose is evidently to reward the male hero for successfully defeating other males. We have feminists to thank for raising our consciousness to this problem, but it has nothing special to do with sexual portrayals. The solution lies in continuing to press for a reasonable balance, over all the media *as a whole,* of depicting women in a great variety of roles, with a great variety of human qualities, interests, and abilities.

It is true that pornography is primarily a male interest and also, as a consequence, that the specific kinds of sexual themes it contains are largely those that appeal to males. (More details as we continue.) This is hardly an objection to it—remember those romance novels for women. But it is also hardly inevitable. The laws of the marketplace decree that a larger female interest in sexual portrayals would change their content—a process that has already begun in the case of video movies. In any event, this brings us to a second special influence on feminists' beliefs about pornography. In the eyes of many of them, virtually all differences between the sexes are bad; the ideal of gender equality requires strict sameness. In particular, some find the dissimilarities in regard to sexuality threatening. Since to them "different" implies "inferior," and since they would not say it is women who are inferior, it is the feelings of males that they attack. As an expression of this type of sexuality, pornographic performances and representations naturally become the target of their anger.

There is a legitimate concern here, but also a fundamental error. On the one hand, differences often make it difficult for people to understand one another, and they can lead to conflicts and inequities. On the other hand, many dissimilarities are harmless, or even salutary. One does not have to deny the existence of skin color in order to oppose racism. (And like rejecting the value of the physical, denying the worth of differences between the sexes leads to the absurdity that being heterosexual is evil.) Indeed, equality in the morally significant sense often requires that people be treated differently in order for those with different needs to be equally fulfilled. Here again, fallacious association seems to be the reason why all gender differences are found threatening. The fact that many such differences in the past have been detrimental to women has given some people feelings of suspicion toward all the others as well. At least, this motive seems reflected in many feminist statements. Whatever may be the latter's motivations regarding gender differences in general, the sexual ones are indeed threatening to many women, including nonfeminists. Since the resulting conflicts are so significant to the issue of pornography, we must now take a closer look at them.

CONFLICTS OVER SEXUAL DIFFERENCES

Let us first consider the visual attraction of males to female bodies and sex organs, which is a crucial reason for both male attraction to pornography and female objections to it. Unless one were to hold the grotesque view (as some appear to) that sexual arousal to bodily appearance is evil while sexual arousal to bodily touch is not, the most that could be said in this regard is that it is unfortunate men's and women's sources of such arousal are not more alike. Even that is surely not true, however. In the present respect, be it remembered, the evidence is clear that nature originally gave males and females complementary rather than identical erotic feelings. This difference between them need not be a source of conflict but can instead be one of pleasure for both sexes. The real cause of problems here is the cultural inculcation of bodily shame. As Friday and other women writers have suggested, the basic reason many object to pornography is the deep-laid belief that their sex organs are unclean.

Even so, given those reactions, a woman or man exposed to same-sex nudity can be caused to feel personally shamed and vulnerable. Fortunately, such feelings can be overcome. Just as there are former porn stars (such as Linda Lee Tracy) who claim to have seen the light about the defiling nature of explicit nudity, there are other women (such as erotic artist Betty Dodson) who report it was precisely through pornography that they came to appreciate the wholesome beauty of their entire bodies.[2] There is certainly no obligation for any given person to try to overcome these emotions, even though it would be wise. Others should respect the sensitivities of those who feel them, just as the latter should respect the feelings of those who do *not*. Nonetheless, it is a serious mistake for society to keep on reinforcing bodily shame. The reason is simply the perennial pain and conflict they cause, both within individuals and between men and women. When blind superstition collides with natural needs, everyone gets hurt.

Sometimes, the complaint against pornography is not really about the display of sex organs, or even about the attraction to the body in general, but concerns its idealization. The women of, say, *Playboy* have faces and figures that the average woman cannot match, it is said; hence comparison with them can only make her feel inferior and insecure. (Harsher versions, such as "Porn says a woman is worthless if she's not young and beautiful," are rhetorical falsehoods like others already discussed and so will be ignored here.) Feminists' concern in this regard has been heightened because, in our culture and most others, physical attractiveness is considered more important for a woman than for a man. This means that lack of beauty can be a special source of distress to women. It is also a source of special pleasure for some; in fact, a lot of men wish women would show more excitement over male looks than they do. Nevertheless, the problem is real. Is it a legitimate objection to pornography?

The problem is obviously not an objection to the nudity involved; at best it argues for greater variety in the women recruited. (Those portrayed in hard-core porn are typically of no better than average appearance.) That evidently would fail to satisfy many who voice these concerns, for they do not make such charges with equal force against similar idealizations elsewhere in the media and the culture. For example, the children on TV family shows are nearly always cute and charming. Then there are all the attractive women in other kinds of media portrayals, such as women's fashion magazines. And how is the average man to feel when he compares himself with the male stars of movies, popular music, and so on? He certainly cannot match their looks, status, and glamour. Male anxieties involving competence, like those of females regarding beauty, are largely the result of the opposite sex's idealizations. On a related matter, it is revealing that in a society where women spend billions on cosmetics and other things to improve their appearance and where portrait photographers often use the airbrush or other techniques to the same end, *Playboy* alone is routinely excoriated for touching up its models' pictures. We do not see stretch marks and cellulite on those in women's publications either, including *Ms.* magazine.

However, the fundamental point for our purposes is that the media, and especially pornography's small corner, do not create this tendency to idealize. They evidently influence the types of things found most appealing, within limits, but that does not alter the fact that humans find some things more beautiful than others. Every culture has its standards of physical attractiveness, causing those who fall short in one way or another to feel inadequate. The problem will exist whether or not there is soft-core pornography, for attractive faces and figures can be seen nearly anywhere. As for the problem's stronger impact on women, that is the result of their traditionally not being allowed (or required, it might be added) to excel at other things. Women's overconcern with their appearance in this culture stems largely from its having been their main asset. The problem must be solved by ensuring that women have other sources of personal pride, not by trying to deny the value of physical beauty to human beings.

Now let us turn to another sexual difference, the stronger desire for sex that male interest in pornography reflects. This too seems to be partially innate—or more correctly, perhaps, females' sex "drive" is more easily repressed or prevented from developing fully. *This* difference between the sexes is not complementary, not inherently benign. It is a chronic source of conflict. But there is nothing in that unfortunate fact to suggest that either way of being made is morally superior to the other, or that either way *by itself* is bad. To the point here, the expression of needs and desires in fictional portrayals is not somehow made objectionable by the fact that the needs and desires of others are different. Male-oriented erotic productions are no more degrading to women than, say, the romance movies and novels that so many women dote on are degrading to men. There is no more justification for telling men to stop having so much sexual interest in women than to demand that women feel *more* sexual excitement over *men*.

It must not be forgotten, however, that this conflict too is largely if not completely the product of anti-erotic training. The repression of female sexuality in this society has been deplored by many women, including the pro-sex feminists, who see overcoming it as an essential part of the emancipation of their gender.[3] The feeling that females are degraded by sexual openness, that sex is something they give up rather than something they get for themselves, that strong desire for it is unnatural or unwholesome in a woman—all these beliefs, they hold, have harmed women greatly. Learned shame and disgust have not only denied them much of the pleasure of sex; they have also made the experience joyless and even traumatic for countless women in the past. Progress has been made in changing this in recent decades, though sex-negative feelings still claim many victims. Of special relevance to our subject is the fact that greater sexual openness in all the media during that time has helped produce the change, narrowing the eroticism gap between men and women. Those who denounce sexual frankness in the name of gender equality are worse than sadly mistaken; they are hurting their own cause.

The foregoing has prepared us to consider another objection some feminists and traditionalists raise against pornography, namely, that the women it depicts are usually sexually assertive and uninhibited. This misrepresents women's real nature, it is claimed. (In its nastier, sloganized form, the charge is "Porn lies.") It is true that the women of pornography are usually idealized in this second way as well. That, however, is largely what fantasies are for—to imagine things as being better, vis-à-vis someone's desires, than is the case in his or her real life. Women in pornography are sexually uninhibited because that is the sort of women the men and boys who seek it out fantasize about already. Women also create fictional men matching *their* ideals in their fantasies; female-oriented love stories portray men tailored to those special longings. To demand that fiction simply mirror current realities, sexual or otherwise, is absurd. In fact, such demands themselves tacitly ask us to misrepresent an important fact about human beings: the nature of their fantasy lives.

The crucial point here is this: it is false that male-oriented erotic stories "stereotype" women *in general* as being like their uninhibited women. As a wish rather than a claim of fact, they do not make assertions about women in general in the first place, any more than a romantic movie with Robert Redford says all men are like *that*. Heterosexual pornography no more tells the "lie" that all women are promiscuous than gay porn tells the "lie" that all men are homosexual. (It is clear enough who the real liars are.) Indeed, patrons of pornography often seek it out precisely *because* the women they know are not like that; it is obvious to them and nearly everyone else that standard sexual materials do not even pretend to describe the everyday world. Even so, there is a sense in which pornography is refreshingly truthful. The women of many cultures *have* had the enthusiasm for sex of those it usually portrays; this fact suggests it is not erotic presentations but our society that "distorts female sexuality." Indeed, one could say that by traditionally avoiding overt eroticism, the mainstream media have stereotyped women and men alike as *non*sexual. The frankness and disinhibition of pornography perhaps help to make our total picture of ourselves *more* honest, and more true to our real selves as sexual beings.

Part of the conflict between men and women over sex has its origin in another unfortunate difference between their desires, namely, those involving love and long-term commitment. That on average females feel a greater need in these respects has already been noted; young men especially are interested less in love and permanence. As was also mentioned in Chapter 1, there are indications that even this difference is partly the product of culture. If so, however, it involves structural features of the society, features that may be much harder to change than attitudes toward sex. In any event, that further difference in needs is also a serious source of conflict and misunderstanding. The net result of the two gender differences (the one involving sexual "drive" and that involving love) is that one winds up being pitted against the other. Consequently, many women regard sex as a threat to love and commitment. It is not difficult to see how all this affects attitudes toward pornography, at least unconsciously: its commitment-free sex symbolizes their difficulties in getting what they need from men. Anything that affirms sex to be valuable for its own sake is apt to be found threatening. Indeed, the love-lust conflict appears to be a major source of sex-negative attitudes among women, second only to their antisexual raising. And each of the two influences reinforces the other.

It is not at all clear, however, that such fears are justified. Blaming lust for lack of interest in love represents yet another case of guilt by association, rather than genuine knowledge of a causal link between the two. There is no reason to believe that suppression of the one need in men liberates a need for the other, even though it certainly may influence their behavior. On the contrary, it is precisely the inability to fulfill a desire that makes it loom large in one's consciousness. What is true is that if getting either sex or love is made a precondition for giving the other, a conflict is created. That sort of bargaining, alas, occurs constantly on both sides. Perhaps it is inevitable, at least to some extent. Perhaps male and female needs cannot be made to match up perfectly; nature does some things like that. (See Donald Symons's book regarding conflicting evolutionary "strategies.") If this is so, however, it is not the fault of either side. The problem of being unable to get what one needs from the opposite sex is mutual.

Unfortunately, that is not the standard response; people blame one another for the problem. Much of the hostility that exists between men and women is because each side is trying to punish the other for failing to meet its own expectations. The fair way to negotiate would be to say, "Others' needs are as important to them as mine are to me, but *this* is what *I* must have." Instead, both sexes use manipulative devices. One that is employed mostly by women is particularly relevant to our issues: minimizing the value of sex in order to enhance that of companionship and love. The more trivial or ignoble a woman portrays sex to be, the better her needs appear in comparison; the more of an imposition on her she can make it the more she can demand in return. (Though that is apt to take a toll on her own capacity to enjoy sex.) So this is a major reason why very many women, and many men as well, denounce strong sexual desire, along with low desire for long-term companionship or affection, as immoral or emotionally defective ("animalistic," "shallow," "immature," "exploitive," and so on and so on). In other words, the familiar charges against things that are more characteristic of male sexuality are in part an attempt to gain advantage in the "battle of the sexes."

They are not just directed against men, of course. It is harder to withhold sex in order to get emotional or economic security if other women breach the cartel, so those who give sex to get sex must be ostracized. As for other targets of such charges, often it is easier to direct the attack at an impersonal one—notably pornography—than at real people in one's life. This tactic seems to have succeeded rather well in maintaining an antisexual orientation in our society, but it evidently does nothing whatever to reduce male sexual needs. Similarly, no amount of contempt, from others or from oneself, will put into a person needs that nature left out, or left at a low level. Ploys like this one are likely only to make people deceive each other and themselves about their true feelings, and to produce destructive self-blame. Perhaps it is too much to expect that people will ever come to bargain fairly and honestly for the things they want, but one can always hope. Learning to understand and respect one another would be so much better than this kind of manipulation.

In summary, various reasons explain why some women oppose sexually explicit materials. In each case, pornography is not really to blame. That opposition is only a symptom of deeper problems between the sexes—problems that need to be faced more honestly than by attacking a symbol.

SEXISM AGAINST MEN

The foregoing discussion has led us to an ironic conclusion. Not only is it false that pornography per se is sexist; but as has begun to be revealed, the shoe is on the other foot. The antipornography campaign itself represents a pernicious sort of intolerance against persons with certain types of sexual needs and desires, the great majority of whom are males. Though the movement's focus is on media expressions of those feelings, the broader message is inevitable: "Your needs and emotions are evil and must be repressed." One cannot rationally say that sexual portrayals degrade women without holding that typical male feelings do the same thing; whether he uses sexual substitutes or not, a man is being told that an inherent part of himself is bad. Coming from women who do not share that nature (more shortly on men who say such things), these charges are blatant sexism. For what is the core of sexism, racism, and other forms of bigotry, after all? It is the attitude, "You're different from me, therefore you're inferior."

Once again, the opposition to pornography is only one manifestation of a wider set of attitudes. Though ours is a pluralistic society, and though it has changed its views about sex somewhat in recent decades, it still contains powerful antisexual currents. These hurt both males and females, to be sure; the "double standard" has included a double dose of sexual guilt for many women. But antisexualism is apt to cause the most pain to those whose erotic desires are strongest. Moreover, females are not raised with the tradition that their natural feelings toward the opposite sex are exploitive and objectifying. Yet from the time a boy is very small, he is sent the message that his desires toward a female's body are nasty and degrading to her and that in any sort of sexual encounter he would be an offender, she his victim. Most women do not seem to appreciate what this can be like. (Women often congratulate themselves on being more sensitive than men. Perhaps so—and perhaps, like people in general, they are mostly just more aware of sorrows like the ones they themselves have to face.) Incredibly, in fact, some go about talking as if sexual guilt were directed only at females.

One marvelous exception to this rule is Nancy Friday, whose book *Men in Love* is full of insights into male feelings. She describes such a young boy, "angry and forlorn in the knowledge that [his sexuality] is unacceptable to women. . . . Women have placed his body at war with his soul. Only when he gets out of the house, only when he discovers that other little boys are just like himself, does he get enough reinforcement to bear being *bad*." A commonly expressed fear from the antipornography camp is that little girls may suffer distress and damage to their self-image from the sight of the naked women in pornography. The real source of any such reaction would be the sex-negative emotions they have previously been conditioned to have. In addition, the author of this book can report the effect such exposure had on his self-image as a little boy: aside from satisfying some powerful yearnings that had been denied, it gave him the reassuring feeling that at least some people did not regard him as evil for having those desires.

Of course, not all males have consciously felt this pain or realized its source, any more than all females have been aware of suffering from the discrimination toward them. The former have historically failed to recognize the sexism against them for basically the same reasons as the latter once did, and they need to experience the same sort of "consciousness raising" to do so. The sad fact is that both sexes are to a great degree the puppets of our culture's attitudes, its codes of propriety and honor and morality that they have not created but merely inherited, which are very often contrary to their interests and their real desires. It has already been stressed that people can be socialized into accepting almost anything; most males (also females, of course) have just accepted and internalized the sexual guilt thrust upon them. To see in further detail why men have traditionally acquiesced or even participated in condemnations of their sexuality, let us look at some special influences.

To begin, they use a variety of psychological defense mechanisms to maintain their self-respect. For one, there is simple denial, for example, deceiving oneself by saying, "It's really love I feel, not lust." Another sort of unconscious defense is compartmentalized thinking and avoidance. The latter is sometimes reflected in replies to attacks on pornography that fall back on appeals to freedom of expression, rather than denying pornography is bad and hence risking tacitly admitting they have the sort of sexual feelings that are under attack. Yet another such mechanism is reaction formation: the zealous way in which certain men denounce sexual feelings that are natural for males smacks of an attempt to atone, to relieve their own sense of guilt. And so on. Even the exaggerated laughter and wide-eyed leering young males often display over sex (including those offensive catcalls, be it well noted) is an attempt to release this anxiety. To whatever extent any of these defenses succeed, they prevent men from acknowledging their emotional pain. As always, real moral awareness has to overcome a powerful array of psychological foes.

Some of the tactics people use in psychological self-defense reveal how intolerance directed at one group can come back around to harm others. (Feminists should note this well.) One of these is compensation: made to feel morally inferior over sex, many men will cope by developing feelings of superiority over women in other respects. Another one is transference of blame. Instead of contritely accepting the guilt, some men will feel it is women's fault for producing such nasty feelings in them. The latter idea has a long theological history, one in which women are regarded as temptresses who cause men to have impure thoughts and stray from godly behavior. Finally, being branded as morally deficient by and on behalf of women can cause smoldering unconscious resentment, an emotion that might manifest itself in various ways. To name one: at the first sign that a *woman* has strong sexual feelings, the compliment is returned with a charge of "Slut!" This, of course, will only go around again in a vicious circle as she defends *her* personal dignity by condemning male feelings. One way or another, antisexualism hurts everyone.

Another aspect of this problem is that not all men experience the degree of sexual urgency and visual arousal that produce the appeal of sexually explicit materials to other men. Hence some men, like most women, have difficulty understanding the feelings involved. Yet it is so easy to go along with accusations of evil when they are not directed at oneself. Indeed, it is apt to be an occasion for feeling morally superior. (That is especially so among those who have come to feel, quite mistakenly, less masculine because of having different needs.) A classic example of this sort of response came out of the degradation of blacks in the U.S. South: socialized to accept their inferiority as a fact, they developed their own hierarchies in which the lighter-skinned negroes looked down upon and discriminated against the darker ones. In fact, the common wish to be superior to others is felt particularly among members of each gender. And one of the main things "intermale competition" manifests itself over is desire for the approval of women. Thus in a culture where male sexual feelings are often regarded as degrading to women, a convenient way for a man to make himself appear superior to other men in women's eyes is by attacking those other men and their feelings—even if it happens to mean being untruthful about his own.

In addition to simply having been indoctrinated with traditional attitudes, men face other forces keeping them from defending their self-dignity in this matter. Many have been frightened into silence by fear of even greater censure, directed at them personally, if they should speak out. Another major problem lies in the same conflict between sex and other needs already discussed regarding women. For instance, for many men jealousy is a stronger motivator than sexual desire. Fearful of a partner's infidelity, they unconsciously feel that a positive view of sex is a threat to their own security—enough to outweigh any personal pain that denigration of their sexual feelings may entail. Or they may have a need for love-bonding that is greater than their need for sex; convinced the two are incompatible, they also disparage and repress their own sexual nature. Finally, there are those who have somehow missed out on the type or degree of sexual fulfillment that, though perhaps they would not admit it, they would have wanted. To assuage the pain of loss, they feel compelled to deny the value of what they have missed, one way or another.

Perhaps the greatest reason for men's acquiescence in attacks on their sexuality involves the wider gender role they are standardly and strongly socialized into, though it may have a biological basis as well. Part of the problem is the attitude that men are supposed to be tough. "Real men don't whine"—certainly not to women, who should be chivalrously patronized instead. For a man to admit his pain, then, is to risk losing others' respect for him *as a man*. "Those nasty names don't hurt *me*," he winces. Given the resulting stereotypes, he is not apt to be believed, as a woman would be, even if he did reveal that he is hurt by such things. The requirement of toughness stems from the traditional male roles of provider and protector for women and children. This leads us to the other part of the problem, which is the felt need to "protect" women from anything, such as sexual openness, toward which aversion is for any reason already felt. (In regard to physical dangers, such protectiveness makes sense; but it is very doubtful that men are less vulnerable than women are to emotional pain.) As well, here can emerge the desire to be superior to other men, superior this time in the protector role, defending women against those nasty *other* men. In the inverted logic that results, a man can feel downright proud to say that women are pure whereas men are unclean; he is getting his glory by defending their honor.

Ironically, these days the attitude of male protectiveness is reinforced by awareness of how male domination has denied women some of their dignity. This can make it even more difficult for men to defend their own dignity regarding their sexual feelings. For one thing, it is easy to conflate real discrimination against women with things we have merely been socialized to consider harmful or disrespectful to them. For another, that awareness can make it more difficult to object to injustices suffered by males. It is apt to seem petty to complain that, after all, men have suffered too. Nevertheless, to give in to such feelings is to be guilty of simplistic black-and-white thinking. Injustice must be rooted out wherever it is found, whoever the victims may be. The plain fact is that men have also been victims of sexism, both social and legal. In addition to that involving sexuality, and another sort of antimale sexism to be discussed in the next chapter, there is the traditional and continuing discrimination against men in child-custody cases. In recent years this has led to the formation of hundreds of fathers'-rights organizations.

"But men have all the power in society," it is often objected. "How could there be any real discrimination against them?" Men's domination of women is a regrettable fact of history, one that we must all continue working to overcome. Yet it does not automatically give men all the advantages, for a variety of reasons. For one thing, in some ways women dominate men. Humans are highly social beings, beings whose behavior is often more influenced by the opinions of others than by superior physical strength. In the matter of controlling others through approval and disapproval, women exercise very great power. (Warren Farrell's book contains some interesting insights about how each sex's expectations strongly influence the other, so that real power—the ability to gain what one wants in life—is often more appearance than reality for men. Sarah Blaffer Hrdy's book also has some revealing data on the ways in which females achieve their ends.) This influence is especially great in the formative years of early childhood, since the bulk of socialization at that age is done by women: mothers, day-care workers, school teachers, and so on. In fact, an effective way of exercising power over others is precisely by exaggerating one's lack of power, by playing victim. Social reality is much more complex than feminist theories generally allow.

That this society's sex-and-love standards match the needs of its typical females better than those of its typical males is itself a good illustration of the great influence women often wield. It is the male needs that are traditionally downgraded as less important, less noble, and downright ignoble; they are even suppressed by means of the law. In the last century, the women's "purity crusade" created laws against pornography, prostitution, and male homosexual acts. Without a single vote, the women involved were able to shame male legislators into doing what the crusaders perceived as being in their own best interests as women.[4] As Symons points out, the different pairing styles of male and female homosexuals reveal what happens when there is no need to compromise with the opposite sex: the lesbian pattern is much closer to heterosexual norms in our culture than the gay one is. This again indicates which sex has had the greatest success getting its needs protected by official teachings and social institutions, at least in the present respect.

A second crucial point here is that "male power" is far from evenly distributed. The males who run government and big business are a small minority of all men. The average man has no more control over social institutions than has the average woman: one single vote, one small voice. Nor do the dominant males readily share their privileges with other males; intermale competition assures that. On the contrary, they often use their power to claim exemption from the very rules they help to enforce on other men, for example, those in regard to sexual behavior. (The inde-cency-denouncing politician caught *en flagrante* is revealingly common.) Moreover, one of the ways in which women have always controlled men is by getting powerful men to do it for them, from gallant knights vying for their favors to modern politicians vying for their votes. Finally, male officials and lawmakers may be especially apt to have the traditional at-titude of protectiveness toward women. Indeed, it is likely to be com-pounded, these days, by feelings of guilt over their own special "male" advantages. The result of all this is that there has been real pressure to redress only one side of the historical sexist discriminations.

Ironically, some men's reason for condoning attacks on male sexuality is to maintain dominance over women. For many of them, to reveal they can be hurt by such attacks is to compromise their feelings of superiority. To argue that their own needs and dignity should be given equal consid-eration with those of women is to admit they have to ask women for their rights, rather than being the ones in control. Threatened by the prospect of gender equality, such men would redouble their commitment to the male-protector role by joining the attack on male nature. They are evi-dently willing to make a trade-off: "We'll grant the claims of male sexual nastiness, among other things, if you'll accept our superiority in the major affairs of life." Interestingly, belief in the moral superiority of women may have arisen in the first place, in the minds of men and women alike, partly to compensate the latter for their lack of status in other respects. At least, so it would appear from accounts of the Victorian view of women as "special creatures" who are too pure to dirty themselves in the world of men. When the day comes that men in general get as upset over antimale sexism as it deserves, we will know they genuinely regard women as equals.

Though feminists have been adamant in rejecting all the traditional dis-criminations against women, they have not been so quick even to recognize those against men. To cite just one example of many, some of them are hyperbolically sensitive to stereotyped and unflattering portrayals of women while quite ignoring such depictions of men. Evidently, to admit the existence of any social unfairness to males raises (mostly unjustified) fears that their own issues will be seen as less serious. In any case, they tend to label talk of men's rights "backlash" against those of women, rather than seeing it as part of the same effort to end gender injustice. Unfor-tunately, the topic of current and traditional discrimination against males is far too large to be discussed here. If these women are sincerely opposed to sexism and not simply pursuing their own self-interest, however, let them show it by publicly opposing that against men as well. That includes objecting to the degrading attacks on male sexuality.

SEXIST EXTREMISTS

One branch of the feminist movement, the one that has been most strident in attacking pornography, is in a category by itself in this regard.

These feminists can only be described as blatant sexists, and are sometimes simply vicious. They make such charges as that all men consciously use the threat of rape to control women, that all men feel rage at women and desire to degrade them, that all men are inclined to be child molesters, that all men are by nature violent . . . the sickening list goes on.[5] These extremists also see antifemale messages everywhere, like Reds under beds. This is reflected particularly in their attitudes toward male sexuality, and toward everything associated with it. In their eyes, sexual comments are never appreciative but only hostile, sexual humor is not just for enjoyment, or even a way of coping with sexual anxiety, but always a put-down of females. A special manifestation of this mindset is their view of pornography. They claim not only that it degrades women, but that that is its very purpose; it is not sexual desire but contempt for women that leads men to make and consume sexually explicit materials. Alternatively, they say that pornography is just another expression of the male desire to subordinate females, not of the desire to have, much less to share, sexual pleasure.

It is difficult to say what a male should find most offensive in allegations like these, the arrogance of pretending to read his mind or the libelous claim of finding such evil there. If he wanted to dignify them with a reply at all, he could point out some obvious realities. There is, for example, the remarkable similarity and complementarity of many female sexual fantasies to those of males. They are often so much alike that reviewers cannot tell which is which. Does this mean all those women hate women?[6] Or he could note the large percentage of pornography of the male homosexual variety, whose various forms are basically identical to the corresponding heterosexual ones (a fact the extremists studiously ignore). Do these men wish to subjugate men, or even to be subjugated themselves? Then there is the point that women in so many male-oriented erotic stories act sexually like men. Do men despise their own sexual nature?

Such claims are as absurd as would be one that women only want babies in order to have a weaker person over whom to exert power. When any reasoning at all is offered in support of the preceding charges, it displays thinking errors even worse than those already discussed here, such as an extreme capacity for guilt by association. "Men subjugate women, and men like pornography; therefore pornography is subjection of women" is often the implicit argument. Writers like Beatrice Faust and Nancy Friday have suspected that the real source of all such claims is a projection onto men of their authors' own sex-negative feelings. That is, since the extremists themselves find sexual explicitness degrading to women, they assume men do so as well and must like it for that very reason. All things considered, their charges of male hatred of females look like nothing so much as a projection of their own hatred of men.

No less extreme in their attitudes than this type of feminist are the right-wing traditionalists, who are also prominent in the crusade against pornography. They are not motivated by animosity toward men, of course, though many of the ideals they support are in fact harmful to males, as many others are to females. Like the extremist feminists, however, they are highly intolerant of those whose sexual needs or practices reflect a difference from their own repressed nature. For example, their rhetoric is full of hostility toward homosexuals, and even toward heterosexuals who engage in such "filthy perversions" as oral sex. It is also equally filled with distortions about those whose moral beliefs differ from theirs. For instance, they often charge that pornography is produced as part of a conspiracy to weaken the family or the nation, and that those who defend the legal right to use it are in conscious league with Communists or organized crime. Underlying all these charges, very clearly, is a general antisexualism. They tend to consider sex education about as evil as pornography, and they are constantly working to censor sexual knowledge out of the lives of young people.[7]

What is most relevant to our present topic is the far right's attitude toward women. The right-wing traditionalists share the extremist feminists' belief in the moral superiority of females, especially in regard to sex. Where they differ from the latter group is in what they think this implies about the sociopolitical status of women; their attitude is generally that expressed by the dictum, "Women are better than men and we aim to keep them that way." It is precisely this sort of view that causes many other feminists, even many who are themselves rather antisex, to fear the antipornography movement. They are keenly aware that historically, special protection for women has often included special restrictions on them. This has been particularly true in regard to sexuality. The desire to keep women (or at least "good" women) minimally sexual is a central motive for the traditional denial of their autonomy; once more, many of both sexes have seen full equality as a threat to their ability to control the sexuality of women. (For one illustration, it appears the far right opposes economic independence for women partly out of fear they will be more likely to engage in premarital and extramarital affairs.) Yet the pretext for the restrictions has often been to protect women from being degraded by the nastiness of sex.

The other feminists' fears of a return to that repressiveness appear to be well founded. For example, one recently proposed law supported by both the political left and right wings would effectively deny women, but not men, the legal right to make contracts to participate in producing pornography. Like children and idiots, women are not to be considered competent to make decisions involving their own lives—and their own bodies.[8] When police and judges crack down on "obscenity," they inevitably include the art and literature of lesbians and of many feminists. Ironically, even feminist antipornography propaganda is often caught up in the sweep: *Not a Love Story,* the production of which was financed with Canadian taxpayer money, has been banne in Ontario.

The right-wing and feminist extremists are a small minority, but they are nevertheless capable of having a huge influence, and have already done so. The reason is that the so-called sexual revolution did not destroy this culture's basic sex-negative attitude; there remains a deep well of guilt and ambivalence for them to exploit. Add to this the special myth that sexual explicitness degrades women, in the context of traditional feelings of protectiveness toward women, and people's thinking on this subject can easily be manipulated. As will become more evident in the next two chapters, the extremists have propagated some serious falsehoods about the purposes and contents of pornography, and they are being believed. In recent years they have managed to convert many moderate feminists and traditionalists, and others, to some of their distorted views. It is high time for concerned women and men to be talking back.

5

Portrayals of Violence

The rhetoric of the extremists, though directed against everything from pinups to hosiery advertisements, nevertheless reminds us of an issue that is a very large part of the current furor. "What about all those depictions of violence in pornography? Surely that is degrading, surely that is evil, is it not? And especially those involving women—doesn't that prove the claims of woman-hating in pornography?" This topic has been put off until now for the sake of treating more general issues first. But it is of the greatest importance to discuss it carefully. Few social issues involve more dishonesty and more irrational fear than that of sexual materials portraying pain or aggression. It is time to set the record straight here as well.

MISREPRESENTATION AND HYPOCRISY

The first point to be made is in regard to the relationship between this category of materials and pornography in general. The current campaign against sexual explicitness is characterized by a constant attempt to link all pornography in the public mind with the violent sort; it is a massive effort at guilt by association. This fact could be illustrated at great length from newspaper articles and columns, pamphlets and slogans ("Pornography endorses violence against women and children"), television "documentaries," and so on. The typical exposé boils down to saying, "See how evil pornography is?" and then showing or describing a particularly violent film or magazine that is also sexually explicit. The unspoken message of this propaganda is that there is some sort of special connection between media sex and media violence. And sometimes it is spoken, as in the slogan "Pornography is part of the continuum of violence against women."

Such tactics are beneath contempt. It is as if one were to cite the devout racists of South Africa to prove that Christianity in general is racist, or parents who abuse their children to show that parenthood itself is corrupt, or a book like *Mein Kampf* to argue that publishing is intrinsically evil. Sometimes this manipulative device is taken to absurd lengths, as when the antipornography movie *Not a Love Story* tries to associate sexual explicitness in the minds of viewers with such things as the African custom of infibulation. (This is particularly bizarre because the purpose of that practice is to suppress female sexuality, not to celebrate it. Of course, those who make this association ignore similar barbaric rites performed on males, such as Australian penis mutilation.) If violent pornography is indeed evil, it is because it is violent, not because it is pornographic. That some sexual materials are violent says nothing whatever about the moral status of the rest.

As a general rule, people resort to illegitimate means of persuasion when they sense that their honest arguments are weak. One can only suspect that many who present the issue this way realize the old "explicit sex is dirty" charge would not sufficiently motivate the average person today, so they resort to fear-and-smear tactics. Now, we will look later at the question of a causal connection between portrayed sex and *real* violence; the issue before us in this chapter is a widely alleged special link between depicted sex and depicted violence. We will be viewing this charge from various angles, but the most fundamental point to make is simply that there are no valid grounds for claiming such a link. Indeed, proponents of the claim rarely cite any (which is precisely what makes it a case of guilt by association rather than a legitimate argument—in case that point wasn't obvious). The charge seems to rest instead on the vague notion that one nasty thing is just naturally like another. But it takes a terribly distorted view of reality to see healthy consensual pleasure as differing only in degree from violent assault.

Moreover, it is certainly not the case, as some have alleged, that most pornography is violent; only a very small percentage of it is so. In fact, surveys by various researchers have consistently found much *less* violence in sex movies than in others; and the most sexually explicit, the "hard-core" shows, have the least violence of all. (It is Hollywood movies, not porno flicks, that most like combining sex with violence.) For instance J. W. Slade, who has conducted surveys of sex films and videotapes in Times Square since 1979, reports that there is now and has always been far less aggression in such movies than in socially respectable ones. Another study by T. S. Palys in Vancouver, then the "porn capital of Canada," found that only about 6 percent of the sex scenes in hard-core pornography

contained violence. The bulk of that, in spite of deliberate attempts to
discover especially brutal sex films, was mild aggression such as verbal
threats and slapping. A survey in Ohio in 1980 found twice as much violence
in G-rated "family" movies as in X-rated ones. There is evidently more
aggression in cartoons and adventure movies by Disney than in the average
sex movie.[1]

Some have pointed out with alarm that the amount of violence in pornography increased during the 1970s. That is seemingly true, though no
fully comprehensive, long-term data have been collected to verify it. (What
actually happened to Hollywood movies was that the amount of sex in
violent ones increased. The lurid realism of the violence has increased in
all types of movies, tracking cinematographic technology.) If it *is* true, it
may be simply the result of sadomasochism coming out of the closet in
that decade—more on this subject shortly. Beyond that, the main motive
could easily have been a desire to diversify the contents of sexual materials,
making them more like the rest of the entertainment spectrum. There are
also indications that the amount of aggression in pornography has decreased in more recent years.[2] In spite of what many would claim, no
legitimate grounds exist for saying portrayals of sexual pleasure have an
inherent tendency to become violent.

Some of those who focus solely on violent erotic materials in denouncing
pornography have simply defined the word "pornographic" to include
aggression, that is, to mean "sexually explicit and violent" or the like.[3]
That is an altogether arbitrary addition, once again, for the dictionary
meaning contains no such element. Even those who use such a redefinition,
however, are not acquitted of sophistry in the matter. By way of analogy,
suppose some group of antifeminists on their own decided to redefine the
word "feminist" to mean, say, "sexist man-hater." That description does
indeed fit some who label themselves feminists. But it certainly does not
fit all or even most of them, and it is not what has standardly been meant
by the term "feminist" in the past. Such a redefinition would be recognized
by all as a transparent case of *semantic* guilt by association, an attempt to
discredit the movement as a whole via Newspeak (a belief further confirmed
if this hypothetical group, in their public denunciations of "feminism,"
usually didn't bother to mention their changed meaning). However they
are interpreted, the ongoing attempts to link media sex with violence are
dishonest.

A second major point about violence in pornography is that the campaign
against it smacks heavily of hypocrisy. At the very best, it is morally
inconsistent. For as a rule, the campaigners are silent about all the *non*-
sexual aggression in the media, no matter how extreme. This argues that
decrying the portrayed violence is largely a pretext for attacking the sexual
explicitness. How many people are going around saying, "Family movies
are evil because of all the violence they contain"? And when we consider
that all of us, including impressionable children, are exposed to vastly more

nonsexual aggression in the entertainment media, the selective concern over sexual violence is even more revealing. Some people are not being honest about their real motives. Of course, many today are indeed alarmed about media violence in general. But far more vocal—and inclined to use actual violence in support of their ends, in a few cases—are those whose only mentioned concern is the pornographic variety.

For just one instance in which this conclusion of hypocrisy suggests itself, consider the following passage from Canada's 1983 "Throne Speech": "Hard core pornography, which often emphasizes violence and degradation of women, has no place in Canadian society." That media violence is bad is here implied by its use in indicting pornography. "So we're going to outlaw portrayed violence, right?" "Wrong. We're only going to prosecute pornography—all hard-core pornography, whether it's violent or degrading, or not!" If the violence is in fact not the real motive, it would not be very surprising. The United States and Canada have a long history of suppressing sexual explicitness, but not violence, in the media. In the former country, sex can be considered legally obscene while violence has been declared constitutionally protected; in the latter, violent sex is the only sort of portrayed violence that is explicitly illegal. For the majority of traditionalists, at least, it is crystal clear which of the two elements disturbs them most.

SEXISM REGARDING VIOLENCE

This last point must be modified in one important respect. It is only the portrayal of aggression against men that has been considered socially acceptable in the past. That against women has been found highly objectionable, and there has been little of it. In the era of gangster movies, with all their violence against men, a scene in which Jimmy Cagney pushed a grapefruit into a woman's face was met with a storm of public protest. This has changed quite a bit in recent years, of course, as new attitudes about sexual equality have taken hold. But the old attitude is far from having disappeared. This is revealed, for example, by the Throne Speech quotation, which does not mention degradation of, or violence against, men. One can find illustrations of this double standard everywhere. Consider that famous scene from *Butch Cassidy and the Sundance Kid,* which has since become commonplace in movies, in which a man is kicked in the groin and doubles over in agony. It is presented as comedy, and the audience reaction is one of high humor. We do not see any analogous events involving women in socially acceptable movies; and if we did, the reaction would be outrage rather than laughter.

Recent years have also witnessed an upsurge in vocal denunciations of violence against women in the media, and the birth of numerous organizations to oppose it. In fact, those involved in this are much the same individuals publicly opposing pornography. For example, their usual re-definitions of the word only class as "pornographic" those sexual portrayals that contain violence toward or degradation *of women*. The clear impli-cation is that only they are worthy of condemnation. Incredibly, these people often talk as if there were *less* concern in society over real or depicted assaults on women than over those on men. It is certainly true that in the past, many of both sexes did not realize the trauma of the crime of rape. But both have always been far more sympathetic to female suf-fering, once they recognized it as such. And in many places, historically, the homosexual or heterosexual rape of a man or boy has not even been classed as a crime.

Let us illustrate this mentality with a pair of Canadian examples; many, many others could also be given. An Ontario judge banned an erotic video movie showing two scenes of consensual sexual spanking—of a man by a woman and vice versa—on the grounds that it contained "violence against women," while movies like *Scarface* were playing openly across Canada. The latter is full of graphic violence against males, including glimpses of a man being cut up with a chain saw, but almost none against women. About a year later an issue of *Penthouse* magazine was banned all across the country over photos by a Japanese artist of bound naked women. The public uproar was deafening; it was "degrading to women." At about the same time, a movie was run on the government television network showing a naked man being tortured. In this case it was the silence that was deaf-ening; there were no police raids, no screaming accusations about degra-dation of men.[4] (To allude to yet another Canadian incident, you can bet there would be no cries of public delight if someone firebombed a video store for carrying a few films showing violence against men.) The portrayal of male pain and humiliation were not even thought worthy of mention, let alone considered worthy of attention by the same legal system.

In this second respect as well, then, people exhibit a remarkable degree of selectivity in the examples of violence they denounce. Furthermore, as anyone can tell, violence is still much more commonly inflicted on males in the entertainment media. About 90 percent of it is against men, by some estimates, and the rate is even higher for the more brutal and deadly portrayals. The sole exception to this rule involves the recent generation of blood-and-horror ("slasher") movies. Even in that case, the apparent reason is instructive. Reactions to violence toward men have been desen-sitized because its portrayal is so common; since violence against women is considered more horrible than that against men, then, films whose very goal is to produce feelings of horror are bound to portray a high proportion of female victims. (Even at that, it is more often threats to women than real harm that is shown.) As for movies that contain explicit sex and violence, this genre too may contain as much or more aggression against males; scenes of women being raped tend to be matched by those involving the nonsexual brutalization of men.

What could be the reason for the special focus on violence against women, completely ignoring that against men? There are several possible explanations, each of which, evidently, applies to some of the many who display the reaction. To begin with, this focus is a manifestation of a more general mindset, the old chivalrous attitude of greater concern about the welfare of women. To be sure, women often need special protection to provide them with an equal level of safety. However, harm to a woman has come to be seen as much *more* serious than equal harm to a man. (This is very possibly another aspect of the trade-off that gave greater power and freedom to men.) From the men who drowned on the Titanic while the women were rescued ("Save the women and children first" is still the international law of the sea) to those who are sent off to the horror of war while the women remain safely at home, men continually see their safety and well-being accorded less concern than those of women. To this day, news commentators make a special point of mentioning it when some tragedy befalls "even women and children." It should not have to be pointed out, these days, that all this is sexism. A man's safety and dignity are every bit as precious to him as a woman's are to her.

Now, this first motive applies mostly to traditionalists; the next two apply mainly to the feminist extremists. One of these is paranoia. From many of their statements, it seems these extremists really do believe violent presentations involving females represent a hate campaign against women. How they can reconcile this belief with the fact that there is far more media violence against men is quite unclear, unless they are simply blind to the latter. (Nor is it true that more of that against women is "endorsed" by the portrayal; more about this in Chapter 11.) Perhaps the fact that such media content involving women was formerly much less common is part of the reason it stands out more glaringly now. Another explanation for the exclusive focus on violence against women stems from the feminist extremists' general view of relations between the sexes, an adversarial us/them mindset. It is clear from their own statements that some of them simply feel a sexist greater concern for their "own kind"—"Let men worry about violence against men." Fortunately for us all, the large majority of women and men are too sane and compassionate to share that attitude.

Yet another motive for this type of sexism rests on the legitimate complaint that men have most of the power in the world, including greater control over the media, and that most of the real and portrayed violence is performed by men. But the idea that these things justify a special concern over violence against females is fallacious. It stems from the inability to see people as individuals—with individual virtues and vices, individual joy and pain—rather than merely as members of a social class. Is one person's suffering to be ignored because of some morally irrelevant similarity, such as gender or skin color, to other individuals, to those who have power or those who make movies or those who are violent? Is a person somehow to blame for his own victimization if he is of the same race or sex as his attacker? The average man has no more control over the media or over the government or over violent thugs than has the average woman. This tendency to see people only as groups rather than as individuals is at the heart of sexism, racism, and like "-isms." For example, it is what lies behind the feeling of white indifference as long as only ghetto blacks are attacked by black criminals, which turns to offended rage when the latter start attacking whites. "After all, they're all alike, they're all in cahoots. If they harm one another, it's not our concern."

A final explanation for the attitude under discussion lies not in the issue of media content per se but in the possibility that media violence will instigate real assault, to which women are generally more vulnerable than men. This fear would be generated especially in the case of sexual violence, since in the real world it is usually women who are the victims of such assaults. The effect of portrayed violence on behavior is an issue to be discussed later, but the answer to this thinking already seems clear. Women's greater vulnerability does in one sense warrant greater fear about their safety, but hardly the exclusive concern over depictions of violence against them that so many display. Their lack of concern for men is especially inappropriate because, once again, the great bulk of depicted aggression is directed at men. Moreover, most real crimes of violence are committed more often against men. For example, in the United States a man is three times more likely than a woman to be murdered and two or three times more apt to be violently robbed or assaulted.[5] Finally, in general a man is as helpless as a woman against such things as a sudden attack or a weapon. Men have traditionally been discouraged from admitting their fears and traumas, while women have not; but the dangers men face are no less real.

In summary, there seems to be no way of justifying the highly vocal campaign against media violence that focuses solely on that involving women. One way or another it is sexist; it is wrong.

REASONS FOR THE VIOLENCE

The fact that sophistry and sexism pervade the issue of sex and violence does not answer the question of whether there is something intrinsically immoral about pornography that portrays harm, pain, or coercion (or about nonsexual portrayals of violence, for that matter). That it is evil, independently of any effects it may have on behavior, is widely taken for granted. Is such a view justified? This is a difficult question. Real violence, unlike real sex, *is* intrinsically bad; but it is not so clear what to say about depicted violence. Of course, if depicted violence is degrading to someone, it surely is morally bad. But that is not more clearly the case for portrayals of sexual violence than it is for many other portrayals of violence. A more specific question can perhaps be answered, however: Is it true, as is so often alleged, that violent pornography is hate-mongering—against women or anyone else? Though it would be unwise to make a pronouncement covering every instance, in general the answer is negative. Once again, the rhetoric we have been hearing so much lately is without foundation.

To begin to explain, let us note that portrayals of violent sex fall very roughly into three or four categories. One of these is that involving mild violence: scratching, biting, spanking, and so on. Though it seems strange to many of us, particularly those with a low pain threshold, the simple fact is that a large part of the human race can find this sort of "violence" highly sexually stimulating. For example, over half of Kinsey's respondents stated that they enjoyed being bitten, and couples often report that they achieve greater sexual satisfaction by making love right after a fight. In many cultures, moreover, various sorts of mild and consensual sexual violence are engaged in by all couples—and often the woman inflicts all the pain. The roots of such behavior may go deep into our evolutionary past, since mild aggression is part of the mating behavior of many species. Given these psychological facts, the appearance of such "violence" in erotic depictions should not be surprising. A few years back, fashion advertisers began experimenting with portrayals of sexually tinged soft violence: some biting, slapping, a woman's spiked heel on a man's bare chest. The response from the groups opposing violence against women was vociferous, and it was effective. Meanwhile, however, other women rushed to buy the items thus advertised, and sales shot up dramatically.[6]

What all this means is debatable (not fully clear). The most plausible explanation of the sex-violence link is that another sort of excitement—notably from pain, fear, or aggression, provided that they are not too extreme—can somehow enhance sexual excitement. Whatever its physiological and psychological origins, the important point for our present purposes is that the sex-violence link does not represent hatred. The desire to give or get small amounts of pain or fear is produced by the desire for sexual enjoyment, not by a wish to cause or receive real harm. It is true that a standard claim of Freudian psychology—which other psychologists maintain is mere unsupported dogma (along with a lot of other Freudian claims about sex)—holds that all erotic desire involves hostility toward the partner at a deep subconscious level.[7] Even if this claim were true, the point here would be unaffected because it indicts real as well as portrayed sex, and because it does not refer to the ordinary unconscious and conscious motives we can influence.

Also in this first category, it seems, is what we might call mock coercion, notably pretended force and pretended resistance. A high percentage of the population reports sexual excitement from this sort of thing as well. Its roots may also go deep into our biology, for in many animal species, mating is preceded by a ritualized flight and capture. Anyone who has watched a little girl tease a little boy, then run screaming in mock terror to get him to chase and grab her, may suspect that the reasons transcend culture. Now, it may be possible to think of fantasies of rape as being a variety of mock coercion, since they are not the real thing. In any case, such fantasies and their embodiment in novels and films are found enjoyable by a sizable minority. And this is not just a male predilection; indeed, surveys indicate such enjoyment is much more common among females. Nancy Friday reported that the fantasy most frequently submitted to her by women was that of being raped. Women's romance novels that prominently feature rape or ravishment—"Sweet Savagery," the category is called—sell millions of copies.[8] One researcher who tested women's reactions in the laboratory found such scenes were as exciting or more exciting to them than consensual scenes of lovemaking.[9]

One must forcefully stress, however, that women who enjoy these stories rarely have any desire to experience the real thing; it is *only* a fantasy. Some of us find it difficult to see how anyone could get pleasure from imagining what in reality would be horrible, but such is the case here. (In fact, attempts are often made to rationalize that it is not really rape that is being fantasized. It is not vicious and brutal, as the real thing often is, but it plainly is rape.) Likewise, few male rape fantasies represent a real desire to subjugate a woman or to violate her will. In fact, different studies have found that in close to half of such male imaginings the men are being raped *by* women; only in those of women is the man nearly always the aggressor.[10] Further evidence for this conclusion is that in the great majority of them, the woman is portrayed as becoming aroused and orgasmic; the ultimate result is pleasure, not pain or degradation.

Then what *is* the reason some people have such fantasies? Aside from the one already mentioned, several explanations have been suggested. One of these is that this element of the fantasy is a way for women to assuage the guilt felt over having sexual imaginings in the first place—"See, it's not my fault!" Some writers claim the real intent is for the woman to be forced to experience sexual ecstasy which she would not otherwise have permitted herself to feel. If this is so, then the occurrence of rape fantasies, in men and women alike, is another consequence of the latter's being conditioned to repress sexual desire. It is certainly true that liberation of a woman from her inhibitions is the wishful theme of many pornographic films and romance novels, including those involving rape. However, the most common explanation given by those who have such fantasies is this: they are a symbol—not to be taken literally—of overwhelming desire, *and* of the wish to *be* overwhelmingly desired. In other words, women's rape fantasies reflect a wish to be so irresistible as to make a man lose all control.

Whatever the full explanation may be, at least this much is true: there is no real evidence, from fantasies and pornography involving nonbrutal coercion or mild violence, for the sorts of malevolent motive that are so often charged. (See Chapter 11, however, for possible effects of such portrayals.)

A second category of sexual violence can be distinguished from this first one, namely, that connected with sadomasochism. Actually, that term is used loosely to describe a wide range of desires and activities rather than a single homogeneous phenomenon. Most of what is so labeled is evidently just a stronger form of using other kinds of excitement to enhance sexual arousal. The extreme and sometimes ritualistic nature of the remainder, by contrast, is indicative of emotional disorder. The average person knows little about "S&M": the whips and needles and so on. It is understandable for ordinary people to be repelled by the thought of getting pleasure from giving or getting emotional or physical pain. Whether and to what extent it is mentally unhealthy is much debated by psychiatrists and psychologists, however; in other respects its practitioners usually seem completely normal. (See Chris Gosselin and Glenn Wilson's *Sexual Variations* or Thomas Weinberg and Levi Kamel's *S&M: Studies in Sadomasochism.*) Indeed, only in a tiny minority of sadomasochists is there any wish to receive or inflict serious harm. Their encounters tend to be carefully scripted and controlled, usually with real concern for the well-being and pleasure of both partners.

A small number of sadistic murderers and sadistic rapists terrorizing the land has produced high levels of public fear in regard to this subject, so such facts must be stressed. These twisted minds are sexually aroused by extreme brutality; they are a grave threat to the safety of women, and sometimes men. But it will not serve the public safety to confuse those individuals with people whose activities are always fully consensual and not genuinely harmful. Note well, too, that the motive for the latter sort of behavior is sexual pleasure, not hatred. Sadomasochism is an emotional variation or abnormality of some sort, not a desire to give or get harm for its own sake. So S&M pornography is employed by these individuals for vicarious sexual satisfaction—it is evidently not made or used in order to vent feelings of hostility. Nor, once again, does it make any general statement about what women *or* men really want.

True, even in the case of mild sadomasochism it is possible that at some deep psychological level, the association of pain with sex represents real anger. If so, it would evidently have to include anger against oneself or against one's own sex—not just the "misogyny" we hear about so much— since masochism and homosexual sadism are as much a part of it as heterosexual sadism. In fact, there are more masochists than sadists, and a majority play *both* roles. It is correspondingly reported (e.g., by Slade) that there is more heterosexual sadomasochistic pornography in which the paingiver is a woman. Furthermore, a high percentage of sadomasochists are homosexual or bisexual, making the claims of opposite-gender hatred even harder to take seriously. As is the case with paraphilias (popularly called "perversions") in general, from rubber fetishes to erotic cross-dressing, most sadomasochists are male. But those who are female again give the lie to claims of woman-hating; see for example the lesbian S&M book *Coming to Power,* by the Samois collective.

A third general category of media portrayals of sex and violence together unites them for a very different set of reasons than the first two. First, blood-and-horror movies and comics are common and popular these days; consider *Friday the 13th,* and *Halloween.* Here, again, is a case of many people, most of them young, getting pleasure from something they would not really want to experience. Whatever the psychological reasons, they like the excitement of portrayed violence. Second, a lot of people like the excitement of sex. These being the two primary sources of thrills for movies and books made it almost inevitable that they would sometimes be combined. Shocking and disturbing though such movies are, surely no more complex or sinister reason for them need be sought in most cases. If we want something to blame, we might consider our traditional acceptance of violence in the media. Not that any *further* blame is justified. Getting excitement and enjoyment from watching a woman being raped is no more objectionable, morally, than doing so from watching men being killed and maimed.

Another factor in producing this combination is the human desire for novelty, as constantly evident in the entertainment industry as it is in fashion and the arts; that alone would induce the less inhibited to produce such movies and books. Yet another apparent motive for uniting sexual titillation with aggression lies in a common horror-show technique: employing a contrast with pleasure, innocence, or helplessness to heighten the feelings of evil and terror. (Recall all those movies about satanic children?) This is evidently the purpose in films of the *Toolbox Murders* ilk. Indeed, on the traditional definition of pornography as material intended to appeal to sexual feelings, such movies are not pornographic at all, since their goal is a different sort of emotion. This fact is conveniently ignored by the same people who insist that nudity or sex in art is not pornographic on the grounds that sexual arousal is not the aim.

Other reasons for the production of and interest in sexually violent materials involve this culture's deep-laid sexual guilt. One especially troubling possibility concerns the case of implicit or mildly explicit sexuality coupled with really brutal violence—the stock-in-trade of "detective" magazines, which are read by many adolescents. It may just be that the violence in them is a substitute for more explicit sex. Since the latter is less available to young people, and since they have been trained to find aggression far less guilt-inducing than sex, it is possible that their desire for sexual arousal is being channeled partially into a different type of excitement—the psychological result being a taste for eroticized violence. If this is so, then campaigning against nonviolent sex but not against nonsexual violence in the media, and doing so on grounds of concern over real sexual violence, is counterproductive as well as morally inconsistent.

Next consider a second way in which sexual guilt might help explain why some sexually frank productions contain violence: the unconscious sense of sinfulness seems to lead some of its makers to feel sex may be indulged in only if it is ultimately punished or else associated with other horrid things. In other words, the violence eases their conscience about the sex. Alternatively, perhaps the violence is intended to mollify the censors, who see it as socially redeeming content for a sexually unrepressed person to come to a bad end. In fact, such an outcome was required under the Hays Code, which used to govern all Hollywood movies. Even today, punishment for sexual misbehavior is a central element of teenage "slasher" movies: "bad" boys and girls get killed by monsters like Jason. So we meet an irony we have seen before and will often see again in the course of this book. The very attitudes the antipornography forces represent produce many of the evils sometimes associated with sex and with its portrayal.

The point of the foregoing brief discussion has been to display the real reasons for the joining of sex and violence in the media. However ignoble or benign those motives may be, they evidently do not involve hatred toward anyone. It certainly cannot be ruled out that such hostility is sometimes involved, of course. Indeed, it will later be suggested that this may be so in some cases, and one explanation for it will be offered. But those who constantly level the charge of woman-hating are reacting from an ideological bias, not looking honestly at the evidence. They rarely consider any other explanations for this sort of literature and movies; it's all just "hate propaganda" to them.

The dishonesty in this view is sometimes so blatant one can scarcely believe it. Even mild violence in a magazine edited by and intended for women is automatically labeled "misogyny." While often insisting that women's rape novels and fantasies are no sign of real desires, or even suppressing the fact that they exist, those who charge woman-hating take rape in male-oriented pornography to be clear evidence of a desire to do it *and* to be a propagandistic statement that all women want to be raped. As is their habit with media violence in general, they usually ignore sexual violence involving men on the receiving end, such as "gay" sadomasochism and male heterosexual masochism. To mention its existence would sabotage the charges or insinuations of hatred directed uniquely at women. But those who do mention pornography showing women or men hurting men are remarkably unfazed by it. They claim that shows hatred of women too, that, for example, the man is simply "in the woman's place"! In fact, they persistently ignore the psychological reality of paraphilias altogether, so they can charge deviant pornography with being designed to degrade and threaten women.

What is alarming about all this is that they are getting away with it. Such is the conditioned fear of sexuality in this culture that all sorts of otherwise reasonable persons are believing the distortions chronicled in this chapter. One can only hope that people will eventually wake up to recognize that aspect of the campaign against pornography for what it really is.

6

Degrading Content

Another special issue often aired regarding sexual portrayals is that of degradation. At least, the degradation of women is an issue. Just as there is a tradition of special concern over violence against women, there is a wider view that affronts to the dignity of women are more reprehensible than those affecting men. Now, the primary topic discussed in this book so far has been whether or not sexual openness or explicitness is degrading in itself; that general question will receive no further treatment. Beyond that claim, however, it is often charged that much pornography is debasing for reasons other than its sexual frankness. Indeed, many antipornography groups claim they are not opposed to portrayals of nudity or sexual behavior as such; they abhor only the degrading ones—though they insist the latter are very common. For example, the conservative Commission on Pornography that did its work under U.S. Attorney General Edwin Meese declared in its *Final Report* that nonviolent but degrading material "constitutes somewhere between the predominant and the overwhelming portion of what is currently standard fare heterosexual pornography."[1] That charge, involving as it does specific types of sexual depiction, does require further analysis.

Actually, this new claim is very often highly misleading, if not deliberately deceitful. "We're only opposed to *degrading* sex" certainly sounds reasonable, and it is manifestly designed to reassure the public that its makers are not just motivated by traditional prudishness. When we read the fine print, however, it frequently turns out that most of what they include under this rubric *is* objected to for its sexual content: scenes that are at all explicit (e.g., with genital close-ups) rather than soft-focus or merely suggestive, or scenes that do not portray sufficient aesthetic content or affectionateness, or scenes whose sole purpose is to display nudity (pin-ups). Some of those making this new claim are simply not honest about their views. Others' attitudes do differ from traditional ones, but only in degree, only in the amount of explicitness or disinhibition or unredeemed sex they find tolerable. In any event, we will now look in some detail at the standard claims of special forms of degradation.

HIGHLY SEXED WOMEN

One charge in this category derives from the fact that the women of pornography typically display strong sexual desire or responsiveness; they show high levels of excitement and enthusiasm, engaging in sex readily and enjoying a variety of sexual acts. And they do this without the pre-condition of love or long-term commitment, often with a stranger or with more than one partner. In short, they value sex for its own sake. The accusation is made, not only that this misrepresents women in general, but that it is degrading to them to be portrayed in such a manner. Often those who make the charge engage in hyperbole or distortion, saying pornog-raphy views women as "dirty whores," or at least as "nymphomaniacs" who are "hysterical" over sex. (There is a lot more exaggeration *about* standard sexual materials than *in* them.) Once again, some even insist the debasement is deliberate, motivated by a desire to degrade all women. As already pointed out here, sexual fantasies do not make a statement about any real women, much less about all. But what if they did? Are such depictions really degrading to anyone?

What is most astonishing about these accusations in this day and age is their totally unself-conscious endorsement of a sexual double standard. The men of pornography are equally randy and uninhibited, a fact the accusers occasionally admit, as an afterthought. But it is usually only com-plained that women are shown as "sexually undiscriminating" and "hy-persexual." And only women are ever said to be degraded by being so portrayed. In the eyes of both sexist traditionalists and sexist feminists, it would seem, it is degrading *to a woman* to be sexually *like a man*. It is even alleged that such depictions will lead to a loss of respect for women (but not men) in general, hence to sexist discrimination and mistreatment of numerous kinds. This is absurd. Such treatment certainly might be caused by the double standard these people tacitly endorse, but it can hardly be blamed on portrayals that treat men and women alike. Actually, it may well be that some who make the charges do not really feel women are more degraded by this type of portrayal. Perhaps they merely realize that to say it debases *everyone* would have less impact on the hearer, and they wish to invoke either traditional protectiveness toward women or modern concerns over sexism against women to censure pornography. In that case, they are guilty of a highly dishonest and manipulative tactic.

The main point here, however, is that it is not at all genuinely degrading, to a man *or* to a woman, to be or to be seen as highly sexual. A strong love of sex is no more evil than a strong love of sports or music. To have erotic desires that are lower than average may or may not be unfortunate, but no one considers it morally evil; an unusually high enthusiasm for sex should be regarded no differently. Only those who find such a characteristic bad would object to anyone's being "stereotyped" as having it; otherwise it would be no worse than being represented as intelligent or as liking lasagna. As usual, the reactions under discussion are a product of this society's traditional anxiety regarding erotic feelings and behavior, notably the belief that sex is itself debasing to women.

One thing that helps to reveal this source of the reactions is the very different attitude found in many other cultures. Readiness to have "casual" sex, for instance, has been standard among the single people of many times and places; such behavior is perfectly healthy and wholesome for human beings. Among the Mbuti, for just one example, work expeditions of young people frequently turn into happy orgies on the trail. Even in our society, it is obvious that a majority feel desires of this type, at least at times. For a variety of reasons, such as moral training and fear of others' jealousy, most do not act on those desires but restrict them to fantasy. But pornography *is* fantasy, after all, a fact that its opponents seem to have difficulty keeping in focus. As for the question of exuberance and disinhibition in enjoying sex, the Western fear of unseemly enthusiasm in such matters again contrasts sharply with the vigorous physicalness of many other peoples. When a husband and wife reunite after a long absence, the Mangaians joke, it is necessary to "tie the house down" that night. Nor are the multiorgasmic women of Mangaia derided as "insatiable"—a popular put-down of the women in pornography.

Regarding sexual assertiveness, it has already been noted that our traditional attitudes are harmful to women, who must passively wait for male initiative in matters of sex. (Indeed, such views are part of a larger pattern that was traditionally implanted at an early age; consider, for example, those dainty little girls disdaining the boisterous boys at their physical games.) Interestingly, this point brings us close to one final source of that "object" rhetoric. In part, women see themselves as sex objects precisely because they are not sexual *subjects*. They are trained to be passive, like an object, rather than active in regard to sex. Hence the only way they can exercise autonomy is by saying *no*. In spite of stereotypes, moreover, surveys reveal that only a minority of men dislike sexually aggressive women. More important, many women have found that taking the initiative made a big difference in their own sexual enjoyment. Finally, sharing the risk of rejection and accusation that such initiative entails, finding out what males have to face, can only enhance empathy and communication between the sexes.

For several reasons mentioned earlier, it must be granted that the sexual behavior in some pornography is exaggerated by any standard. An additional reason is overcompensation. Deprivation of any sort is apt to result in fantasy wishes that go beyond what is really desired. In particular, the common male longing for women to be more sexually aggressive and responsive can easily get carried away. Arguably, a parallel overcompensation occurs in female love-fantasies. Is the prince on the white horse who goes through fire to win her love degrading to men? Yet another cause of exaggeration lies in the fact that sexual sensations can only be felt, not shown on the screen; in an attempt to convey their intensity, unsophisticated moviemakers resort to scenes of ejaculation by males and noisy vocalization by females. The result may be a foolish failure, but that hardly makes it evil. A similar problem, that of portraying emotion, infects the fully clothed love scenes of TV and Hollywood movies: the goo-goo eyes and passionate clinging may or may not be silly, but they do not degrade either gender.

A different type of exaggeration is that occurring in comedy, which makes up a high proportion of sexually oriented entertainment. The much maligned and admittedly unsophisticated movie *Porky's* was very popular among teenage boys because of its use of humor to allay anxiety toward their three primary sources of anxiety: adult power, acceptance by peers, and sex. Taken literally and seriously, the film would have to be regarded as more degrading to adolescent males than to anyone else. In reality, by this viewer's lights, the only degrading scene of the film is one in which fun is made of a homely overweight girl. In a similar vein, consider the television commercial in which Michael J. Fox is so euphoric over an attractive neighbor that he performs acrobatic feats and risks his life in traffic in the dark to get her a Diet Pepsi. There have not been long lines of people saying this commercial is degrading to men. Nor should there be—*perhaps* it reinforces an unfortunate stereotype of males, but it is only comedy, after all. As much as anything else, what antipornography ideologues lack is a sense of humor.

Any way it is looked at, for a man or woman to be portrayed as highly sexual is not degrading. As usual, in fact, the shoe is on the other foot: it is those who express such extreme intolerance of people with greater sexual needs or lesser sexual inhibitions who are doing the degrading, not movies and magazines that portray such things in a positive way. To say it is nasty for a woman to be unabashedly sexual is degrading to the many women who *are* that way. It is also degrading to men: part of the sexism of the double standard is the attitude "You *expect* such awfulness from men; one can't degrade creatures who have already thoroughly degraded themselves!" Few of those who make the charge under discussion would go so far as to call the sexually uninhibited people of other cultures "animals" or "sluts"; that verges too close to racism. It is very sad that only in regard to race and culture have many people realized it is evil to despise other people for being different.

Actually, it is contrary to the policy of both sexist feminists and chivalrous traditionalists ever to blame women for anything; females are only the victims of male domination or exploitation, you see. So these people usually do not accuse sexually free women of degrading themselves but insist they have been manipulated or pushed into such nastiness by men. (The old sexist attitude toward "bad women" at least credits them with minds and wills of their own.) Nevertheless, the inevitable result of their pronouncements that sexual disinhibition degrades women, ignoring men, is to reinforce the double standard, and hence to reinforce the societal blame directed at women who violate it. This is ironic, since in other contexts feminists spend so much time decrying both the double standard and traditional attitudes toward "fallen women."

EXPLOITATION, SUBORDINATION, AND HUMILIATION

Let us turn to the claims that certain types of portrayal in pornography are debasing for reasons independent of the sexual content. The Meese Commission listed three general kinds of depiction that they saw as encompassing the "degrading" category: portraying persons as "existing solely for the sexual satisfaction of others" or as being "in decidedly subordinate roles" or engaging "in sexual practices that would to most people be considered humiliating." As described, such scenes might indeed be objectionable; it will be of value for us to consider these cases one at a time.

That first phrase, unfortunately, is more rhetorical than descriptive: it is not at all clear what it comes to, and no examples were given. Others who level this charge, however, sometimes do apply it to specific kinds of pornography, including ordinary pinups. Their accusations are generally absurd. Though posing for a photograph of any kind typically involves making oneself as appealing as possible, only in the case of pictures of nude females is this considered a sign of existing merely to satisfy others. Notice that feminists who make the claim are often guilty of doublethink: deliberately revealing dress on a woman does not announce that she exists for men's pleasure, on their doctrine, but sexy pictures in a men's magazine do. Traditionalists who say this sort of thing are equally mistaken, but at least they apply it consistently. Another standard complaint is about portrayals of fellatio. Those who make it are usually stone silent about portrayals of cunnilingus, even though they are also a staple of hard-core sex films and books, for that shows a man giving pleasure to a woman. But neither act is at all totally one-sided, since such a large factor in sexual excitement is the excitement of the other person.

In other contexts, what is seemingly meant by exploitation rhetoric like this is the flip side of that "nymphomaniac" charge. On the grounds that no woman would for her own enjoyment engage so readily in sex, or in so much sex or in certain types of sex, it is concluded this time that she is doing so only to satisfy men. That is to say, many critics insist on reinterpreting scenes of highly sexed women as cases of the women merely accommodating the men. They are reading traditional stereotypes of females as compliant and nonsexual into scenes where they are obviously anything but. The "nymphomaniac" charges are exaggerated but at least more honest. Quite naturally, now, men fantasize about women who enjoy sharing things they themselves would like. Yet equally, women's romantic fantasies typically have men engaging in and enjoying things that the women want. So the main problem here is that in some sexist eyes, a fantasy interaction between the sexes is exploitive unless it involves men's desires becoming like women's, rather than the other way around. But there is nothing genuinely wrong with either.

This is not to deny that a one-sided selfishness is ever found in pornography—or in real sex. There certainly are men and women whose pleasure in receiving things from the opposite gender (security, financial support, affection, *or* sex) is not contingent upon the latter's pleasure. But only a small proportion of pornography genuinely reflects these attitudes. This is so even though the making of such materials, unlike that involving women's fantasies, has been left largely in the hands of people whose social sensitivities are not very keen. Even though certain depictions do contain a one-sided concern for male pleasure, however, to describe them in terms of "existing only to serve men", or even to consider them degrading rather than merely selfish and inconsiderate, is gross exaggeration. Indeed, they are not different in principle from many a romance novel whose "success-object" male conquers the world *for her,* then courts, flatters, and pampers her. Further, the one-sidedness of that type of pornography is hardly worse than the message of this society's chivalric sexism, that women's needs and wishes are more noble than those of men. Indeed, it is precisely the failure of pornography to accede to the latter social attitude that so distresses sexual traditionalists and many feminists.

Actually, the charge under discussion here is only one manifestation of a wider distortion in the views of sexist feminists. They talk as if women in this society are constantly serving men, whereas men never do anything to help or to please women. This is a complex topic, but there is far less truth to that allegation than is commonly charged. Indeed, their perception of such things often contains a further double standard. If men are shown being solicitous to women—for example, opening doors for them or paying their way—the "message" is that women are helpless children; if females are shown doing things for males, it is that women exist only to serve. In summary, this first category of "degrading" pornography is almost wholly the product of the paranoia and excuse-fishing we have encountered before. We will have to look elsewhere for examples of genuine debasement.

Let us turn to the second alleged type of degrading portrayal, that in which someone is shown in a definitely subordinate role. Objections to this kind of thing arise from concern over traditional male dominance and female passivity. This is a problem that must not be taken lightly. The power imbalance between the sexes is responsible for most of the inequalities women have historically faced, and overcoming it is essential to eliminating those inequalities. Unfortunately, some have become hypersensitive to the issue, reading such imbalances into innocent situations. The more extreme feminists tend to see male domination everywhere. They do this with a vengeance in the case of pornography, charging that subordination of women is endorsed in all or most male-oriented materials.

It is often claimed, for example, that emotional passivity, not just the physical stillness required in posing for a camera, is reflected in ordinary pinups. And a reclining nude is said to be doubly passive and helpless— never mind that the only comfortable way to have sex is lying down, to them the posture represents submission, not sexual invitation. (On the question of whether the "missionary position" subordinates women, of course, the extremist feminists and the traditionalists part company.) With the typical pretense of mind-reading, one prominent feminist denounces photos that clearly reveal the female genitals as degrading, doing so on the grounds that it is not sexual desire but the wish to subjugate women that makes such things attractive to men.[2] (In light of such charges, one reason why some women enjoy displaying their bodies to men is especially interesting: they report that part of the thrill results from the feeling of power over the men it gives them.) Like others we have examined, this mindset regarding power leads to some revealing doublethink. If, for instance, a male is shown having mutually consenting sex with two or more females, they are automatically his "harem"; if a woman is shown with two or more men, the scene is "gang rape."

One of the more incredible charges of this type is that sexual portrayals of interracial couples are racist, no matter how equally they are actually depicted. (This is also ironic, since in earlier years a common objection to men's magazines was that they were racist for only showing white women.) The rationale here is that the social power imbalance between the different races means that any such depiction inherently involves dominance. If that conclusion followed, it would bode even worse for a *real* sexual relationship between members of different races, including marriage. What makes this claim especially disturbing is that abhorrence of interracial sex is such an integral part of real racism. "Would you want your sister to marry one?" used to be the presumed clincher in defenses of segregation. Under Hollywood's old Hays Code, not only sex but any depiction of interracial couples was strictly prohibited. If racial dominance is really endorsed, be it in pornography or anywhere else, that is very wrong. But the idea that depicting interracial sexuality is inherently evil is itself tinged with racism.

False charges aside, it certainly is true that some pornography depicts men who are dominant and women who are passive to one degree or another. This, however, merely reflects the reality in our culture; from dating to kissing and embracing to sex itself, males are still forced by female passivity to take the controlling role. (Notice how this particular objection clashes with an earlier one; it comes dangerously close to complaining that pornography is *too* true to life.) Moreover, sexual depictions of this type are only doing what other depictions often do, from adventure stories to romance novels. To single out sexual portrayals for special blame for something that is so universal reveals once more that the real objections lie elsewhere. The footnote on page 330 of the Meese Commission's *Final Report* suggests that they were desperate to find power imbalances. The allegedly common theme in pornographic scenes, "He is ready to take. She is ready to be taken," describes equally well the large majority of love scenes in romantic novels and movies. In fact, however, pornography on the whole treats women and men more alike and more equal than the entertainment media in general do. So far from just doing what they are told, once again, most of the women portrayed in pornography are sexually assertive.

This was borne out by the study of hard-core videotapes made in Vancouver. The survey found that in only 14 percent of the sexual scenes was the activity less than completely mutual; in these, the team of male and female coders felt that at least one of the participants was playing "a more dominant or directive role," "a more assertive role in directing the course of the interaction." In half of these cases, moreover, a woman was the more dominant party—which would seem rather more egalitarian than mainstream movies. Note also that this description does not sound particularly serious; extreme subordination was evidently quite uncommon. That being so, it is not clear that even this much dominance is very objectionable. Many independent women report that they sometimes like to be dominated in the bedroom—"but not anywhere else!" Evidently, they do not see this as having consequences for the nonsexual aspects of their lives. If they are right, a mild power imbalance in depictions of sexual activity is not a threat to women's equality. Notice finally that this desire appears to be part of a more general one, for women often speak of the emotional value of being held by a man, but not of *doing* the holding. It is not clear that anything is bad about that, however; only those who feel threatened by all gender differences will automatically reject it.

What about the few instances of extreme dominance in sexual portrayals, then? They fall into several categories that will need to be considered separately. To begin with the case of rape scenes, what was said under the topic of violence should be recalled here. Given what usually motivates them, it is not in the least clear that rape fantasies in general should be regarded as degrading; as with other types of portrayed violence, whether a given scene is degrading would depend on its details. On the specific question of subjugation, we have already noted that that is usually not part of the motive for rape fantasies. The charge is often made that the *only* motive for male rape fantasies is power over females. That is belied by the fact that the men who have them, unlike the women, tend to imagine themselves as both rapist and rapee. Revealingly, those who make this claim never grant that the greater numbers of women who get pleasure from such imaginings do so because they want to be subjugated and degraded.

Next consider a certain type of macho novel in this regard. Liberally sprinkled with scenes of rape and men pushing women around, they certainly are objectionable for their portrayal of women *and* men. Whether such portrayals should be considered downright degrading to anyone, however, is a difficult question. In this more general case as well, most of those who fix that label on depicted victimizations of females never use it to describe those of males. If coercion in general is degrading, moreover, an awful lot of what is on television nightly falls into this category. In any case, the large majority of these stories would not rightly be classed as pornography, since sex is not their central focus. As for those that would, the point here is that they are only the erotic segment of a larger category of fantasies, those expressing the power desires of lower-class males. Denied access to the money and status of successful men (and to the women money and status attract), these men compensate with a tough-guy self-image. So the characters in the stories ride roughshod over other males as well; general dominance is the theme, not just the subjection of women. To pretend, as many do, that this mistreatment of women is a natural outgrowth of the portrayal of sex is a serious distortion of the facts. Its cause and cure lie elsewhere.

Another variety of genuine subjugation involves a special paraphilia. What is known as "dominance and submission" is practiced by a tiny sexual subculture. (*The Story of O* provides an extreme illustration. This and another paraphilic specialization, "bondage and discipline," are often both classed as subcategories of sadomasochism.) The causes of such desires are obscure, though their milder forms are readily explained in terms of transfer of excitement from the feeling of power or that of powerlessness. The Freudian hypothesis that they trace back to the love-and-helplessness relationship of a child to its parents is plausible, but hard evidence is not easy to get. What does seem clear is that they are not in general produced by a wider desire to subjugate women, as some have charged. Indeed, the majority of the males in this category desire the submissive role. (They want a "dominatrix.") This may even be true of the sexual materials published for these people: in a survey of such magazines, one researcher found roughly 30 percent more submissive males than submissive females.[3] (In a different store, however, another survey got the opposite result.) The extremist claim that "porn is about power, not about sex" is absurd, once again; but it is even false in regard to paraphilic dominance and submission. For the individuals who have these feelings, power or its lack is what *causes* sexual arousal. The former is only a means to the latter—just the reverse of their charge.

Is not that sort of activity, or its portrayal, evil nonetheless? To answer, we must realize again that paraphilic behavior like this is playacting; it is practiced by mutual consent and for mutual enjoyment. Moreover, its practitioners' nonsexual lives tend to be quite normal. Disturbing to others though they naturally are, these desires are not in general a reflection of forces or feelings that are a threat, to women or anyone else. And they certainly are not common. One study of "adult" book shops in New York City found that about 17 percent of their magazine covers depicted bondage or domination; a larger survey, by not counting more debatable instances, arrived at a figure of just over 9 percent for bondage and sadomasochism. Yet even the latter figure is misleadingly high, for several reasons. First, materials that cater to more unusual sexual tastes are concentrated in these stores; the big-selling sex magazines are sold in more socially acceptable outlets. Second, the paraphiles who consume such materials gravitate to major cities like New York; they also use more pornography than ordinary people owing to their difficulties in getting real sexual activity of the type they desire. Finally, these particular surveys counted titles, rather than separate issues or the number of copies of the latter. This overestimates the percentages, since, among other things, publications portraying more deviant activities tend to be produced only once (in spite of the "Vol. 1, No. 1" they may carry).[4]

To return to the general problem of male dominance, let us recall our earlier observation that women also exert much power over men, notably in regard to sex. A point not made then concerns the way in which men's greater need for sex puts control into the hands of women. "All that power," marvels Nancy Friday in describing the influence this gives adolescent females over their male peers. Some women are oblivious to the situation, while others exploit it—just as some males exploit females' greater need for love. The manner in which this particular power imbalance affects sexual fantasies is extremely important to our present topic. For once more, their purpose is often to make the world seem better than it is in real life. Hence it is not surprising that some men's fantasies would "turn the tables" in this relationship. Those scenes in which a woman is so strongly aroused that she begs for sex make a transparently clear statement of male powerlessness. Similarly, pornographic portrayals in which men dominate women—*and* those that are the other way around—appear to represent varying attempts by males to cope with the feelings of helplessness and frustration. Such things must be understood for what they really are, not simplemindedly denounced as yet another manifestation of patriarchy.

As always, however, the important point is not whether men or women have more power in this respect, but that both are robbed of control over their own lives by antisexual attitudes. Indeed, as the pro-sex feminists have long since realized, it is the very people who level the false charges of one-sided power in pornography who are trying to limit women's autonomy in regard to sex. This is especially clear in the case of those who say portraying sexually uninhibited women is degrading to women in general; they do not want to allow individual women the choice of being that way. And speaking of power, false principles of morality often arise precisely because they are a particularly potent way of controlling other people. Given their own belief in male dominance, the use of this "subjection of women" argument by right-wing members and staffers of the Meese Commission is especially brazen.[5]

The third category of degrading pornography proposed by the commission is that involving behavior which most people would find humiliating. This is a troubling idea, for it implies that anything a majority thinks is degrading really is so, no matter what its objective nature may be. Such a doctrine ignores all the blind and arbitrary influences that go into making something seem shameful to a given society, and how quickly they can change—that is, unless they are cemented into the law. This has already been discussed, but it will now be of value to pursue the matter a bit deeper. Consider the ancient Polynesians again: they perceived very little involving sex to be humiliating, but (Hollywood movies notwithstanding) they regarded kissing on the mouth as terribly disgusting. It takes little thought to realize what many in this culture would say about people kissing had they been raised with the same emotional response: "Another attempt to degrade women!" (And when you consider all that mucky, germ-filled saliva, it would be especially hard to change their minds.) On a more serious note, one has only to read certain accounts by educated whites in earlier centuries, descriptions of how repulsive they found the faces of other races, to realize how dangerous it can be to trust one's gut reactions.

The problem is not these emotional feelings themselves, which to some extent are involuntary. Rather, it consists in reifying them, in supposing that subjective responses faithfully reveal objective moral truths. Alternatively, the problem lies in assuming them to be fully *inter*subjective, in projecting one's individual reactions onto others. For an illustration that closely parallels the kissing case, it is as if antipornography writers say things like this to themselves: "I find semen dirty, therefore that couple must do so as well; so if it goes on her body or in her mouth, she's feeling degraded and he's doing it to degrade her." This much maligned type of scene, be it noted, occurs in homosexual as well as heterosexual pornography; it is evidently *not* done to degrade the opposite sex; it is evidently not done to degrade anyone. A lot of us find the thought of many actions personally repugnant, from eating insects to homosexual acts, without being upset by the knowledge that others like them; the inability to distinguish individual or societal taste from morality is a central characteristic of bigotry.

Speaking of homosexuality, some of the cruelest people loose in society today are the "gay bashers," a class of hypermacho males who feel no compunctions about beating up or even killing an innocent human being. Why do they do it? The reason is highly instructive: they feel personally shamed by the knowledge that members of their own sex should be so unmasculine, or that other men should engage in acts they themselves find repulsive. In their eyes, male homosexuality is degrading to men. As for female homosexuality, right-wingers consider lesbianism at least as degrading to a woman as being "hypersexual," but of course the extremist feminists do not agree. The two types of ideologue differ largely in regard to just which sorts of harmless behavior they consider obviously revolting. The Attorney General's Commission avoided mentioning homosexual behavior per se as humiliating, even though most people would find it degrading to personally engage in such; nor did they cite oral-genital acts, which most would have found humiliating a few decades ago.

None of this is meant to say there is no such thing as real degradation; far from it. But the question is, what constitutes it? In general, what debasement consists of is bringing severe disrespect or shame on someone, making some person or group seem worthy of contempt. A given thing might be bad in a variety of ways, but to be bad in *this* way essentially requires that it elicit strong feelings of inferiority by or toward someone. Now, it has been argued here that behavior toward which people have been conditioned to feel aversion, in itself, should not be seen as doing this; it is the conditioning alone that is to blame. No matter how shameful certain things (sexual acts, skin color, and so on) may seem to others, if those actually involved have no such conscious or unconscious feelings, then they are not really degrading. By contrast, any words or actions that really express the message that someone lacks human worth certainly do qualify under this category. With these things in mind, let us look at a few more claimed illustrations of humiliating behavior in pornography.

The main author of the commission's *Final Report* cited a number of sexual scenes that he considered degrading in the extreme.[6] One of these depicted the behavior of a rare paraphilia (urolagnia), a general category that will be considered shortly; two others portrayed physical and non-physical coercion, which has already been discussed. The remaining scenes involved open labia, the shaving of pubic hair, more than two persons relating sexually, someone watching others have sex while masturbating, and ejaculation on the body. In truth, not one of these things is degrading in itself. Of course, any one of them *could* be portrayed in a demeaning manner; that depends entirely on whether feelings of shame or contempt are also conveyed. But the same may be said of everything else that might be depicted, sexual or nonsexual, for just about anything can be done in a way that expresses such feelings. (The only other scene mentioned was so unusual there has likely been only one like it: it involved the wearing of a dog-costume. Though that would not likely be seen as degrading in a nonsexual or a male-only context, it plausibly was intended to be so.)

The plain reason why things like these seem debasing to so many is this culture's entrained anxiety toward sexuality in general. People are hypersensitive to the possibility of sexual degradation because sex itself is so shame laden. What in other contexts would be considered merely playful or creative, or different from one's own taste, or at worst desperately dumb, is suddenly threatening because it involves sex. It is also threatening because women are involved; all sorts of behavior that would not be regarded as degrading if only men were portrayed are so judged if women are. As already noted, moreover, it is a very effective tactic to call just about anything one wishes to oppose "degrading," especially to women. Revealingly, the commissioner's list deliberately omitted any scenes in which the males involved might have been regarded as being humiliated. Yet as two other members of the commission reluctantly reported later, its own survey found that a higher percentage of portrayals were degrading (by their standards) to men.[7]

To be sure, rationalizations are always at hand. It is charged, for example, that shaved pubic hair on women is an attempt to treat them like infants. Never mind that most women in this culture prefer men with clean-shaven faces—are they trying to turn men into little boys? The actual reason in both cases is that some people find what the hair conceals attractive. Against such determined illogic, perhaps the best defense is to point out how many of the behaviors commonly labeled "degrading to women" are to be found in women's own sexual fantasies, engaged in for their own pleasure. A recent survey in conservative Ontario found the following percentages of women in its sample had fantasized about the corresponding acts: cunnilingus, 66 percent; rape, 51 percent; fellatio, 49 percent; intercourse with a stranger, 46 percent; doing a striptease, 37 percent; watching a male masturbate, 33 percent; sex with many men, 29 percent; sex with inanimate objects, 23 percent; sex with others watching, 21 percent; gang rape, 18 percent; anal sex, 17 percent; group sex, 16 percent; incest, 14 percent; sex with an animal, 9 percent; sadomasochistic acts, 7 percent.[8]

One special category of pornography is standardly accused of involving humiliating acts, namely, that associated with various paraphilias. The things that are sexually arousing to certain individuals are sometimes so unnatural they would be repellent to any healthy person (e.g., those involving defecation). Yet even these do not in general include any desire to degrade or to be degraded. Indeed, they are not usually seen *as* degrading by these people themselves, at least consciously. It is only some error in their psychological programming that makes paraphiles find such things powerfully desirable. Now, there are paraphiles of one special type who do get sexual pleasure from giving or receiving degradation itself. Even in their case, however, it is not because of any hatred for themselves or others (unless, once more, it is at a subconscious level). The most likely cause of this particular condition will be discussed shortly.

Should these deviant feelings nevertheless be condemned as morally evil? Certainly not; no more so than other mental or emotional disorders, though they can sometimes be successfully treated. Most paraphilias harm neither the individuals themselves nor anyone else; the former are more likely to *be* harmed by others or by the law. And in spite of the punitive medieval attitudes of many people, such tendencies are not acquired by choice. No one decides freely to have needs or feelings that will make the world despise and pity him. Correspondingly, there are no adequate reasons for condemning the sorts of sexual portrayal that cater vicariously to their needs. On the contrary, compassion would seem to dictate that they be allowed access to whatever will reduce their distress, provided there is no reason to suspect this will bring harm to anyone else.

REAL DEGRADATION

The upshot of the preceding discussion is that most sexual depictions standardly labeled degrading are not anything of the sort. Of course, there certainly are some that would fit the description to one degree or another. Even so, the reasons for their existence are revealing. To begin with, the standard explanation for why certain paraphiles find degradation sexually arousing is that they were raised to believe sex itself is degrading. In a culture where children are so often taught that erotic thoughts and actions are filthy, it would hardly be surprising if dirt and shame became eroticized for some vulnerable individuals, either by associative learning or through an unconscious defense mechanism. In the former case, the person has been made to feel it just is not sex unless it *is* degrading. In the latter, the subconscious mind says, in effect, "You can't destroy my sexual desires by telling me they're debasing—I'll just proceed to *enjoy* degradation!" Alternatively, having been made to feel like dirt over their sexual attraction to others, they unconsciously defend their personal dignity by seeing the others as also degraded; if sex is dirty, then those who attract one sexually are dirty. To a lesser degree, presumably, normal persons would also be influenced in these ways, and this might be reflected in their fantasies.

A second source of degrading depictions is much more conscious; it just reflects the satisfaction many people get from jeering at those who have maligned them. This is evidently the motivation of the likes of Larry Flynt and his readers. For example, that infamous meat-grinder cover on *Hustler* was a mocking response to antipornography "pieces of meat" rhetoric.[9] (Equally grotesque pictures involving males have also appeared in *Hustler*, it should be noted, such as a huge penis on a platter. A general proclivity for taboo-breaking, not "hatred of women," is its raison d'etre.) A more general and more serious reaction of this type might well be a result of our culture's continuing denigration of male sexual feelings. This important topic will be explored in Chapter 12; the constant message to men that their desires are degrading and exploitive is bound to produce feelings of hostility in some, feelings that could express themselves in mental images that really are degrading. A few pornographic portrayals give a distinct impression of a desire to prove women are not such paragons of purity after all, to bring them down to the same level as the nasty animals we have always been told men are.

One way or another, then, such real degradation as occurs in pornography may be entirely the product of traditional antisexual attitudes. The irony in this should be obvious: the very views that motivate the charge that pornography in general is degrading are what produce the real degradation.

However, it must be stressed again that there is little of the latter. Public perceptions on this matter have been manipulated by the sophistries of those who actively compaign against pornography. As they do in the case of portrayed violence, they pick out instances of genuine debasement and pretend it is representative. They suppress the existence and nature of paraphilias (e.g., such facts as how frequently it is a male who is receiving the unpleasantness), so they can pretend that type of portrayal represents hatred of women. They also tend to ignore all the nonsexual degradation in all the entertainment media—at least that experienced by males. Finally, they find vast amounts of degradation that does not exist, manipulating the sexual anxieties of the general population to raise anger against pornography. As we have seen with other claims about pornography, those involving the special issue of degradation are shot through with half-truths and outright falsehoods, sexism and antisexualism, illogic and groundless fears. Even a little honesty and good will would go far toward curing that condition.

7

Alleged Ill Effects from Use

To summarize what we have discussed so far, the belief that pornography is evil in itself is simply wrong. This leaves open the important question of whether it has effects on the user's attitudes or behavior that are harmful to anyone. Charges that this is so are continually being made, so in the next four or five chapters we will explore that issue. It will not be a simple one, since it involves all the complexities of human psychology. Though some things about human nature are fairly obvious from introspection or daily observation, others are extremely difficult to find out. And in many ways, the behavioral sciences are still in their infancy. Noting this warning, we will survey the major kinds of evidence currently available in regard to the influence of sexually explicit presentations. We will begin in this chapter by considering a number of standard charges, falling roughly into three categories: claimed effects on general morality and character, on personal relationships, and on the family.

One particularly profound problem involves the issue of human agency. Now, some people are logically inconsistent in regard to this issue. In response to the suggestion that a violent criminal was made that way by a traumatic childhood, they invoke a notion of absolute free will: "His circumstances are not to blame; he *chose* to let them affect him!" But let the subject be something as comparatively minor as exposure to words or pictures, and suddenly the same people insist on a causal influence. The perennial debate over freedom of the will can hardly be discussed here. But one thing is perfectly clear from all the evidence: heredity and environment have a powerful influence on human behavior. The only room for rational debate is over whether that influence is total (deterministic) or not—and, once more, over just how much effect different types of causal factor exert.

Added to the difficulties in getting knowledge about a terribly complex subject are all the logical fallacies to which humans are prone, especially when they have had no training in specialized reasoning. These have seriously infected the long debate over pornography. We will continue to expose bad logic here, but the best general advice for all of us is simply caution in drawing conclusions. As has been noted before, it is very easy to believe one has factual knowledge when one does not. Indeed, to some people the very idea that good evidence is required for holding a belief seems quite foreign. They speak as if the answers to the most scientifically difficult questions were "just obvious," out of the thin air of ideology or what "everybody knows." In other cases, what are taken to *be* potent reasons are equally valueless, for example, the ever popular *"post hoc, ergo propter hoc"* fallacy. ("After this, therefore because of this.") Consider an illustration: "The United States is a Christian country, and it has a high level of violence; therefore Christianity makes people violent." Even if the conclusion happened to be true, or could be argued for on reasonable grounds, this argument for it, on these grounds alone, is simply absurd.

Perhaps the greatest impediment to clear-headed assessment of the evidence is emotion. No issue that did not affect our emotions in some way would seem (or *be*) important enough to discuss in the first place, but strong emotions induce people to commit errors to which they would not otherwise be prone. It has been said that claiming to have knowledge one clearly does not have is a form of lying—the polite phrase is "intellectual dishonesty." (This includes the case of deceiving oneself.) By that standard, there is a lot of dishonesty in the claims commonly heard about ill effects of pornography. The preexisting desire to find something about it to attack has led to much distortion and pretended knowledge. In fact, in those claims it is almost always clear from the context that the speaker or writer believes pornography is *intrinsically* evil. The underlying motive for such charges is very often nothing but religious or political dogma, not scientific evidence. "It's degrading and ugly, so it *must* have horrid effects." By no means are the bad reasoning and bad faith all on one side, however. Many who defend sexually explicit materials as harmless are motivated more by sexual liberalism or dislike of censorship than by the evidence. We will have to examine each issue on its own merits.

THE DOMINO THEORY OF CHARACTER

The first of the claims we will discuss is usually expressed in vague generalities; it is basically the charge that use of pornography tends to produce all sorts of wrongful behavior. From the rhetoric some of its proponents employ, one would swear they believe sexual thoughts that are not strictly confined will create a desire to rush out and break windows or steal cars. It is as if they retained the primitive belief that individuals are motivated by only two basic desires—to do good or to do evil—rather than by a complex panoply of needs and emotions. In the minds of some, this idea seems to rest on the conviction that one sort of corruption just naturally leads to others. Few, if any, scientists take such ideas seriously today; "degeneracy theory," with its concept that physical, psychological, and moral defects are all bound together, was popular in the last century but died with the rise of psychology and scientific medicine. In the rest of the population, unfortunately, notions like this one linger on.

The more specific suggestion is sometimes made that "losing self-control" in regard to sex—as allegedly might be precipitated by the use of pornography—produces a general lack of self-discipline, hence a tendency toward selfish libertinism or worse. This sort of thinking has a long history. In Victorian times, married couples were advised to limit the frequency of their sexual activities strictly lest they lead to a weakening of the will and of general character. And the myth that sexual excess brought about the decline and fall of Rome has been around for centuries, having come down to us with those old suspicions about bodily pleasure. (Never mind the gladiators and slavery and brutal imperialism; sexual pleasure was Rome's real failing.) Part of what is involved in the thinking, evidently, is an inability to distinguish between the very specific matter of sexual "permissiveness" and the rejection of *all* restraints on behavior. Alternatively, it is a confusion between a strong interest in sex and a failure to care about any other sources of happiness, or else a tendency to be concerned only with one's own happiness or with the pleasures of the moment. Such tendencies are certainly bad; for example, a person or nation fixated on momentary satisfactions will lack the discipline to plan for and protect future happiness. But there is no reason to suppose that sexual desires are any more apt to have such consequences than are other strong desires.

As usual, it is revealing to point out the inconsistency between these concerns and the lack of fears associated with other needs and pleasures, say, those involving food, love, religious devotion, or the arts. How many are alarmed that our lack of eating taboos—so common in other cultures—will lead to a general obsession with the happiness of the moment? Perhaps we should ban the Wednesday food section in the newspaper, with its seductive pictures and emphasis on the pleasure of eating over its utilitarian function. How many suppose that getting great enjoyment from music or dance will lead to a general lack of self-discipline, or to a disregard for the welfare of others (say, of those who perform them)? The rhetoric about the perils of "pleasure-seeking" is remarkably selective in regard to which pleasures it notices. The real source of this belief, it seems clear, is the sexual anxiety with which so many are raised; it produces the fear that something terrible will happen if one should ever "let go."

The most important response to such charges, however, is that those who make them do not have a shred of genuine evidence. They have been accepted and repeated endlessly, like so many other cultural beliefs, without critical examination. In earlier times, when racism was more socially acceptable than it is now, mixing of the races was often alleged to have brought about the decline of Rome and other civilizations—on the basis of the same worthless *post hoc* reasoning. (In the course of criticizing certain historical writers for irresponsibly parroting such sentiments, Dr. Bullough remarks that the Roman empire actually became less sexually permissive with time, not more.) Certain commentators have claimed to have evidence from one or two studies that reported finding a statistical association between exposure to sexual materials and juvenile delinquency in the United States.[1] It could well be true that in this society, there has been a tendency for those who lack the traditional sexual attitudes to reject other social standards as well. The former is easily explained as a result of the latter, however: those who have been less well socialized into or have rebelled against the system as a whole will naturally be among the ones whose sexual behavior is less constrained. Alternatively, those whose needs have led them to break one social taboo will feel less threatened by other societal rules. These points will be discussed in greater detail later on.

Of course, that a belief is held for bad reasons does not mean there are no good reasons for it. Nonetheless, it can be said without hesitation that the evidence available is strongly against the "domino theory" of character. One has only to consider the cross-cultural picture to begin to realize this, say, the promiscuous children and youth of Mangaia or the Trobriand Islands or the Muria villages, who grow up into hard-working adults who have internalized all of their society's moral standards. More generally, there is no indication that sexually positive cultures have greater amounts of antisocial behavior. In fact, one cross-cultural survey found significantly more personal crime in groups where premarital sex is strongly punished than in others.[2] (The fact that the crime rate in permissive northern Europe is much lower than that in the United States may already be known to the reader—but beware of *post hoc* thinking.) The belief that gratifying sexual feelings tends somehow to turn into a general state of moral corruption, or even to damage one's capacity for self-discipline, is sheer superstition.

What looks like a special version of this "generalized corruption" belief is involved in the charge that much pornography is controlled by organized crime. Actually, very little of it clearly has such links. (Mafia informants insist that particular organization is quite puritanical in matters of sex, and refuses to get involved with sexual materials.) Like so many other claims against pornography, this one has been grossly exaggerated to frighten the public. In fact, the same kind of semantic cheating used elsewhere in the debate is employed here. Here is the reasoning of one of the key officials who make the charge: pornography is produced or distributed by an organization (which could hardly be otherwise), and it might somewhere be judged legally obscene, which is a crime; so pornography is *ipso facto* controlled by organized crime.[3] Since that is not at all what the ordinary person understands by the phrase, this is a blatant attempt to deceive the public. If religion were illegal here—as it has been in some places—then religion would be "organized crime" in the same sense.

In a similar category are the stories one hears about individuals being coerced and mistreated in the making of commercial pornography; these stories are also told in order to discredit the "sex industry" as a whole. In response, numerous erotic models and actresses have come forward to insist that cases of genuine mistreatment are rare. In fact, they often say, they are accorded more respect than women tend to get elsewhere—and they make much better pay than the men.[4] (In the same vein, there evidently never has been a *genuine* commercial "snuff" movie, though a couple of psychotic killers have made videotapes of their ghastly crimes.) Presumably, some of the charges of abuse are true. But people with an axe to grind will readily fabricate or exaggerate, especially when they know there is an audience eager to hear such stories. For whatever it means, the standard tale of mistreatment sounds remarkably similar to acclaimed ballerina Gelsey Kirkland's exposé of American ballet: naive young girls given harsh training in unnatural movements that can cripple them, taught to use their bodies but not their minds, and just generally exploited. The result, she says, is rampant anorexia and bulimia, and drug abuse. All this for the pleasure of upper-class women! Consider how quick the public is to believe the porn stories in contrast to this one—whatever the actual truth may be. When movie actresses become victims of the fast life, Hollywood's image may suffer but not that of motion pictures per se; it is very different for sex movies.

However, what is of interest here is not the precise facts but the conclusions that are drawn from such claims. Though the point of these arguments is usually not made explicit, it often appears to be the claim that sexual entertainment has a natural tendency to attract lawless people or to incite exploitive behavior. If so, this is another piece of *post hoc* reasoning. It provides as much reason to regard pornography as inherently evil-inducing—that is, none at all—as it does for so regarding the labor movement, small businesses, and many other enterprises taken over by organized crime. This claim is as irrational as would be one that agriculture is evil, promoted on grounds of the cases of worker exploitation and even slavery that periodically come to light from that quarter. (Speaking of moral character, two things that have made the Mafia so strong are the much admired qualities of loyalty to tradition and family closeness. Does their association with organized crime mean they are bad?) One has only to reflect on recent horror stories of the kidnapping of babies and mistreat-

ment of unwed mothers, committed to provide children for desperate in-
fertile couples, in order to realize that corrupt individuals will exploit any
strong human desire.

What *has* sometimes attracted criminal types to pornography, then? The
answer seems transparently clear. First, there is the fact that highly explicit
materials are already on the fringes of social respectability: ordinary businesspersons hence tend to shun them, leaving a vacuum to be filled by
those with fewer scruples. Being on the fringes of legality has an even
stronger effect, as those involved search for protection from the police.
According to *Time* magazine, for example, the U.S. Supreme Court's
"local community standards" approach to obscenity left producers of erotic
materials at the mercy of the law in every conservative hamlet in the nation;
so some of them turned the more explicit ones over to organized crime to
distribute rather than risk going through legitimate business channels. Finally, the big profits to be made can attract the criminal element. And
what makes the profits big is just pornography's social and legal status
again. Instead of normal competitive pressures to bring prices down, there
have historically been the sort of black-market and gray-market influences
that push prices up.

All these things would happen to any other strongly desired product that
was treated as sexual materials have been. We have seen the same type
of thing happen repeatedly, in fact. Both before and after Prohibition, the
liquor trade in the United States was controlled by socially respectable
businesspersons (and this in spite of the fact that liquor genuinely does do
extreme amounts of social harm). Yet in between, the mob acquired vast
power as a result of alcohol's illegal status. When prostitution was made
widely illegal and quasi-illegal about a century ago, the women were forced
to leave their own neighborhoods and emotional ties for the anonymous
life of the streets. For protection and a measure of emotional support, they
turned to men who were willing to live, and profit, outside the law—and
we have all heard the rest of that horror story.[5] In a similar vein, the high
crime rate often found in the vicinity of porno shops exists for precisely
the same reason as it does in the neighborhoods of degraded ethnic groups.

Ironically, then, it is not sexual explicitness at all, but social unacceptability—the very attitude motivating these arguments—that has put some
pornography, with the money and power it produces, into the hands of
criminal types. Indeed, many of those who use such arguments are determined to make a much greater proportion of pornography illegal, and we
can predict the result. Of course, no one would suggest that all possible
products and services be legal in order to avoid giving power to criminals.
Whether explicit sex or anything else should be prohibited is a matter to
be decided by weighing any harm it may produce against that caused by
its criminalization. The point here is simply that another common argument
against pornography is completely without merit. To use "the crime con-

nection" as an argument for suppressing sexual materials, when suppressing them is what has produced that connection in the first place, is nothing less than insane.

PERSONAL RELATIONSHIPS

A second variety of claim that pornography has ill effects is that its use tends to damage personal relationships between men and women. This charge takes several different forms, including some that are bizarre (e.g., the idea that many men prefer it to real women and hence will avoid relationships with them if given that option). The simplest of these allegations, however, just points out that numerous women are upset by their partners' interest in pornography, so that it becomes a source of conflict. Part of the problem here is jealousy: the mere biologically normal fact that the partner is attracted to other persons is threatening to some, even when it is all fantasy. But that is evidently not the main difficulty. Few men feel upset over their partners' interest in love stories, say, in soap operas, with their romantic hunks and adulterous love affairs. The real problem seems to be the woman's aversion to nudity and sexual openness.

That being so, this argument presupposes that pornography is hurtful rather than proving it. For it could equally well be said that it is the woman's prudishness, rather than the man's interest in pornography, that is "the real" source of the trouble; which it is would have to be argued for rather than just assumed. Mention to the feminists and religionists who employ this objection that women's liberation or religious devotion has broken up many relationships, and they will make the same basic point. Given the conclusions already reached in this book, moreover, it seems clear which one is the real culprit. In earlier years, the attitude that explicit sex is offensive to women led men to go off by themselves to watch "stag films"; what could have been an enjoyable shared experience became a source of alienation. Although female interest in such things might never approach that of males, the ones who divide the sexes are those who say, "My desires are noble and yours are nasty," not those who believe in the equal worth and dignity of the needs of both.

One special argument of this kind alleges that pornography harms relationships by its overemphasis on sex, and also by its underemphasis on companionship or romantic love. It is said to "teach men" to value the former too much and the latter too little. With its culture-bound and egocentric notions of how much emphasis is too much or too little, this claim ignores the possibility of keeping the sexes in harmony by teaching women to want sex in the same way. Its biggest error, however, lies in assigning to media depictions far more power to influence basic desires than is at all justified. As usual, those who make this claim express no similar beliefs about the persuasive powers of the constant barrage of love songs and love stories in all the entertainment media. If such exposure were really so effective, one would think, we would all be incurable love-junkies by now. In any case, there is certainly no lack of publicity promoting love and companionship in our society. Moreover, male sexuality is not detectably different in cultures without appreciable amounts of pornography; indeed, it is evidently very much the same the world over.[6]

What really underlies this claim is an old problem: the unfortunate fact that, on average, men's and women's needs in regard to love/commitment and sex are not well matched. Unable—or perhaps just unwilling—to believe men could ultimately have such different needs than they themselves do, some women suppose it must be the different amount of stress on sex or love among men that does it. One common response is simply to deny that men are really different. For example, these women say men just *think* they have a strong need for sex because advertisers keep telling them they do. Others grant the reality of male sexual responses but do not want to believe they are natural. (Among feminists, this is just part of the wider conviction that there are *no* innate differences between the sexes except anatomical ones.) Yet those who make both claims insist it is men who have been most affected by culture in this regard. Over and again, without offering any argument as to which is cause and which effect, they assert that men would not be so interested in sex, or so attracted to female bodies, if only there were not so much emphasis on those things in this society. Besides projecting their own responses onto male nature—responses that are themselves largely culture-conditioned—the women (and sometimes men) who make such claims are somehow blind to all the societal efforts to suppress male sexuality and promote female needs.

What is true is that a double standard is still taught to adolescents in our culture. But it is glaringly false to say that it encourages males to be sexual; it merely discourages them less. Consider the common charge that "this society" teaches young males they have to "score" to be real men, for example. In fact, you will not find this preached by any of the major socializing institutions, not by church, government, school, family, *or* the media.[7] Even that small segment of the latter that celebrates sex overtly cannot really be said to do this—and it is standardly maligned and even banned by the society at large. The one place where such a thing is taught is in the peer groups of some young men as they themselves rebel against society's teaching on the subject, trying to justify their own needs and feelings. However all this may be, the point remains that pornography is not the cause of male sexuality. It has again become a scapegoat in connection with male-female conflicts whose real causes lie in biology, or at least much deeper in the socialization of men—or of women.

A different type of argument in this category grants that pornography does not cause basic male desires or misperceptions of them by males but holds that it can give men unrealistic expectations about fulfilling them. It involves the idealization charges discussed earlier; this time the claim is that the beautiful and highly sexed women in pornography can make men dissatisfied with the bodies or the sexual behavior of the women in their lives. Sometimes the reason given for the former is that they mislead men concerning what the average woman's body is really like. But that is wholly implausible. There is ample opportunity to learn what shapes most people come in, especially at swimming pools and beaches. Any misleading that is done in this regard is being done—often quite deliberately—by clothing, not by nudity.

What is true is that being exposed to more attractive individuals can make one's own mate seem less appealing, at least temporarily. This is but one manifestation of a common experience, the contrast effect: lukewarm water will feel cool to a hand recently immersed in hot water, warm to one from cold water. But pornography represents an extremely small portion of most people's exposure to attractive members of the opposite sex; those who single it out for blame in this regard are getting desperate in their search for raps to pin on porn. Certain recent experiments have indeed indicated that men exposed to attractive pinups will for a short time afterward find ordinary women, including their mates, less physically appealing. Other experiments, however, involving nonvisual sex and nonnude physical attractiveness, make it clear that the nudity involved is not part of what produced those results. (The recent book by Edward Donnerstein et al., *The Question of Pornography,* provides a good discussion of this and of much other research on the effects of sexual materials.) Finally, the things women are exposed to daily that can make their partners seem less appealing are too numerous to list: handsome, high-status/high-competence males in advertising, soap operas, romance novels, and so on.

As for the dissatisfaction erotic portrayals might produce with a partner's sexual desire or behavior, here the objection is on firmer ground. It is still not very likely, however, that being deceived concerning the average woman's libido is the reason. It is indeed less easy, in the case of sexual desires, to get good information about other people's feelings. Even at that, normal persons are not apt to be misled by what are clearly fantasy escapades. To the extent that any are misled, moreover, we should blame the sexual ignorance in which our society keeps everyone. Myth, projection, and wishful thinking will always rush in to fill a knowledge void, whether or not commercial fantasies exist. In fact, traditional social dogma about sex is full of distortions about real needs and feelings. (When it comes to distorting reality, nothing can compare with the asexual view of life traditionally presented to impressionable children.) Furthermore, the intrinsic danger of sexual fantasies misinforming men about the opposite sex's feelings is no greater than that of romantic ones doing the same to women. Indeed, condemning or suppressing the fantasies of only one sex is a good way to mislead the other one about their desires. Finally, what a person's sexual desires *might* be like, if she or he were not freighted with inhibitions, is another question. In this regard it has already been argued that, in general, pornography does not distort the truth.

Some have claimed there is scientific evidence that standard pornography causes misperception of other people's sexual desires. In a certain type of experiment, volunteers are exposed to a presentation of some kind and then asked questions about their beliefs or attitudes. (A subterfuge is used to keep them from realizing the true purpose of the test.) In one version of this test, subjects who have been shown sexual materials indicated they regarded women (as well as men) as somewhat more sexually liberal than did subjects who had not been shown the materials. In itself, this is no evidence of misperception; the former might have been closer to the truth than the latter. In any case, the result is not in the least remarkable. A recent or extended experience of *any* kind looms large in one's consciousness. Hence just about any book or movie, *or* real person that one has recently met, would have a similar influence on one's other judgments, temporarily. For a more striking example, one who has just seen a scary movie is much more likely to look under the bed before retiring at night. The effect soon fades, however; it is swamped by that of subsequently encountered books or movies or real people. And most of the latter tend to promote the culture's current party line on sex, just as they do on other subjects. Except in unusual circumstances, the conclusion remains: sexual entertainment will have little effect on perceptions of reality.

A variant of this objection says that the ecstatic pleasure often portrayed in pornography will tend to make the readers or viewers disappointed with their own sexual experience and, hence, with their partners or their partners' performance. (Although it is women who standardly complain about the latter, this new claim is usually framed in terms of male dissatisfaction.) It is not always clear whether those who present the argument believe ordinary tepid sex is really all that is possible—the half-hour orgasms of Mangaian women argue otherwise—or whether for some reason they just think it unwise to aspire to greater enjoyment. In any case, few people would be misled even by genuine exaggeration, which is an extremely common part of life. Does the hysterical euphoria of the consumers in commercials for hamburgers and soft drinks make anyone seriously expect them to taste different? Once again, the only reason for possibly being misled in the special case of sex is societally imposed ignorance. And it is people who use arguments like this one who often want to keep young people in that vulnerable state.

Even without misleading anyone, of course, pornography might make men dissatisfied with ordinary women by awakening repressed desires or by making them aware of appealing new possibilities. Stories of uninhibited women can indeed engender disappointment concerning other women's degree of sexual interest and enthusiasm (something tales of the South Seas have done for generations of men). But notice the argument's sexist presupposition that only male expectations should not be raised. By the same token, women's traditional complaint that men are not affectionate and attentive enough is apt to be sharpened by their reading romantic novels or listening to some current media heartthrob croon love ballads to them. More important, however, neither of these results is necessarily bad. To the extent that they help people get in touch with their own feelings or communicate them to others, media idealizations can aid in changing things for the better for both sexes. But do not expect the people who use this argument, with all their professions of concern about interpersonal relationships, to endorse real openness. Many of those who say they wish men would be more expressive about their feelings react with instant condemnation when those feelings turn out not to be politically correct.

One final argument claiming harm to relationships from pornography rests on the charge that conflict often results when a man wants to try out activities he has seen in sex movies but the woman does not. Aside from sexual acts that are dangerous or intrinsically repulsive, it looks once again as if the real villain here is learned sexual aversion. (Given the standard report of prostitutes that a majority of their married clients come to them for the oral-genital sex their wives will not engage in, that is presumably the most common such desire.) The usual unspoken sexist assumptions are also operating here; if he didn't want to share something she wished to do, guess who would be the unfeeling beast again. In any case, it is odd to put blame on the thing that merely gave him the idea, which could equally well have been a sex manual or a friend. The implication seems to be that sexual awareness itself is a bad thing and should be suppressed. "Knowledge is dangerous—keep people ignorant."

A special form of this last argument concludes that pornography is evil on the grounds that some men try to force their partners into the activities they have seen in sex films.[8] It is difficult to know how much truth is in the premise here, since in the vocabulary of some who assert it, men never seem to make sexual requests but only "demands." In any case, it is again strange to suggest that knowledge of something that is not bad in itself is made morally blameworthy by the fact that coercion is sometimes used to obtain it. It is as if one objected to teaching about driving or the value of money, on the grounds that he might then go out and take an automobile or money by force. The problem is not the knowledge of possibly desirable things but the existence of unprincipled persons. (Of course, pornography that portrays coercive acts may be a special case; we will be looking at it later on, along with charges that portrayals of consensual sex can themselves inspire coercive acts.) Men *or* women who use coercion or violence against their partners are to be deplored and stopped. But that problem is one that is not at all unique to the sexual context.

Most of the foregoing claims about pornography's "effects" assume that too much stress on sex is dangerous to an intimate relationship. That can certainly be true, but the proper balance of emphasis between sex and other needs in that context is one that requires sensitive exploration, not dogma. In fact, those who give these fallacious arguments typically overlook the opposite problem. Surveys and clinical experience have long revealed that a high percentage of couples have unsatisfying sex lives. That is a major destroyer of relationships in itself. There are many reasons for this, but a serious one continues to be the sexual inhibition this society inculcates, with its *negative* stress on sex. Conversely, once more, countless women have discovered that sex could be a joy rather than a burden, and they have done so precisely by learning to become more sexually assertive and more adventurous in bed.

What is especially relevant to our purposes about the latter fact is that pornography has often aided in the process. Large numbers of people have reported that it has helped their sex lives and hence their relationships. In one survey of couples who went to sex movies together, for example, 42 percent made that claim.[9] In her beautiful little book on female sexuality, *For Yourself,* Dr. Lonnie Barbach tells how women have overcome difficulty in getting sexually aroused, or in having orgasms, by learning to use fantasy and pornography. Indeed, it has become standard practice for therapists to use sex films to treat the sexual disabilities of individuals and couples. The ways in which they help are very revealing in light of what has just been discussed: they aid in overcoming inhibition, enhance arousal in preparation for sex, and introduce ideas and techniques that bring freshness to a stale routine. So far from harming intimate personal relationships, pornography can have the very opposite effect.

MARRIAGE AND THE FAMILY

A third general charge of social harm from pornography has been put forth, mostly by traditionalists. Its use is seen as a threat, not to love and personal relationships as such, but to marriage and the family. The basic claim is that by celebrating sex for its own sake, pornography entices people to leave or refrain from entering committed relationships—"Why be married if you can get sex without it?"—or else leads to their breakup by encouraging extramarital adventures that result in jealous conflicts. This is a serious charge indeed. The legalistic concern some have with marriage ceremonies is highly questionable; but the family, in its role of raising children, is of crucial importance. And divorce, with its adverse effects on children, has become increasingly common in recent decades. Such a large and complex topic can hardly be explored adequately here, but we can address two relevant questions: Is a positive attitude toward sex for its own sake necessarily a threat to marriage? And is pornography an appreciable factor in promoting that sort of attitude, hence itself such a threat?

The answer to the first question seems to be negative. For one thing, there have been many cultures with a stable family life and also an accepting attitude toward nonmarital sex. In fact, prior to the rise of the world religions and the empires that spread them, socially sanctioned premarital sex may well have been the cross-cultural norm.[10] It has even been suggested that such behavior contributes to later marital stability by providing young people with experience on which to base a wiser choice of mate. In any case, it does not speak very well of marriage to suggest that, given a choice, people will reject it. As a matter of fact, most do have a strong inclination toward pair-bonding. Since they do not marry just for sex in the first place (and *shouldn't* do so), liberal sexual attitudes are not likely to dissuade them; only the timing is apt to be affected. In addition, there are many good reasons for not forcing young people to rush into marriage by making it the only way they can get sex.

As for the case of *extra*marital sex, where it has been socially sanctioned and controlled, it too has not been a serious threat to the stability of the family. It is true that jealousy is a powerful emotion. But it is also true that humans are far from being strictly monogamous in their feelings. Although our culture has traditionally taken jealousy as morally justified and condemned extramarital desires, others have done just the reverse: they have sought to mitigate the conflict between the two emotions by controlling the former more than the latter. And the anthropological reports indicate that they succeed rather well. It just may be, for all we know, that their system works better than ours in this respect.[11] In fact, it can be argued that our unbending attitude toward sexual exclusivity contributes to marital breakup by creating unrealistic expectations. The offending party may not want such a break but feel it is necessary to satisfy other desires; and the offended one may fear loss of face in not avenging the act, or else think there must be something wrong with one of them or with the marriage for such a thing to have happened.

However all this may be, it is not the immediate question here. For us the issue is whether pornography is in any of the ways suggested a threat to the family in our culture. In spite of what many assume, it is far from obvious that it is. Indeed, it may be more likely to act as a "safety valve" for preventing marital breakup by providing a substitute way to satisfy nonmonogamous desires. Many cultures of the world have had special festival times and special locations in which the usual sexual taboos could be broken. (For just one example, consider the temple "prostitution" of the ancient Near East, in which all men and women took part.) The seeming value of such institutions in maintaining both monogamy and mental health has been noted by many students of the subject. The fact that such large numbers of strictly monogamous couples in the present time have come to use sexual entertainment together hints that it can serve the same purpose. Given the strong biological urge to have more than one sex partner, this may be an extremely important consideration.

Furthermore, pornography can help to preserve marriages by means of the positive effects listed earlier. As for the chance that it can also have the opposite effect, it might be suggested that romantic love stories present more of a danger to long-term pairing by awakening desires that many a marriage gone stale cannot satisfy. After all, falling in love with someone else is more likely to produce the wish for divorce than is a one-night stand. In any case, factors other than sexual fantasies have been vastly more influential in creating marital instability. The data indicate that such things as the following have been responsible for increasing divorce rates: greater independence for women (most female advocates of long-term commitment do not assail *this* causal factor), changes in laws and attitudes regarding divorce, unemployment and other financial troubles, and the greater mobility of the population, which has led to a loss of controls by the extended family and the community.

To really answer the question before us, however, we must consider the possible dynamics. Exactly how might pornography produce the allegedly destabilizing desires? Those who make the charge sometimes talk as if it is just a matter of arousing feelings that would not otherwise exist. But that is *their* fantasy, for biology can quite adequately do so. It does not take "outside agitators" like pornography to produce lust and wandering eyes. There is one thing, however, that pornography certainly can do, and that is to thwart attempts to suppress such feelings. Efforts to promote one moral point of view are indeed apt to be hampered when people are allowed to become aware of other views as genuine alternatives. This is just to say, however, that freedom and knowledge are an obstacle to attempts at thought control. "How're you gonna keep 'em down on the farm, after they've seen Paris?" asks an old song. It was not only the pill, but the loosening of restraints on sexual content in the media, that launched the reassessment of traditional sexual attitudes that occurred in the 1960s.

So there is a much broader point here that is very important. It is clear that formal and informal education—learning more about the world—tend to make people more tolerant and liberal in their views. For just one apparent example, surveys have revealed that half the readers of sex magazines are college educated, in contrast to a third of the readers of magazines in general. Ideologues, however, do not like such tolerance; what they are opposed to at bottom is the right of other people to make up their own minds. (From Moscow to Washington, they answer, "Don't *let* 'em see Paris.") But it cannot easily be argued that keeping people in ignorance of different ideas is best for them. As Carl Sagan pointed out in *Cosmos,* science has flourished at those times and places in history where there have been the greatest social openness and freedom. So it is for good reasons that we have our tradition of freedom of expression: aside from the great value of liberty itself, we have a better chance of discovering truth in a "free marketplace of ideas" than in conditions where only certain beliefs and attitudes may be extolled.

In particular, our best hope of working out the most viable social arrangement concerning sex and the family is to allow an open dialogue in which all human needs are given consideration. It is just as wrong to censor portrayals of alternative sexual lifestyles as it is to suppress those of different political or religious systems. In all likelihood, given the large range of human differences that exists, the best system in the present regard is a pluralistic one that allows individuals to discover the different modes of living that maximize their fulfillment. To rigidly impose the same kinds of relationships upon everyone (on homosexual and heterosexual, pair-bonder and non-pair-bonder, and so forth) surely does not serve the best interests of individual people. And the common assumption that it is best for society as a whole is the product, not of a careful study of alternatives, but of the very prejudice that censors consideration of alternatives. Socially enforced error is self-perpetuating.

A related problem that needs comment here is that of unmarried pregnancy among juveniles. Teenagers in this culture are generally unprepared, emotionally and otherwise, to cope with pregnancy and childbirth. This is largely the result of modern technology and social structure; under the type of society in which humans evolved, adolescents did the same work as adults and had extended families or the whole tribe to help care for their children. For us, by contrast, teenage pregnancy is a serious problem. For reasons similar to those already cited, however, it is unlikely that pornography has a significant effect in promoting adolescent sexuality. Aside from the fact that other media and social institutions are much more influential, to make young men and women find sex desirable does not require such material. Indeed, it is romance novels and magazines that most stimulate the sexual feelings of teenage girls.[12]

Should we nonetheless try to keep young people from acting on those desires by preventing positive messages about sex from reaching them? Absolutely not. The sexual ignorance and guilt traditionally imposed on adolescents are harmful in countless ways. (More on this as we continue.) In fact, they are highly counterproductive; they are what prevent large numbers of teenagers from using adequate contraception. For one thing, to take such precautions means admitting in advance—to others *and* to themselves—that they have sexual plans, rather than having the excuse of being carried away by the passion of the moment. ("Nice girls don't use birth control.") Other industrialized countries with greater acceptance of adolescent sexuality have a much lower level of unwed pregnancy. In the permissive Netherlands, for example, where use of contraceptives is strongly stressed, the rates of teenage childbirth and abortion are only a tiny fraction of those in the United States.[13]

Here again, then, we see that the antisexual attitudes behind the anti-pornography movement are themselves a cause of serious social problems. Indeed, appealing to the problem of teenage pregnancy verges on being another rationalization for those attitudes. For some who do so, manifestly, the main concern is a metaphysical worry over teenage "chastity," not the very real problems resulting from such pregnancies. It is not the fear that sex will lead to unwed pregnancy, but the fear that contraception will lead to unwed sex, that really motivates them. The only moral wrong involved in teenage sex, or any other kind, lies in taking an appreciable chance of bringing harm to another—not in sexual activity per se, nor in the desire that leads to it. If our society's moral condemnations were placed there, where they belong, some of the serious social problems we now face would be vastly reduced.

8

Sex and Psychological Health

In addition to calling it morally wrong, humans have another familiar way of denouncing something they wish to oppose; they charge mental illness or emotional maldevelopment. "That's sick" and "you're immature," for example, often replace "that's wrong" and "you're immoral." In fact, this tactic is very often more effective in influencing others' behavior, for many are more afraid of being considered emotionally ill or inadequate than of being thought evil. Consequently, such charges are continually being made, made by people with no knowledge at all about whether or not the attitudes or activities in question are psychologically healthy. Distressingly, this sort of thing happens even among professionals; there is a long history of value-beliefs being masqueraded as science or medicine. In Victorian times, many doctors and psychologists who felt that "woman's place is in the home" preached that females were constitutionally unable to stand the emotional strains of higher education. They even managed to find lots of "examples," such as young women who had to drop out of college with health problems.

But it was in regard to sexuality that medical doctors of that earlier era, even including Freud, were most thoroughgoing in "medicalizing sin." They identified as maldeveloped or mentally ill a wide variety of sexual feelings and practices, and did so in a way that mirrored faithfully the attitudes of their day concerning what was moral and proper. For one illustration, they inflamed the traditional moral fears about masturbation by insisting it caused a whole raft of mental and physical ills from insanity to syphilis. Although there was no evidence worthy of the name for such claims, they were widely accepted, and they did vast amounts of harm. Even today, a lot of what passes for knowledge about healthy sexual development and functioning is nothing but disguised moral dogma. The mental-health attacks on pornography that we so often hear by laypersons and even by specialists are in this same category. In many ways, in fact, the current campaign against sexually explicit materials is just a modern version of the Victorian one against masturbation.

CHARGES OF EMOTIONAL HARM

It is alleged, for example, that erotic portrayals are likely to cause an unhealthy degree or type of sexual feelings. Alternatively, the charge is that interest in them already reveals immaturity or an unnatural preoccupation with sex. Let us begin with the latter claim. As pointed out earlier, the use of sexual fantasy, and its extension to erotic portrayals, are perfectly natural; this fact argues that they are both signs of psychological health. Indeed, on the same grounds, it is those who have a compulsion to avoid sexual images who are emotionally unhealthy in this respect. It might be supposed that people who turn to fantasy do so only because they are sexually deficient. This is presumably true of some; but scientific studies of the subject have concluded that higher rates of sexual fantasizing correlate with good sexual health, not inadequacy.[1] Though we are all familiar with the description of fantasy as "escape from reality," it has become increasingly clear to psychologists that this activity is an important part of human mental life. That includes, but is not limited to, helping those who are deprived or inadequate to compensate and to adjust. Revealingly, those who see the use of pornography as a sign of maladjustment seldom say the same about the *non*sexual imaginings of fictional plays and movies and books.

It is true there are men who consume large amounts of pornography; there are also women who read great numbers of paperback romance novels. (Many of the latter go through two or three books a week, leading the publishers to turn out new ones like tires off an assembly line.) Though this may indicate a less than ideal balance of interests in life, it need not signal any emotional problem, only a high libido. It should be reiterated here that individuals can differ greatly from one another. What *would* be highly unnatural for one may be perfectly healthy for another, though in their egocentrism humans are prone to ignore this possibility. To one with a total lack of interest in stamp collecting, for example, a person who dedicates large amounts of time to it might seem unbalanced or even obsessed. It is a truism that anything can be carried to excess, but once again, those who make the mental health charges are usually in a poor position to judge what is excessive or inadequate in regard to sex. They know when something exceeds what they have been conditioned to accept but have little objective information regarding what is natural and healthy.

Turning to the charge that sexual materials cause mental or emotional harm, it comes in several forms. For example, it is often claimed that pornography's "overemphasis" on sex produces an obsessive interest in the subject. Alternatively, the charge is that it threatens to destroy interest in sex altogether. Those who make such claims say nothing about the massive numbers of love stories and love songs on radio and TV, for example, that they will lead to obsessive interest in or jaded unconcern with romantic love. Nor do they mention our constant exposure to talk of and pictures of food, friendship, and so on. To be sure, genuinely obsessive desires and associated behaviors do exist, from compulsive eating to excessive love-dependency (recently treated successfully with drugs that affect brain chemistry) to sexual obsessions. The question is, what causes such conditions? It seems very clear that the answer is rarely if ever simple overemphasis on the desire in question. Human appetites are equipped with satiation mechanisms to prevent unhealthy excess; in other words, when we get full, we lose our hunger. (This is true in the case of natural needs; things like recreational drug use represent a very different situation.)

It has been noted by students of Polynesian culture that, for all their overemphasis on sex by Western standards, those people were not in the least obsessed with the subject; they just treated it completely naturally. (See Bengt Danielsson's *Love in the South Seas* for a good discussion of their attitudes and mores.) In fact, the compulsive search for pleasure generally begins with pain. For example, compulsive eating is often an attempt to compensate for emotional privation of some type. Moreover, experience with eating disorders like anorexia reveals that repressing natural appetites, not satisfying them, is what perverts those appetites. It is the chronically hungry or unloved who are obsessed with food or with love—if anything leads to obsession it is deprivation, not "letting go." If an excessive interest in sex is sometimes reflected in the use of pornography, therefore, the latter is a symptom rather than a cause of the former. Instead, it has likely been caused by this culture's very attempts to suppress sexual feelings.

Sometimes the claim is that pornography itself is addictive. Now, the word "addiction" is used very loosely by some of these people; thus labeling a strong interest in sex is the latest trendy version of the charge of emotional ill-health. But cases of obsessive interest in sexual materials have been reported by psychiatrists. Does this prove such materials are dangerous to mental health? Hardly. People can and do become addicted to just about anything. Jogging is an example of current concern, and pathological levels of love-attachment represent another (e.g., those emotionally unstable fans who constantly harass the media stars with whom they are infatuated). There is a multitude of reasons for such problems in this neurotic society. One might legitimately worry that there is danger in the use of substitutes. In general this fear seems groundless, however. Should we fear letting a little girl have a doll as a substitute person to love? When excessive attachment to some such thing is discovered, we realize that the problem lies elsewhere. Even if some substitutes are dangerous, moreover, that argues not for suppression of the surrogate, which all by itself would just increase the deprivation, but for enhancing opportunities to get the real thing. Revealingly, the sexual conservatives who voice this sort of concern do not suggest *that* solution for highly sexed teenage boys.

Another charge often heard is that use of pornography produces the desire for stronger and stronger sexual thrills, leading eventually to the wish for violent or deviant sex. There is no evidence worthy of the name for such allegations. In fact, it seems highly implausible. Why wouldn't engaging in real sex produce the same obsessive quest for ever more perverse thrills? In sex, as in anything else, humans do require a certain amount of variety to prevent boredom. Within a limited range, the degree of arousal a stimulus provides will change if there is greater or lesser exposure to it. (It will do so temporarily, that is: after miniskirts were out of fashion for a time, attractive thighs became more exciting to men again.) But the *basic* kinds of things that "turn on" normal individuals are remarkably stable through life. As for paraphilias, psychologists report that they are also very stable over time; one does not move continually from one kinky obsession to another.[2] Certain sadistic individuals do become progressively more violent, but even in that case the *desire* for extreme violence is found to have been there all along.

One recent study some claim gives evidence for the "stronger and stronger thrills" charge does nothing of the sort.[3] Experimental subjects who were first shown large amounts of ordinary pornography were, on one brief subsequent occasion, more likely than others to peruse "uncommon sex" videotapes (S&M, bestiality, or bondage) instead. The obvious explanation for this result is simple curiosity, together with the prior disinhibition of viewing sexual materials in general and the prior satisfaction of curiosity about ordinary erotica. In other words, the subjects were not as apprehensive about either kind after viewing the ordinary porn and were still inquisitive about only the more heavily tabooed type. It may also be, of course, that they were still somewhat satiated with the common porn. That, however, does not mean they would find the uncommon stuff at all sexually arousing, or any more so than they would have in the beginning. One of the researchers who performed the experiment has also claimed that the boredom of monogamy would tend to lead married couples into sadomasochism—if sexual entertainment is a threat to mental health, so is marriage. (Even more so, in fact, since the greatest need for sexual variety is in regard to partners, not acts.) In reality, neither one will change one's basic erotic desires.

The existence of sexual deviance is a favorite scare tactic of the antipornography forces, who are constantly hinting or claiming outright that use of sexual entertainment leads to perversion and sexual psychosis. Such charges have about as much evidence behind them as the claim that reading the Bible is what produces the psychoses of the Reverend Jim Joneses of the world. (Remember Jonestown?) That fantasies can become unhealthy is no evidence at all that fantasies or fantasy aids themselves are unhealthful. The clinicians who treat paraphilias have never found any evidence to suggest that ordinary pornography was a factor in causing these conditions. On the contrary, studies have found that sexually deviant desires begin at a much earlier age than that of first exposure to pornography.[4] In fact, the standard treatments for paraphilias employ nonparaphilic sexual materials in the attempt to condition the patients into normal sexuality.

To counter irrational fears on this subject, it will be worthwhile to say a little about what is known concerning the causation of paraphilias. There are two main proposed explanations, both of which have some clinical support—perhaps both etiologies are at work in different cases or some of the same ones. The compensatory account suggests that the perversion is a defense mechanism, the subconscious mind's way of maintaining sexual desire in spite of traumatic events that threaten to destroy it. The "imprinting" theory holds that salient features of the circumstances of sexual arousal in early life become a permanent part of the paraphile's mental "lovemap." It posits a kind of one-shot conditioning that is perhaps reinforced through time. (Some writers still talk as if ordinary "classical" conditioning could explain paraphilias, but its effects are too weak to account for the data. For example, sexual perversions have a strong resistance to "extinction.") Either way, the damage is done by important events early in life, when the person is first experiencing sexual reactions—though neither theory can claim to know for sure what other factors, such as high suggestibility or a fragile ego, make one particularly vulnerable. Finally, in a certain category of cases the cause of the distorted sexuality is brain damage or chemical imbalance in the brain.

All this raises the question of whether pornography that is itself deviant (depicting fetishes, sadomasochism, and so on) might produce actual paraphilias. But here, too, many absurd claims have been made. For example, the fact that many pedophiles make sexual photographs of children is frequently presented as evidence that such photos produce sexual interest in children in the first place—even though they were clearly made after the interest existed. Obviously, those with nonstandard sexual desires will have fantasies to match and hence an interest in the corresponding type of pornography. So we must have more than that correspondence to argue that the pornography might cause the interest. Is there any such evidence? Certain psychologists have hypothesized that deviant depictions of sex might be able to produce actual paraphilias, at least in sexually inexperienced young men. The data so far weigh against so easy an origin, however; no actual case with such a cause has ever been identified.[5] Now, some clinicians do believe that deviant pornography can help to maintain deviant desires once they exist. But there is not any clear evidence of that; and even if it should be so, the paraphile's own imagination is quite adequate to do the same thing. Here again, those who register such fears tend not to make the parallel suggestion that young people be allowed to have "straight" pornography, or real sex, in order to preempt the possibility that they will succumb to whatever it is that does produce deviant desires.

HARM FROM ANTISEXUALISM

To summarize the discussion of the last section, the persistent charges of emotional harm from pornography, and from "overemphasis" on sex in general, are without justification. Indeed, a considerable body of evidence indicates that the very reverse is true. The traditional sex-negative attitudes of this culture appear to be a significant causal factor in emotional problems involving sexuality. Little of the data can be presented here, but a few special points are worthy of mention. Anthropological researchers have often commented on the virtual absence of sexual dysfunction (impotence, frigidity, and inability to orgasm), and of paraphilias, in sex-positive cultures. For example, Malinowski reported that there were no such problems among the Trobriand Islanders—with the exception, that is, of homosexual activity among heterosexual youth put into gender-segregated schools by missionaries. Similar reports have been made concerning the Polynesians, the Micronesians, and various others.

To look specifically at the matter of dysfunction, one study of thirty cultures found a strong correlation between sexual restrictiveness and impotence; another such survey got the same result for sexual disabilities in general.[6] Turning to our own culture, Alfred Kinsey years ago found a high correlation between sexually restrictive raising and orgasmic difficulty in women. This finding was later confirmed by William Masters and Virginia Johnson, and by many sex therapists since. In fact, it is often remarked that a major function of such therapy is, not to teach erotic skills, but to give the patients "permission" to enjoy sex; even many married people have been unable to shake their entrained conviction that sexual desire and pleasure are morally bad. Recall that a common tool used by sex therapists for overcoming the learned fear and disgust and shame is pornography. Sexually explicit films, with their tacit message that sex is not bad but good, seemingly can help undo the original negative training.

Returning to the case of paraphilias, the evidence that sexual repressiveness is a factor in producing them is also quite impressive. In the words of Chris Gosselin and Glenn Wilson, "One of the most consistent findings to come out of research on sexual deviation is that people who develop unusual sexual patterns are likely to have had a more restrictive than average upbringing." As Dr. Money puts it, parents who severely punish their children's expressions of sexuality "sabotage the lovemap," distorting their subsequent psychosexual development. Once again, the causation of sexual "perversion" is a much debated subject. There is little certainty in regard to the details. Yet it is widely accepted that neuroses often result from inner conflict—and sexual guilt has long been a major source of such conflict within individual members of this society.

Let us consider a few theories about those details. The case of individuals who find degradation sexually arousing has already been mentioned. For another example, there is wide agreement that exhibitionists tend to come from sexually puritanical families. It is believed by many psychiatrists that this compulsion to display their sex organs represents a subconscious reaction against the unacceptability of their own visual desires.[7] There are also such theories concerning extreme sadists and masochists, notably that the pain or punishment they find sexually arousing is a symbolic payment they subconsciously feel is necessary to expiate the sin so sex can be enjoyed. Such theories have also been proposed to explain some fetishes. This time the suggestion is that our culture's taboos concerning certain body parts make them threatening to susceptible persons, so that the natural interest in them is displaced onto other things instead, such as adjacent clothing. Typically, antipornography crusaders also rage against sexual "perversion." When they finally meet the enemy, he will turn out to be them.

It may even be that our general mental health has been adversely influenced by negative sexual feelings. Malinowski reported that his Trobriand Islanders were psychologically very healthy; it was only among the nearby Mailu and Amphlett Islanders, so similar to the Trobrianders in race and custom but authoritarian and sexually repressive, that he found nervousness, obsessions, and deranged violence.[8] Similar claims have been made by others who spent years living in sexually permissive cultures. As Danielsson remarked, "Most of the well-known complexes and maladjustments from which our children suffer are still unknown in Polynesia; I have not yet been able to discover any serious cases of thumb-sucking, contrariness, bed-wetting, day-dreaming, nervousness, nail-biting or stuttering on the islands, where I have lived long enough to know the conditions well." It must be stressed again that these are all uncertain matters. Human psychology is extremely complex and hence very difficult to get sure knowledge about. But this much is clear: there is far more evidence that negative sexual attitudes are emotionally harmful than that open, accepting ones are—and that speaks in favor of the sexual openness of pornography.

A final topic worth mentioning here has to do with physical rather than mental health: that of sexually transmitted disease. Most of what was earlier said about unwanted pregnancy applies in this case as well. It is often charged that pornography promotes such diseases by encouraging promiscuity, but here, too, the blame may be on the other side. Sexual superstition has long been a barrier to the eradication of this type of disease. Both efforts to prevent sexually transmitted disease and to treat it after it is incurred are discouraged by shame and ignorance. This is so especially among teenagers, whose levels of such diseases tend to be much higher than those of older sexually active persons. This topic leads us to what is becoming the most fearful spectre of our time, the AIDS epidemic. At the time of this writing, no one knows for sure how the situation will turn out: whether a cure or vaccine will soon be found, whether completely safe ways to have sex will be developed, or whether it will become the only good reason people have had in a long time for sexual abstinence. As regards the topic of this book, however, the epidemic just might make sexual substitutes more important than ever, for using pornography is a paradigm of "safe sex."

One thing is clear: genuine dangers like this one will not make moral and rational people embrace all the old irrational and immoral attitudes against positive sexuality—though it is certainly relevant to the question of what is moral and prudent to do at present. No one could have foreseen this horrible development; it no more proves that certain sexual lifestyles were evil all along than the plagues of past centuries prove it is immoral for people to live around other people. Consider the fatal diseases that must have been spread in earlier times by the communion chalice. And the Black Plague, which devastated Europe in the thirteenth century, was carried there on ships with crusaders and pilgrims returning from the Holy Land. Those individuals who smugly see AIDS victims as just getting what they deserve are monsters, incapable of real moral feeling.

SEX AND YOUNG PEOPLE

The preceding discussion has skirted the edge of one of the most explosive issues surrounding pornography and sexuality in general: that involving minors. For it is in childhood and adolescence that basic sexual attitudes are formed, and in those years that the foundations are laid for psychological health or maladjustment. For example, the great majority of paraphilias appear then, and the others seem traceable to that period. But it is in regard to sexuality during those years that public attitudes were changed least by the "sexual revolution"; the prevailing feeling still is one of great apprehension or aversion toward nonadult eroticism. Minors these days have more sexual information (and more misinformation), and they engage in much more sexual activity than in earlier decades, but they still suffer from high levels of guilt and ambivalence. Although to do this subject justice would require an entire book, it is essential here to say a few words about one thing: the common idea that there is something inherently emotionally unhealthful about children, or even adolescents, having sexual knowledge or sexual activity. It is widely averred, for example, that they are not "emotionally ready" for such things. Or, in regard to children, that it is not natural for them to have sexual feelings at all.

The latter is a perfect example of rationalization and ideologically induced blindness. It seems clearly motivated by our traditional sex-negative views: "Sexual feelings are tainted, but children are pure; therefore they couldn't have such feelings." And it is flatly false. Even though children learn at an early age to hide and repress their sexual desires in this culture, the fact that they have them could be discovered by anyone. (No, their sexual explorations aren't *just* "curiosity"—the standard euphemism for childhood lust.) Moreover, in cultures where they are not prevented from doing so, they begin sexual activity, sometimes even coitus itself, at a very early age.[9] In fact, such activity long before puberty is nearly universal among primates and very common in other mammals. The idea that it is only because of "overstimulation" by sexual images around them that children have sexual thoughts is a myth. Exposure to nudity or sex does not create such feelings in young people, though of course it can trigger them; it is their biological nature that does that. What evidently *is* true is that for many individuals, owing in part to a greater dependency on genital friction for arousal, sexual "awakening" can be long delayed by preventing the youthful experimentation in which they would otherwise naturally engage.

As for the common idea that sexual awareness and exploration are harmful to children or adolescents, it is no less biologically false. Stories of emotional distress from early sexual experience are often told in this society; but it is clear that the real sources of such trauma, other than those involving unwanted pregnancy, coercion, or disease, lie in the accompanying social attitudes. Ironically, in fact, it is the very fear and guilt that children are taught to keep them from being sexual that cause the problems. Countless stories of adults who waited till marriage for sexual contact and then found it traumatic can also be told. This is especially true of earlier times, when English women were advised that the way to minimize the unpleasantness of marital sex was to "lie still and think of England." The anthropological data are perfectly clear on this point. Breaking *any* serious social taboo can have a devastating psychological impact on those who do so. But the sexual anxiety that is standard in varying degrees in this culture is unknown in those where people get only positive messages involving sex in childhood and youth.

So the idea that sex is bad for young people is at best another self-fulfilling prophecy. To illustrate how easily mistaken such social traditions can be, consider the long-standing Western belief that babies should not be picked up every time they cry. "They will be spoiled," it is piously alleged, "always expecting instant gratification. They won't grow up independent and strong." In recent years it has been realized, partly through becoming aware of other cultures' practices, that the truth is just the reverse. At that helpless age, evidently, children *need* such reassurance and security. It is those whose needs are not met who are apt to grow up anxious and dependent, unable to delay gratification for fear it will not come later.[10] Minors certainly do need guidance and discipline, especially with all the dangers in the modern world, such as drug abuse. But when blind dogma makes us try to fight biology in such ways, the results are often tragic.

As the foregoing parallel suggests, the truth in regard to young people's emotional health may well be just the opposite of the common claim. Among other primates, early sexual activity, like play in general, is a kind of "rehearsal" for their adult roles. And in at least some species, such sex play is known to be required for later sexual adequacy. That something similar is the case for humans has been suggested by sex researchers. (See John Money's book *Love and Love Sickness*. Dr. Money is possibly the world's foremost authority on sexual development in childhood and youth.) One of the reasons for distorted or inadequate erotic feelings may well be that, in vulnerable individuals, healthy sexual knowledge or experiences are not available during the crucial years in which nature intended sexual mental structures to be developing. Prevented from having natural erotic stimulation, the mind may find it in unnatural things, or become obsessed with it, or perhaps never find it adequately at all. For one possible instance of this, there is a strong statistical tendency for men imprisoned for "peeping" to have been late in learning about sex, and late specifically in seeing the genitals of the opposite sex.[11] (They also tend to have had no younger sisters, which could help explain the latter statistic.)

However all this may be, the important point for our purposes is that sexual awareness in itself is not harmful to young people. That fact brings us back to the issue of pornography. Of the arguments standardly used against it, one of the most influential has always been that of protecting children from exposure to sex. Once it is realized that such exposure in itself is not harmful, yet another objection to erotic portrayals is seen to be without merit. It may even be the case, as various researchers have suggested, that there is a valuable place for erotically explicit materials in the education of children, especially given the fact that our society's high degree of privacy deprives them of the exposure to nudity and sexuality they would have in a more natural environment. This does not apply, of course, to depictions of deviant sex. Though it is doubtful they cause actual paraphilias, they still might send very inappropriate messages. But healthy, happy sexual depictions or descriptions are no more inappropriate for them than is the case for those involving other kinds of healthy human behavior.

To be sure, recreational portrayals of sex by themselves are no substitute for a well-rounded sex education. If pornography is the only source of sexual knowledge young people can get, they can be misled in various ways. But if they are denied reliable sources, as is so often the case, they will go on getting it from questionable ones. It is a real tragedy. Despite the great importance of sexuality in human life, this society continues to keep youth in the dark about it. The "official" information they do get, moreover, tends to be all negative, about the perils of disease or molestation, never about the joy of being sexual. The inevitable result is a society in which the *adults* are, in spite of what they assume, both miserably ignorant about and filled with superstitious fear concerning their own bodies and feelings. They raise their children the same way they were raised, and the cycle continues.

One currently popular argument against pornography involves its use by child molesters as "bait" to entice children into sex with them. Now, banning the sale of such materials certainly would not stop this practice, since it is easy enough for such people to make their own or to employ other lures such as candy. In fact, this and similar tactics by pedophiles are possible because young people are prevented from having the sexual knowledge, and the sexual contact with peers, that they naturally desire. (Many of the current efforts to protect children from sexual exploitation are equally counterproductive and terribly harmful—though that is a whole new story.) As for the case where minors are sexually attacked or coerced into sexual activity, note this well: the best protection against psychological harm from such assault is a healthy and positive prior attitude toward sex, not ignorance and shame. In fact, given all the harms that (as we'll continue to see) result from teaching sexual guilt to children, it would be very appropriate to regard such teachings as a form of child sex abuse.

Finally, what about that special category of pornography that has caused so much alarm in recent years, that which itself portrays children? This is another topic that needs far more treatment than can be given here, but a few things can be said. Once more, there is no evidence that such materials *cause* a sexual interest in children, any more than seeing homosexual pornography produces a homosexual orientation. As for those who already are sexually aroused by children, for reasons that have also been discussed, banning it does not prevent them from being so aroused. Even something as innocuous as the little girl in the old Coppertone ads has been reported by numerous pedophiles to be highly sexually stimulating. Note also that in most of the world throughout history, children have gone naked until the age at which they begin to internalize their culture's taboos. This is often the case in modern Europe, where complete nudity for swimming is common for all ages. Moreover, even the possibility that overtly sexual depictions of children elicit child molestation is somewhat disconfirmed by the fact that no increase in police reports of such acts occurred in Denmark during the years there when child pornography was legal and widespread.[12]

There *is* something to the idea that if "kidporn" were legal, it would send the message to pedophiles that their desires are socially acceptable. Even that is unlikely, perhaps, in a society where they are often despised more than murderers. However, there is the special argument that depictions of sex between adults and children can be used to give children the impression that such behavior is socially acceptable. More importantly, there is a serious problem in regard to the photographic making of such materials. Given that children are particularly vulnerable to coercion, protecting them from being pressured or forced into something which, in present social conditions, can be highly distressing or even psychologically damaging is a serious concern (though it is potentially no more so than the practice of coercing them *not* to act sexually). That being so, a case for the legal prohibition of this type of pornography can be made.

The topic under discussion is admittedly laden with emotion, but that is precisely why it must be approached with cool heads and correct factual information. We know only too well the evils to which hysteria leads. Our strong concern for the welfare of children has been exploited shamelessly by the antipornography movement. For example, although strict laws have made it virtually impossible to buy child pornography for some years, these people continue to claim it is rampant, a billion-dollar industry.[13] They have been collecting and parading such materials before the public in an attempt to associate them with adult sexual materials in people's minds, and they are constantly alleging, on the basis of no evidence whatever, that pornography in general encourages child molestation. Once again, a major source of all this irrational fear is our culture's misguided attitudes about sex and children. Until they are revised, our efforts to protect young people will continue to do more harm than good, to everyone.[14]

9

Elicitation of Violence: The Theories

Of all the evils alleged to be caused by pornography, by far the most commonly mentioned is violent or coercive behavior, notably rape. This charge has been around for a long time, but in recent years it has been made increasingly stridently and often. (It is clear even at the outset that most who make such claims have no adequate grounds for doing so. They are motivated instead by the various nonrational influences already discussed. They are also influenced by at least one further thing which seems particularly significant, the scapegoat syndrome (either the sincere-because-unconscious variety or the deliberate one). We all know how this works. The fear or anger produced by a horrible situation of some sort is escalated when its cause is unknown or inaccessible to remedy. So one lashes out at something that *is* visible and controllable—something that has a link, however remote, to the intolerable situation (and more especially if for independent reasons it is already despised)—in order to release the feelings of powerlessness and frustration. That such emotions are currently at work in this society, with its high level of fear over violence in general and sexual assault in particular, seems obvious.

The important question here, however, is not whether the usual motives for blaming pornography are bad but whether there are any good reasons for doing so. What evidence is there in favor of or against the charge that pornography incites coercion or violence? In the next two or three chapters, we will examine the arguments. A crucial aspect of this question is the nature of the alleged causal link: Just exactly how is pornography supposed to lead to aggression? The various groups who make the charge offer explanations very different from one another. The purpose of this chapter is to survey the theories.

STIMULATED SEXUAL DESIRE

What is perhaps the most obvious hypothesis, often cited at least obliquely by traditionalists, might be labeled the "awakened desire" theory. The idea is simply that since pornography arouses sexual feelings, in the absence of a willing partner certain persons will be induced to use force in order to satisfy the aroused desires. A stronger version of the theory, common among right-wing writers, holds that "overstimulation" by sexual materials tends to drive people into a frenzy or to produce sexual obsession. That claim has already been found here to be baseless. Even the weaker version faces various problems, however. For one thing, those who believe strongly in human free will are apt to have trouble with it. Shall we say that people who drive nice cars in public are to blame for inciting car theft or, instead, that the thieves are wholly responsible for their own actions?

Even ignoring that issue, two problems remain. First, the primary effect of pornography could plausibly be just the reverse. Although proponents of such claims seem reluctant to admit it, sexually explicit materials not only arouse but also satisfy sexual desires. Some seek it out, as a substitute, precisely because of strong feelings that already exist. If the latter is the dominant influence in the present regard, pornography might defuse more strong desires than it creates. This suggestion is known as the "safety valve" or substitution hypothesis. (It should not be confused, of course, with the catharsis theory concerning portrayed violence, a theory that is in wide disrepute among psychologists.) The question is, how might we know which alternative, if either, is correct? Secondly, rapists are overwhelmingly young men; their sexual desires tend to be quite autonomous, and are continually being aroused without any help from pornography. That being so, the presence or absence of that particular stimulus would not seem to make much difference, except perhaps as a substitute means of satisfying those excited feelings once again. As psychologists Michael Goldstein and Harold Kant put it in *Pornography and Sexual Deviance* after interviewing many rapists, "In our view erotic pictures, stories and movies simply serve as a substitute for the self-generating daydreams of the pornography user."

It could be replied that sexually explicit materials may at least add to the arousal level of everyday sexual stimulation. This, the reasoning might run, would push "over the brink" certain individuals who were already predisposed toward rape. That idea, however, conflicts with the fact that what it takes to produce strong sexual urges is highly elastic. Thus, as has also been mentioned before, attempts to cool male ardor by covering more of the female body result in enhancing the power of other parts to excite and, conversely, what becomes familiar loses much of its capacity to arouse. To give a personal example, the author's first youthful experience with close dancing produced strong (not to mention embarrassing) sexual excitement. Should that type of dancing be banned as a potential incitement to violence? On the contrary, with continued experience it ceased to be a powerful stimulus. Given the biological realities, the claim before us looks less and less reasonable. Even without pornography, evidently, the same levels of sexual arousal will occur, from such things as the sight of women in revealing dress. Here, again, such views are most persuasive to those trained to fear sexually "letting go."

A somewhat more plausible version of the "awakened desire" argument attributes the problem, not to sexual arousal per se, but to the creation of feelings of deprivation. The suggestion is that sexually explicit materials can produce or heighten the sense that one is missing out on something one desires, which could lead to a willingness to take it by force. In other words, the villain this time is the frustration produced by perceiving how things might be in contrast to how they actually are. (Often, those who use the argument assume this effect occurs because males are led to think their sexual needs are greater than they really are. That claim, too, has already been addressed; it is more apt to be a matter of uncovering repressed yearnings.) Here, again, it is not at all clear that this is a genuine danger. Using pornography may be no more likely to result in violence in this way than is seeing attractive women on the street or at the beach. But suppose there is such an effect. Would that mean sexual presentations ought to be regarded as a genuine evil? Not in the least.

Let us consider a pair of analogies. The speeches of Martin Luther King, Jr., for equality and civil rights were sometimes followed by violence among black people. This was in spite of his own message of nonviolence; it is just a fact of human nature that raising people's hopes and expectations has the potential for inducing antisocial actions in some. In a similar vein, the women's rights movement of the past two decades is seemingly the cause of a rapid increase in crimes committed by women and girls; the rate of increase has been far greater than that among males.[1] It appears that the increased social freedom and assertiveness women have achieved have in a tiny proportion of cases led to license and aggression. Shall we say, given these effects, that such feelings as self-confidence and self-respect, hope, and desire for freedom are pernicious? Or that influences that arouse them should be prohibited? After all, when they are combined with selfish disregard for others, they can indeed lead to wrongdoing and even violence. Surely no reasonable person would say this. We would blame the selfishness, not those other feelings, for the criminal acts. The situation is basically no different in the case of sexual desires, and of things that awaken the hope of satisfying them.

The preceding analysis also suggests a second plausible account of how sexual materials might conceivably lead to rape. However, this account would also not lay the real blame on the materials. This time the key element would be, not desire for sex, but its perceived desirability. If pornography in general can be said to carry any messages, the primary one is that sex is good for its own sake. Of course, such a claim does not in the least justify forcing such activity on anyone. Quite the reverse is true, as we know that for the victim, rape is not anything like real sex; it is a horrible experience. In the twisted minds of some, unfortunately, the idea that something is desirable translates into the belief that compelling others into it is morally acceptable. Sometimes the belief is accompanied by the rationalization, "Once you're pushed into it, you'll like it after all." (Recall the *verbal* coercion used by members of both sexes to get their own needs met.) But that attitude can hardly be blamed on other people's simply celebrating something they consider good, sexual or otherwise. To appeal to another simile, various religious traditions believe they have the key to escaping evil and finding joy; and in their zeal to spread that perceived good, many throughout history have used force and committed great evils. Except for any specific teachings that may endorse coercion, however, this does not reflect ill on religious belief itself, or on books and movies extolling it. The same thing is true in the case of noncoercive sex and also of representations that legitimize it.

This line of reasoning helps us see part of what is wrong with the first "awakened desire" argument as well. For suppose it is true after all that the existence of sexual materials results in greater amounts of sexual arousal in the population at large than would otherwise exist, and suppose that this leads, among those willing to harm others to get what they want, to greater numbers of rapes than would otherwise occur. Only those who see sexual desire as being bad in the first place would assign moral blame to what gave rise to it, rather than merely blaming the willingness to harm others and whatever produces *it*. Conceiving "demon lust" as something that pollutes the soul, rather than as a perfectly legitimate or even desirable feeling, is what underlies their argument. Otherwise, what would be concluded is that it should be made easier for people to get their sexual needs met in noncoercive ways instead—something these traditionalists seldom do. If displaying pictures of food incites hungry people to steal, that is an argument for adopting social policies to end hunger. Likewise, if anything follows from the claim that sexual arousal leads to rape, it is that the societal conditions that produce sexual privation and frustration should be changed.

The point here is more clear when we see what else follows from the antisexual assumptions underlying the argument against pornography now before us. Given such a view of sexual desire, anything that results in increased amounts of erotic feeling (or lessens repression of it) is also to be condemned: sex education, greater enjoyment of sex by women, even talk about sex in a positive way. Although not always frank about their many motives, many who promote this explanation of rape do indeed hold all these views; to them, sex is ugly and dirty. But others should be aware of the logical consequences of the "awakened desire" argument. It leads to the conclusion, for example, that women who dress revealingly or behave suggestively are to blame for other women or themselves being raped. If banning pornography on these grounds is justified, surely so is requiring women to wear clothing that covers their skin and hides the shape of their bodies, like the Iranian *chador*. And surely that is not at all justified.

PROMOTION OF ATTITUDES TOWARD WOMEN

These facts have been clearly perceived in the feminist movement. Consequently, the motivations antipornography feminists propose to explain how it might lead to rape are of a very different type. They blame it instead on messages about women that, they say, are carried by all or most male-oriented sexual material and on the attitudes toward women those messages allegedly create. For example, in accord with the standard denunciations of pornography as "objectifying" and "exploitive," it is said to teach men that women are just objects for their use whose own desires and feelings do not matter. Having already discussed that type of thinking, we need not say much more about it in this new context. Except perhaps in regard to a small percentage of macho movies and books, mostly nonpornographic, the claim is false. Most sexual entertainment no more carries the message that women exist only for men's pleasure than it says that men exist only for women's pleasure—or than romance novels, with their adoring suitors, teach women that that is all men are for.

An experimental study has often been cited in support of this particular charge.[2] It was found that male and female college students who had been shown a lot of sexually explicit films recommended shorter prison terms for a rapist than those who had not. The claim has been made that this study shows that pornographic films cause insensitivity to the exploitation or abuse of women. No such conclusion is warranted, however. For one thing, the average suggested prison term was still long—longer, in fact, than is usually served in the United States or Canada.[3] More fundamentally, there are more likely explanations for the result. One of these rests on the fact, confirmed by various experiments and by clinical experience, that exposure to sexual explicitness makes most people more sexually tolerant. Evidently, the openness about sexuality reduces some of the anxiety the viewers have been conditioned to feel. Now, one effect of that conditioned anxiety has been that crimes involving sex are widely seen in this society as more heinous than equally violent and harmful nonsexual crimes. For example, the historically heavy punishments for rape, which even included the death penalty, were evidently assigned less out of concern for the woman's trauma than out of belief that loss of her "chastity" meant loss of her value. That being the case, coming to have a less negative attitude toward sex itself would reduce the perceived seriousness of sexual assault, bringing it closer to the level of equally violent crimes. If this is the correct explanation, then watching the films did not produce a decrease in compassion for rape victims after all.

This interpretation has been confirmed by other tests, in which being shown sex movies was not found to result in a rape victim's being viewed as less worthy or less injured, or in other calloused attitudes toward such victimization. In fact, some studies of this type have even failed to replicate the result of shorter assigned prison terms for rapists—which reveals how tentative such experimental findings often are. The explanation being suggested here for the original result is also supported by the fact that in sex-positive cultures, rape is regarded as being more like other crimes against the person; in such cultures sexual assault is also evidently much less traumatic to the victim.[4] Since the movies in question reportedly portrayed no coercion or inequality between the sexes, this explanation seems much more plausible. In any event, the experiment certainly does not show that ordinary pornography creates unfeeling attitudes toward women. A recent study of consumers and nonconsumers of nonviolent pornography also found no greater incidence of negative attitudes toward women, including views of rape, among the former. (However, it did find a very small association between such attitudes and use of violent sexual portrayals. More on this topic later.)[5]

Another aspect of that prison-sentence study also deserves comment at this point, though it is far too complex to discuss adequately here. A questionnaire purporting to reveal sexually calloused attitudes toward women was given to the same subjects, and those who had watched the large amounts of filmed sexual behavior got scores a little higher. For several reasons, this writer maintains that the test was terribly flawed. Although an affirmative answer to many of the questions would indeed indicate such feelings, many others would just show a positive attitude toward sex for its own sake and others would merely reflect factual beliefs about the sexual attitudes and behavior of other people. The unjustified interpretation of the questions was clearly influenced by the traditional view that a strong interest in sex by or toward a female is degrading to her. Here too, a more plausible explanation for the experimental result is that watching sexually uninhibited behavior tends to create more liberal beliefs in the subjects. (This might be especially true when such movies are shown by authority figures such as university professors, which hints that it is not so socially unacceptable after all.) Although themselves strong foes of pornography, the researchers involved have since admitted the questionnaire faces such objections, and have agreed to stop using it in their research. Unfortunately, many of the other questions being used by various scientists in similar experiments reveal the same antisexual biases.[6]

A second theory about how pornography might lead to rape by influencing attitudes toward women involves the claim, also discussed before, that common sexual materials promote male dominance and female subservience. That, it is averred, gives men the idea they can take what they like from women. Alternatively, the explanation is that it gives men the desire to "put women in their place," rape then being an obvious way of doing so. It has already been argued here that only a small category of such materials might plausibly be said to advocate male dominance, and that pornography in general is less guilty of this than are other media presentations. Indeed, by treating women more as equals in matters of sexuality, pornography would be more apt to undermine the traditional attitudes that include such dominance. What actually upsets those who make this charge is not any sort of inequality, but the kind of equality that is portrayed in porn, that in which both genders are interested in sex for its own sake.

Many feminists and traditionalists give a third attitude-formation explanation of the claimed causal link, saying that pornography leads to rape by making men feel contempt for women. (The extremists, as usual, say it deliberately teaches such contempt.) It does this, the claim continues, by portraying women who enjoy sex for its own sake—outside a monogamous relationship, and so on. By the same reasoning, however, *real* women who are sexually uninhibited are to blame for getting themselves or other women raped. Indeed, a corollary of this theory is another version of the idea that provocatively dressed women are at fault when they or others are raped. This time, the claim is that they invite it by appearing "loose" and therefore worthy of disrespect. Of course, those who make the charge concerning pornography realize how it sounds these days to say such things about women themselves, so they do not usually follow their theory to its logical conclusions. Even so, the question remains, are there any good reasons for believing it? The answer is *no*.

Experiments designed to test attitudes after exposure to pornography have not found any increased disrespect for women. They have found male subjects inclined to judge an unfamiliar woman, or man, to be a little more interested in sex than they otherwise would have; but only in the eyes of antisexuals does that amount to a "loss of respect." In one such test, young men asked thirty-two questions about a woman's character did not give a more negative assessment when she displayed uninhibited sexual attitudes; on the contrary, she was seen as being a more reasonable person.[7] The truth may be just the opposite of what this theory holds. Once again, pornography use evidently tends to cause *more* liberal attitudes toward the sexual behavior of others, including that of women. Even though the "double standard" is found, to a greater or lesser degree in most cultures of the world, there is far less hostility toward highly sexual women in sex-positive cultures than in others. Consider the attitude toward a "fallen woman" in Middle Eastern countries, for example: She may even be killed, to preserve her family's "honor." It is the very sort of society foes of pornography want that is harshest toward sexually uninhibited women.[8]

The part of their claim that is true, of course, is that it is easier to bring oneself to do harmful things to one who is considered deserving of contempt. Such feelings are very clearly involved in many crimes of violence against both men and women. This suggests a nonculpable way in which pornography might lead to rape. In the eyes of a person raised to believe strong sexual desire is degrading, to see women as having such desires is already to regard them as degraded, hence perhaps to make violence against them seem more acceptable. So by portraying its women as strongly sexual, pornography could presumably trigger these feelings in men who already have certain sex-negative attitudes. (Assuming they also cannot distinguish fantasy from reality, or one person from all others of the same sex). An earlier example may illustrate this point: consider the possible effect on white racists of observing scenes in which white women associate willingly with black men. If hostility is triggered by either interracial or sexual scenes, it is clear where the real blame for it lies. Those preaching that women who enjoy sex for its own sake are worthy of contempt are themselves the ones responsible for any crimes against women caused by such feelings of contempt—and that includes most opponents of pornography.

One further aspect of the loss-of-respect argument must be noted. Once again, it is absurd to say that materials portraying men and women as sexually alike degrade only one sex. Hence there is something very odd about the idea that exposure to such materials would lead to hostility only toward one sex. Any such differential effect would have to be blamed on the existing double standard of the viewers. What an egalitarian portrayal, of any sort, *might* do is to diminish the perceived differences between the sexes. In particular, it might conceivably reduce the feeling that harm to a woman is more serious than equal harm to a man. This in fact is a standard argument by traditionalists against feminists. They contend that by bringing women down from their pedestal, gender equality has been a cause of increasing rape. Whether or not there be any truth to this claim, it is still morally objectionable. Removing special honor for one group is not the same as creating disrespect toward it; it is only what justice requires. And respect for women *or* men should not be dependent on their sexual "purity" but on the fact that they are human beings.

A fourth and final claim about the cause of rape involving attitudes toward women rests on a fourth charge discussed earlier that standard pornography misleads men about women's real sexual desires. Once again, the theory involves the uninhibited sexual behavior portrayed—oral sex and masturbation, different partners, and so on. This time, the conclusion drawn is that the pornography user will be led to believe women really do not *mind* being raped. "If they're so quick to engage in sex anyway, and willing to do all those *other* kinky things, how could they object to a little force?" In fact, it seems clear that some rapists do reason in this manner, from "doesn't mind those other sexual things" to "wouldn't mind being raped." Let us for the sake of argument also grant that some people are appreciably misled by pornography about the sexual tastes of women in general, in spite of getting a very different message from other media presentations and from real life. (Notice that they would also be misled by self-help books urging that "any woman can" get more sexual pleasure by shedding inhibitions.) Shall we say, given all that, that portrayals of sexually uninhibited women and men are morally to blame for some cases of rape? Once more, the answer is negative.

The real villain, as usual, is antisexual attitudes in this society. The problem is that in common thinking various pleasurable, consensual activities have been lumped together with forcible rape. Both are "bad" in a special sexual sense of the word (hence the myth that only "bad" women get raped). But the nonviolent behaviors portrayed in standard pornography, though not everyone's taste, are perfectly healthy and wholesome; they should never have been associated in anyone's mind with genuinely evil things like rape. If they had not been so associated, there would be no special tendency to believe that a person who engaged in them would also be receptive to "other bad things." That is, there would be no more reason to suppose a sexually uninhibited woman would not really object to being raped than that a gourmet who likes a wide variety of foods might not mind being force-fed (or, for that matter, that someone who enjoys more traditional sexual behavior would not mind being raped). In this argument then, the reasoning is again based on antisexual assumptions. In the minds of those who employ it, evidently, little distinction is made between uninhibited consensual sex and rape. But their sex-negative thinking cannot be blamed on sex-positive pornography.

It is also clear who is really responsible if the alleged consequences do occur. It is those who promote the view that there is something unclean about certain kinds of sexual behavior—that only "bad" women do such things—who are morally to blame for any rapes that may be committed because of portrayals of women who engage in them. They are also to blame if that crime is committed because of real women who enjoy them. Those who argue that pornography makes men think women would not mind being raped likewise seldom follow their argument to the point of blaming real women. Even so, their target is not just sexual fantasy; it is obvious they are also promoting a view of what is sexually appropriate behavior. What better way to do that than by instilling fear of rape in women? "This is what happens to bad women." The message may or may not be intended, but it follows logically from their premises. As has been stressed before in this book, the real issue in the pornography debate is not pornography.

Let us pause here to consider a more general question about the nature of rape. Many today, following the feminists, are loath to admit that sexual desire could be involved at all in rape, even in an exploitive way. Instead they insist it always has hatred or the desire to subjugate as its sole motive. Extremist feminists carry the view a step further, claiming that the latter emotions are just part of a wider pattern, a contempt and hatred of women that have long been taught in this culture. It seems clear from the evidence that a minority of rapists, especially among those who use considerable brutality, are indeed motivated mostly by these emotions. But this sweeping claim about all of them is a contemporary rape myth; it conflicts with a lot of clear facts. The arguments given in support of it range from poor to worthless, and the passion with which it is often maintained reveals an ideological need to insist on it—notably, the refusal to believe that sex is a powerful need for men. The claim is of interest to us because it also conflicts with most of the common theories about how pornography would lead to rape, including (as we will see later) those involving portrayed violence; they mostly require the motive to be sexual desire.

In any case, it appears that the primary motivation of rape is very often the same as that of other violent crimes, that is, the individual wants something and, for various reasons, is not deterred by the usual internal and social constraints against using force to get it. Feelings of anger and dominance can indeed help overcome those restraints, but what removes the deterrent must not be confused with what makes the act seem powerfully desirable in the first place. Such emotions can help to disinhibit other crimes as well, such as robbery (including robbery with gratuitous violence, or "mugging"), whose goal is clearly to acquire something desirable. In fact, rapists themselves tend to commit various other crimes. One psychological dynamic is worthy of special note. Many rapists are young men who are seen as undesirable by women, as "losers," and they respond with the attitude, "You can't reject me—I'll have you anyway!" Anger at their situation is what in their minds justifies coercion, but sexual desire is what they are using coercion to satisfy. And pornography is not the cause of either the anger or the desire.

As for those rapists for whom other motives are central, the clinicians who treat the men tell a very different story of origins than do some feminists. So far from having simply been taught to hate women, by pornography or the society or anything else, the rapists motivated mostly by anger tend strongly to have come from brutalizing backgrounds, to have been physically or emotionally abused themselves as children. As for the desire to subjugate the victim, that emotion is widely regarded by psychologists as a defensive reaction against the assailant's own feelings of worthlessness, powerlessness, and victimization. The only individuals who get satisfaction from exerting power over someone obviously weaker are those who themselves feel helpless for some reason. American blacks have a rate of rape about five times that of whites, and interracial prison rape is almost 100 percent cases of blacks attacking whites.[9] The former have not been taught that the latter are their inferiors, who exist to be dominated and exploited; quite the contrary. Note also that both anger and desire for dominance motivate many other violent crimes, against males as well as females. This contentious subject obviously cannot be discussed adequately here. But the extremists' claim of a pervasive atmosphere of "woman-hating" in this culture is a gross delusion—just like their view of pornography.

SEX AND VIOLENCE: A BIOLOGICAL LINK?

Yet another causal connection between pornography and rape that has been claimed to exist involves an alleged biological link between violence and sexual arousal. There are indeed some interesting hints of some such connection in nature. The seemingly innate tendency for mild or mock violence to be sexually arousing has already been mentioned. Moreover, there are data indicating that the same hormones that produce sexual desire are also involved in producing a capacity for aggression. But the biological complexities are sufficiently great to make the total picture at present rather ambiguous. The weight of evidence does not indicate any systematic connection between real aggression and normal sexuality in humans; in fact, the reverse is true.[10] It is well known, for instance, that pleasurable feelings tend to reduce violent ones. Furthermore, the frequency of rape in sexually permissive cultures is evidently no greater than in restrictive ones; indeed, in some of the former, violent sex crimes are said to be unknown.

If there is some such link, it seems likely that sexual frustration, not sexual arousal per se, is the real problem. Among the data arguing for this conclusion are reports from sexually deprived prisoners that they release the frustration by picking a fight. If this is so, it would argue for more sexual permissiveness in general, not greater suppression of such desires. Another possibility is that the emotion apt to lead to violence is not lust but sexual jealousy—the very emotion that ultimately underlies so much antisexual thinking. (This is clearly the main link between sex and violence among other animals.) What is most important for our subject, however, is that this matter has no special relevance to *portrayed* sex. The reason is that any concerns it may raise apply to sexual feelings and behavior in general. If we are not careful, in fact, we could wind up concluding that real sex is especially dangerous, since there is a potential victim already at hand! All these things being so, the suggestion of a special biological link between sex and violence is of no value to the antipornography arguments.

Whatever the facts may be about a specific link, a general connection exists between highly aroused emotions of any sort and violence. For example, strong feelings involving ideology, love, loyalty, self-esteem, and ambition are major sources of aggression in the world. The hatred religious devotion has produced between opposing religious groups over the centuries, and is still creating in various parts of the world today, is a clear illustration of this. Another familiar example is the sort of violence to which love often leads. This powerful emotion can produce equally powerful negative feelings in a variety of ways. When it is unrequited or jealous or when the relationship goes sour, love not infrequently turns into hatred or other violent tendencies. (In one case, a young man distraught from having been jilted went out and killed a policeman, and then himself.) Given the obvious dangers from overwrought emotions of these sorts, do we hear claims that there is too much emphasis on religious belief, or on the importance of romantic love, in this society? Do we get calls for the banning or censoring of religious literature or love stories, demands made on the grounds that such things can lead to dangerously high levels of emotion? We do not. What we do get, once again, is a myopic attack on one sort of feeling, and on the media presentations that express it.

This covers all the accounts commonly proposed to explain the alleged tendency of pornography to promote violent behavior. In summary, they are all either highly suspect or plainly false. None of them has the feature of being plausible while at the same time laying the moral blame on pornography. This matter of explanation has yet to be adequately addressed by those who seek a connection between sexual portrayals and violence. Of course, to point all this out does not by itself show that there is no such tendency. Having an adequate explanation is crucial, especially given that no one is claiming vicarious satisfaction of other nonviolent desires leads to acts of aggression. It is possible, however, to get data arguing for or against causal links without having an adequate explanation. Since direct evidence that pornography produces violence is often claimed, we will now turn to that topic.

10

Elicitation of Violence: The Evidence

Roughly speaking, three types of evidence could be appealed to in regard to the causes of behavior: stories about individual cases, statistical analyses of groups in the population, and experimental studies. Each has its strengths and weaknesses, and we must consider all three.

ANECDOTAL CLAIMS

The anecdotal variety of evidence is perhaps the most commonly abused in everyday thinking, particularly in the sloppy *post hoc* reasoning that has already been described. To put it schematically, merely finding instances of A accompanied by B—for example, women who leave school with health problems—is not legitimate evidence that A causes B. Such thinking has been especially common in regard to the charge that pornography elicits violence. We constantly hear claims about sex criminals found to own pornography—ignoring all those who do not, and all the noncriminals who do. Similar stories of rapists and murderers who were Bible readers can equally well be found, from Albert Fish to Leonard Lake.

Some of the most manipulative uses of this sort of reasoning are to be heard at those perennial governmental hearings on obscenity. Individuals presented as "victims of pornography" tell horror stories about physical and emotional violence they have suffered. It is even sometimes stated that if one does not believe pornography is to blame for the plight of these people, one does not have any compassion for them. Though their experiences are tragic, however, in most of the cases it is plain the sexual materials were present in only an incidental way in lives already disordered and violent for obvious sociological reasons. (In fact, sometimes those testifying merely assume pornography must have been present.) The same may be said of those cases where erotic materials were employed in the commission of an assault, say, where someone was forced to look at them or to participate in making them. They no more support the claim that pornography causes coercive tendencies than the existence of slavery and forced labor argues that labor in itself tends to produce coercive behavior. The fact that some are willing to use force to get what they want does not argue that what they want is itself evil or evil-inducing, be it sex or love or a baby or money or anything else. Yet that is the insane inference that is constantly being drawn.

Some of these stories turn out on closer inspection to involve serious distortions of fact, or even to be wholly fictional.[1] From media reporters pandering to public fears to lawyers attempting to prove a client was not responsible for what he did, people are always susceptible to dishonesty. One must maintain an attitude of critical judgment in such matters. All the same, it is certain there have been instances of pornography triggering violent behavior. The reason is that virtually anything can incite such a response on the part of a psychotic or sociopathic personality. To mention just two infamous cases, the British murderer John George Haigh reported that he had been impelled to his acts of vampirism by an emotionally charging Anglican high mass. Then there was Nannie Doss, who poisoned four husbands in succession; when finally caught, she explained that none of them had measured up to the romantic males she read about in *True Romances*. Nevertheless, if we are to say meaningfully that some type of thing causes violence, singling it out from the multitudes of other elements in life that can incite the unstable, it must be involved in a more systematic way than is suggested by such incidents as these.[2]

One crude type of more systematic evidence are the reports of police and FBI agents who say they regularly find pornography in the possession of rapists. However, these tend to be subjective, nonquantitative impressions, and they are not shared by other police and agents. In fact, some of them are reminiscent of claims, made by certain officials in earlier years, that most civil rights workers were Communists; ideology exerts a powerful influence on what some people will report having found out. A few researchers have attempted to gather data on pornography and violent sex crimes in a more rigorous way by studying cases of rape reported to authorities. In general, these efforts have discovered no good reason to suspect a causal connection between the two. For example, the Williams Committee, which studied the pornography issue for the British government, reported it was unable to uncover any cases of a probable link between pornography and violent sex crime. Instead, the committee remarked, "One can study case after case of sex crimes and murder without

finding any hint at all that pornography was present in the background."
A similar conclusion was drawn earlier by researchers who surveyed juvenile criminal cases in the United States.[3]

Interviews with violent sex criminals themselves have provided another
type of evidence on this matter. One recent survey of a group of convicted
rapists elicited reports from a large number of them that they had used
sexual materials just before seeking out a victim.[4] That certainly indicates
a connection of some type, but the nature of the link is problematic. By
itself, this information may be no more significant than the fact that rapists
think about sex before raping. It is too obvious that a strong desire for sex
could constitute a motive both for using pornography and for committing
a sex crime; there is no reason to suppose it was the former that produced
the latter. In fact, the researcher described many of the rapists as employing
the materials to excite themselves in preparation for the act, so the intention
was evidently there in advance. Without the pornography, they could just
have stoked themselves up on their own fantasies, as rapists so often report
doing.

As for the possibility that these rapists would have committed their
crimes less often without the added stimulation, that encounters another
question we have considered before, namely, how many would-be rapists
have been deterred by the use of a sexual substitute. For all we know,
they more often lose their cravings as a result of masturbating with sexual
portrayals. To speak schematically again, the important question is not
whether A ever causes B but whether it does so "on balance," that is,
more frequently than it prevents it. In this same vein, stories are often told
of rapists who were carrying sexual materials when caught. Doesn't *that*
show a causal link? But by the account some rapists have given, pornography is used as a backup; they masturbate with it if they cannot easily
find a victim. What they might do if they did not have a substitute to relieve
their urges is a serious question. All these facts leave too many questions
unanswered.

What about criminals' own perception of what causes their behavior,
then? In one questionnaire survey of convicted rapists, eleven out of sixty
responded "yes" to the question of whether pornography had had "anything to do" with their being in prison or psychiatric hospital.[5] An even
higher proportion, 39 percent, felt pornography had led them at some time
to commit a "sexual crime." (Note that that vague phrase, given the laws
in the area at the time, could have included noncoercive acts of oral and
anal intercourse.) This is a worrisome result; but as various researchers
have pointed out, it cannot be accepted at face value. For one thing, the
indeterminateness of a questionnaire answer raises issues we have considered before. For example, perhaps the prisoners would have said pornography had something had "to do" with their situation only in the same
sense that any source of sexual knowledge or arousal might have done,

such as seeing women in provocative dress. Questions concerning the latter sort of stimulus are conspicuously absent when rapists are asked about pornography these days.

A much more serious doubt hinges on the fact that violent criminals as a group tend to be very unaware of their own motivations (which may have a lot to do with their being violent in the first place) and highly prone to rationalization. They could simply have been falling back on an "explanation" they have often heard, one that would tend to relieve their own blame, at that. Statements of this type that we occasionally hear from rapists sound very like the politically correct "confessions" that turn up in other ideologically charged contexts (e.g., those old Chinese Communist "self-examination" sessions). Other excuses that rapists commonly give, such as "she led me on," are rightly regarded with skepticism and often clearly false. The notorious Ted Bundy case obviously could have involved such motives, including the desire for a last-minute stay of execution. (Sources close to Bundy have pointed to a broken home and other childhood factors to explain his murderous rage.) If we buy our psychological theories from a certified psychopath, he will be conning us even from the grave.

Quite apart from such doubts, however, there is positive evidence on the other side. For one thing, this survey result conflicts with those of others who have interviewed sex criminals extensively. From their questioning of convicted rapists and pedophiles, for example, Goldstein and Kant concluded that "few if any" had been appreciably influenced by pornography. Instead, they decided, real persons in the environment "are far more potent sexual stimuli" for the sex criminal. In fact, many psychiatrists who have worked with sexually disturbed patients believe that pornography often has the effect of preventing sexual violence. Many sex offenders themselves report that that is the case, moreover.[6] According to Dr. Money, persons requesting help in a sex-offender clinic "commonly disclose in the course of counseling therapy that pornography helps them contain their abnormal sexuality within imagination only, as a fantasy." In fact, in the questionnaire just discussed, 39 percent of the convicts also agreed that pornography "provides a safety valve for antisocial impulses." Overall, this type of evidence provides at least as much reason to believe sexually explicit materials prevent violence as that they incite it.

STATISTICAL ANALYSES

The attempt to solve the problems facing the foregoing kind of data has led researchers to statistical methods. Now, it would not help us to learn that a high percentage of rapists use pornography; after all, a very great proportion of them drink coffee! What is needed instead is a correlation: that more pornography users than others commit rape (or, equivalently, that more rapists than nonrapists use pornography). Schematically, it is not whether or not most A's are B's that counts; it is whether a higher percentage of A's than of non-A's are B's, even if both percentages are low. In such a case, provided the statistics are collected carefully enough to rule out biased data and coincidence, we have good evidence for a causal relationship of some sort between A and B. This relationship, however, could be different things, notably that A causes B, that B causes A, or that A and B are collateral effects of some common cause, C. As an illustration of the latter, consider the operation of a barometer. The falling of its fluid level does not cause a storm to come; instead, a decrease in air pressure tends to produce both a storm and a drop in the barometer level.

So merely finding a correlation does not reveal a cause. With the right kind of further information, however, we can sometimes eliminate the other possibilities. For two obvious cases, if the A always follows the B, it clearly is not a factor in causing B; and if we have *arbitrarily* produced the A's ourselves (the experimental method), we know there is no common cause for both them and the B's. In most cases, however, this is very difficult to do. Sometimes we are able to eliminate all the plausible common causes in other ways, but often we simply do not know which of many possible explanations for a correlation is the right one. Consequently, though the strict absence of a correlation between them guarantees that A does not, on balance, cause B, the presence of a correlation all by itself is very weak evidence that it does.

One important type of statistical survey brought to bear on this question attempts to compare the backgrounds of those who have and those who have not committed violent sex crimes, in order to see if they differ, on average, in their prior exposure to sexually explicit materials. For we would expect a correlation between such acts and some aspect of such exposure if the one tends to cause the other. Five studies of this type were performed at the request of the U.S. Commission on Obscenity and Pornography at the end of the 1960s.[7] To the surprise of many, only one of them found a larger amount of exposure to pornography in the backgrounds of those who had committed serious sex crimes than among those who had not. In fact, three of them, like an earlier study by the Kinsey Institute, found a *smaller* amount of prior exposure among violent sex criminals than in a "control group" of persons not known to have committed sex crimes. (The remaining study was not able to employ a quantitative analysis.) This seems to suggest that sexually explicit materials tend to prevent violence; at least it argues that they do not cause it. But there are various possible sources of error in studies of this kind. For just one thing, they had to depend on memory reports of what had been seen in previous years, which are certainly fallible, and on the answers being honest. Though such results are of some value, then, they are far from conclusive.

Another way to get evidence regarding the influence of pornography would be to compare the frequency of sex crimes committed by offenders who use pornography with the number committed by sex offenders who use none, in order to see if there is any difference. One clinical study of this type, involving rapists and child molesters, has been conducted in recent years, and it found no such difference.[8] (Even if it had, however, that might have been the result of some other common factor, such as a higher sex drive among those who commited more offenses—more on this point below.) Any new result requires corroboration, but this is evidence against the correlation needed by the hypothesis that pornography promotes sexual crimes. Although concerned that violent or paraphilic portrayals might reinforce deviant desires, the authors of this study felt there was no good reason to suspect ordinary sexual materials caused harm. Quite the reverse is generally believed by clinicians who treat sex criminals, in fact; ordinary pornography is standardly used by therapists in an attempt to replace the offenders' perverted desires and fantasies with normal ones.

The evidence on this matter is mixed, however. Two recent studies have found a correlation in their sample between the current use of pornography and coercive sexual acts by the offenders.[9] Though these surveys also face doubts over such things as the reliability of self-disclosure, their results are actually quite plausible. There are a number of reasons for suspecting that sex offenders would use erotic materials more, some of which have already been hinted at. For example, these individuals often have an obsessive preoccupation with sex; this would tend to express itself *both* in acts of sexual coercion and in more frequent use of sex substitutes. A study of men who admitted having raped but had not been prosecuted found they had an appreciably greater felt need for sex than other men, which suggests the same causal influence.[10] Secondly, rapists as a group are known to feel alienated from women; this could also be a partial cause of a greater use of such substitutes as well as of a greater likelihood of hostile interaction with women.

For another such reason, rapists are known in general to come from social and family backgrounds that are less sheltered and stable, less constrained by the prevailing standards of society (e.g., the families are more violent. This was reconfirmed by one of the studies just cited.) Such persons might well be less inhibited about seeking out socially disapproved things like pornography, as well as in regard to the use of antisocial violence. Conversely, those who receive stronger training against harming others are often, in this culture, taught that pornography is degrading to women; they would be less apt either to commit violent crimes, especially against women, *or* to use pornography a great deal. (By way of analogy, in a culture teaching that both theft and eating pork are evil, a correlation between those two things would not be surprising.) This might be especially true for religious groups, which were disproportionately represented in the one study of the five mentioned earlier that did find a correlation between sex crimes and prior exposure to pornography. A society in which sexual openness is considered offensive to women may well display an association between rape and consumption of sexual materials, even if the latter has no tendency whatever to cause the former.

This last comment is the main point of the foregoing discussion. In circumstances where a common cause for two phenomena is not only possible but known to exist, a correlation between them is by itself useless as evidence that the one causes the other. To appeal to another simile, there is a very strong correlation between lying down and dying, but this is hardly evidence that the former produces the latter. Indeed, one who supposed that it did so and tried to avoid death by always standing up would probably hasten his or her own demise considerably. As this example reveals, a correlation between two factors is quite compatible with the one *preventing* the other. Even should it ultimately become clear that rapists and other sex offenders do use more pornography, we would have no grounds to believe that such use in any way causes their behavior unless all the other plausible explanations for the correlation could be ruled unlikely by the evidence.

A different kind of statistical approach looks at the rates of sex crime and of consumption of sexual materials for the population as a whole. One recent study of this type in the United States did find a correlation between rape and sales of big-selling "soft core" magazines; it did so by comparing the rates of each in the different states.[11] Although many sources of error and nonuniformity exist in the reporting and gathering of crime statistics, the large size of the population involved makes the results look significant. On the other hand, as the authors of the study stress, there are various possible explanations for its outcome. For example, most of the "common causes" just considered could apply here. So might such things as a higher percentage of young men in certain states, which would tend to increase both the rate of rape and the consumption of sexual materials, independently. In fact, the researchers later tested a hypothesis of the general-social-disinhibition type, and it seemed to account for the correlation entirely.

The situation is extremely complex, however. Trying to measure causal influences across the whole country requires highly indirect indicators, and it is such a difficult task overall that it is unlikely to produce firm conclusions any time soon. Consider just two complications. A study of the numbers of "adult" bookstores and theaters across the country showed *no* correlation with the reported rates of violent sex crimes.[12] However, a correlation has been found between those rates and sales of the feminist magazine *Ms,* and further, there is an even stronger association between progress in women's rights and sales of sex magazines.[13] The latter fact runs directly counter to feminist claims about *how* pornography leads to rape. Indeed, the other correlation argues that sexual materials incite rape no more than this one argues they promote respect for women's rights. The fact that many states with high rates of lethal violence and Klan membership have the highest levels of religious fundamentalism should also give pause to some who wish to see evidence against pornography in these data.

One way of trying to decide among alternative explanations is to look for correlations through time rather than across space; some of the possible common causes noted here could be effectively ruled out in this manner. In fact, those opposed to pornography frequently claim such evidence, though usually in a very crude form. "There have been large increases in both the amount of pornography available and the number of sex crimes against women and children in recent years," the claim runs, "so the former must be the cause of the latter." This reasoning is so bad it is difficult to know how to respond. One could with equal justification—that is, none— pick out as the cause of increased sex crime any of the multitude of other social phenomena that have changed during the same period, from the cost of living to sales of pantyhose to the rise of feminism to the resurgence of evangelical and fundamentalist Christianity. Part of what is wrong with this thinking is that the data are terribly imprecise. Those who employ it usually have no idea how much the amount of pornography available or of sex crimes committed has changed. In fact, it is notoriously difficult to get reliable statistical data of this type at all. For example, U.S. government surveys that ask people whether they have been the victims of various crimes indicate a large decrease in the rate of rape since 1973, whereas the rate of rape reports recorded by police has increased greatly during that time.

It is instructive to contrast this argument with others that do supply some evidence. The Danish experience with legalizing pornography is particularly noteworthy in this regard.[14] Denmark's homogeneous population, together with the careful gathering of data by the social scientists involved, make one reasonably confident of the statistics. That the increase in availability of erotic materials was so large and so sudden, occurring under fairly stable social conditions, eliminates from consideration a lot of other variables that might conceivably have had a causal role. As is widely known, the rate of reported sex crimes of various types dropped greatly while that increase was taking place. By questioning people about their feelings, the researchers determined that the decline in reports of milder offenses (e.g., exhibitionism) could plausibly be accounted for by a general softening of attitudes regarding their seriousness, rather than by a change in the frequency of the offenses themselves. That is, the milder offenses were simply not reported to the police as often as they had been.

Yet they found no comparable change in feelings about "peeping" (still regarded as a frightening invasion of privacy) or adult-child sex, even though reports of both had declined drastically—by 80 percent and 69 percent respectively—thus indicating a genuine decrease in their occurrence. Lacking any other plausible explanation for such a result, the researchers found it reasonable to conclude that it was brought about by the sudden high availability of sexually explicit performances and materials. In fact, it is known that both of these offenses are often committed by socially inadequate individuals as substitutes for socially acceptable sex; so it is quite plausible that the new availability of erotic materials simply provided a legally safe substitute. Whatever the explanation, given that so much of today's concern over pornography stems from fears for children's safety and women's peace of mind, these statistics are highly significant.

The safety-valve hypothesis thus gained support in the case of certain sex crimes, but this was not so for rape. Through the period of vastly increasing amounts of pornography in Denmark, the rate at which this crime was reported remained at roughly the same level. From this it would appear that the psychology of rapists does not allow for substitution, on the aggregate, of coercive acts by use of sexual materials. But the claim we are considering here is that pornography causes sexual violence, and in that regard, this is a very important result. That under such conditions there should have been no increase in reports of these crimes (and again, seemingly no change in attitude as regards their seriousness) argues against that allegation. In fact, Denmark's continuing low rate of coercive sex crime, in spite of its liberal attitude toward pornography, is itself worth remarking here. To date, this study is the only really careful investigation of the availability of pornography and rape trends over time.[15]

One researcher has claimed that such trends in various countries show a positive correlation. As the Williams Report revealed, however, the researcher's data were incredibly weak and his manipulation of statistics dishonest. His more recent claims of the same type are no better.[16] In fact, data from various nations reveal no acceleration in the existing trend of occurrences of rape when big increases in the availability of pornography took place. This is the case, for example, for Germany and the United States. In the latter and in England, violent sex crime was increasing at the time, but it had been doing so before the proliferation of sexual materials occurred; there was no apparent change in the rate of increase. (See Berl Kutchinsky's article in *Comparative Social Research,* Vol. 8, 1985.) In England, according to the Williams Committee, there was a five-year period during which the availability and explicitness of sexual materials increased but reports of sexual assault decreased; then a crackdown on hard-core pornography that greatly reduced the supply was followed by an increase in such reports. During the first half of the 1980s (before the latest rash of local and federal crackdowns) the availability of pornography in the United States, in the form of home videotapes, expanded rapidly; but the rate of rape remained level or even decreased.

It must be stressed again, however, that we are facing a great deal of uncertainty in all this. There may always be unrecognized social forces at work in producing the net results the statistics reveal, masking the effects or lack of effects of any given factor. At the time of the big increase in sexual entertainment in Denmark, for instance, the more general "sexual revolution" was occurring; the United States was also then experiencing the social upheavals associated with the "baby boomers" coming of age, the Viet Nam War, and the civil rights movement. To mention another problem, the rise in awareness of and concern about rape that has taken place in recent years may well have increased the percentage of rapes that are reported to and recorded by police; if so, a climb in the police statistics would not mean any actual increase had occurred after all. Since the latter rate in the United States is only up to half of that reported to the victimization surveys, this is a plausible reason for the discrepancy between the changes in the two rates.[17]

As a final point, changes in the rate of rape tend to occur in parallel with those in the occurrence of other violent crimes. This suggests that the social influences producing violent behavior in general, for example, those that make people more willing to use force to achieve their ends, are more to blame than anything else. Given the often erratic variation in crime rates from year to year, from a multitude of jurisdictions, it is bound to be possible to find at least short periods in at least some places where changes in the statistics for pornography sales and for various crimes either match each other or fail to, as one chooses. Nevertheless, the best evidence we currently have from crime trends over time, such as it is, weighs against the claim that pornography induces sexual violence to any discoverable degree.

EXPERIMENTAL EVIDENCE

The main weakness of statistical studies in society, their lack of control over possible causal variables, leads naturally to a consideration of experimental approaches. They cannot eliminate, but can greatly reduce, the influence of extraneous factors. The most common type of experiment, repeated in a large variety of ways by different researchers, involves getting the subjects to perform acts they believe are physically punishing another person (e.g., with supposed electric shocks). If those who have first been exposed to a certain stimulus—say, sexually explicit presentations—are on average likely to give more severe or less severe "punishments" than those who have not, it is concluded that something about the stimulus has been a factor in causing this result. What has the verdict been? The researchers have almost uniformly gotten the same result: subjects simply exposed to pornography beforehand are not inclined to administer harsher treatment than those not so exposed.

A variation on these tests was also devised in order to discover whether sexual explicitness would have any effect on persons who already have a predisposition to aggress. This has usually been done by having the target of the intended punishment anger the subject in some way beforehand. In the many experiments of this latter type, the results have been inconsistent. In some, those who had viewed erotic scenes have been more aggressive in giving punishment, on average; but in others, they have been distinctly less punitive than angered subjects who had not been exposed to sexual stimuli. Though there originally was some dispute over how to interpret such mixed results, the explanation is now agreed to be this: those who observed less sexually arousing scenes (still photos rather than movies, notably) were the ones who tended to exhibit reduced aggression. Indications are that it is the pleasurable feelings induced by mild pornography that result in reduced tendencies toward aggression. But what of the other results? May we conclude from them that erotic movies probably do tend to induce violent behavior in real life?

Some have been anxious to do so. (They have not been equally willing to embrace the result that nude pinups reduce violent tendencies, or the corollary that we should therefore spread lots of them around.) But for various reasons, we may not draw that conclusion. For one thing, there is the fact that the laboratory setting, with its authority-given permission to aggress, is highly artificial. It is not at all clear that the same results would occur in "real life." For another, there is the question of whether and to what extent the mild "pain" administered in these tests can be extrapolated to the serious harm done in a real physical attack. Beyond this, we must notice again that what sort of portrayal is found arousing is very elastic, being dependent on what one is commonly exposed to. As if to confirm this, it has been found that experimental subjects who are more sexually experienced, or who have already viewed large amounts of pornography in the past, are not induced to aggressiveness by highly erotic presentations in the lab—a fact that could argue for greater exposure to sexuality in general, if these results seem worrisome.

The most important response to these laboratory data, however, is the one that emerges from discovering the underlying reason for them. Various experiments have made it now seem very clear that the source of the greater aggressiveness induced by sexual presentations is nothing more than the excitement they produce. It is not a feeling of contempt for women, or a special moral nastiness, or anything of the sort; it is just a general state of heightened physiological activity.[18] Similar results of enhanced aggression have been obtained from such excitement-arousing things as exercise and comical films, even without angering the subject first. And the greater aggressiveness lasts only as long as the state of excitement persists: a few minutes.

These facts heavily underscore the question of extrapolation beyond the laboratory. Would anyone seriously suppose that, say, the recent explosion of interest in exercise has increased the level of violence in our society? In any case, the lab results provide no more reason to oppose pornography than they do to oppose jogging. Moreover, it has been discovered that aggression is not the only activity that can be enhanced by a state of excitement. Experiments in which the subject is supposed to reward another person have generally found that excitement, including sexual arousal, also leads to the giving of higher rewards.[19] It would seem that the effect of being excited is to mildly exaggerate *all* of a person's responses—hardly a novel idea. In sum, sexually produced emotional arousal by itself has not been found to be any more dangerous than that induced by countless other experiences in daily life. Yet another type of evidence concerning the effects of pornography has failed to provide any adequate reasons for considering it objectionable.

A different type of experiment tries to gauge the effects of various influences on the attitudes of subjects rather than on their immediate behavior. So far, as has been indicated earlier, no genuinely adverse changes in male attitudes toward females have been discovered in this way. In one test that was widely reported, males who watched certain nonviolent sex films afterwards indicated a slightly higher average level of belief that they might commit coercive sexual acts, provided they were guaranteed they would not be caught. That is a troubling result, but it turns out to be valueless as evidence; the details of this particular study reveal that something went very wrong with it. For one thing, only one or two small categories of viewer showed any such reaction, and they were already in the habit of viewing large amounts of video pornography in their personal lives; it is highly implausible that an hour and a half more of it would really change their attitudes.

More revealingly, these men also reported having already, in the past, committed more sexually coercive acts. Since the acts preceded the experimental viewing, however, they could hardly have been caused by it. In other words, this particular experiment provided no more reason to believe pornography causes a tendency toward sexual coercion than to believe it can change the past. Evidently, either a disproportionate number of males who already were or saw themselves as more sexually aggressive somehow were assigned to watch the films, or else something affected the accuracy of the subjects' answers about themselves. One indication of what went wrong lies in the way the subjects were recruited and instructed: they were given clues concerning the sorts of responses that might be expected of them. Indeed, other experiments in which subjects viewed pornographic materials have *not* found changes in their self-reported likelihood of committing rape.[20]

In conclusion, at this stage of inquiry the experimental evidence that nonviolent sexual materials might somehow lead to rape is virtually nonexistent. What evidence there is is nearly all on the other side. That is also the conclusion we must draw regarding all the scientific data up to the present. The often heard claim that pornography leads to violence is simply not justified on any such grounds. If anything, the evidence we have points more in the other direction. Even if clear evidence of such an influence is eventually found, however, we must remember what we discovered in the previous chapter. None of the ways in which ordinary sexual materials might reasonably be said to lead to rape are of such a nature as to make pornography itself genuinely blameworthy for that result.

11

Portrayed Violence and Real Aggression

Up to now, we have focused exclusively on the effects of sexual explicitness per se. Whether it might have importantly different effects when in combination with other special features is an independent issue. In particular, the issue of pornography that is violent is one that must be addressed.

NONSEXUAL AGGRESSION

The first matter to be explored is whether violent media presentations in general, with or without sex, have any appreciable and systematic tendency to elicit violent behavior. In this case—unlike that of sexual explicitness in itself—there are good grounds for believing it might. To be sure, they are far from conclusive, and the issue continues to be hotly debated among behavioral scientists. Nevertheless, it seems to many that such evidence as we presently have points more in that direction than in the other. We cannot begin to survey the data here, but we will look at a few salient points.

To start with—and again, this is quite unlike the case of sexual explicitness—there are some clear explanations of why portrayals of violence might evoke real violence, explanations that are already reasonably well established in other contexts. For example, there is modeling and imitation. These involve the tendency to do what others in one's environment do and to regard it as normal, acceptable behavior. This is a significant feature of human psychology, one that is extremely important in the case of children. In particular, then, observing violence, especially if it is perceived as natural and ordinary, can lead to acceptance of it. The *type* of aggression seen might be especially apt to be imitated: in the same circumstances, with the same sort of victim, and so on. A second such explanation is desensitization: even if certain behavior is initially considered repugnant, repeated exposure to it can make it come to seem less serious, lowering the barriers to doing it oneself. Of course, that is a good thing if the behavior is good (e.g., the media have in recent years used positive portrayals of minority races and of integration to desensitize racist feelings). To habituate the acceptance of violence is another matter, however. Other psychological mechanisms that might have a tendency to elicit aggression will emerge as we continue.

The evidence that violence is actually caused in these ways comes in several forms. To begin with anecdotal evidence, most of us have heard of such cases. After each highly successful violent movie, stories appear in the press about "copycat" crimes: *Clockwork Orange, Deer Hunter, The Burning Bed,* and very many others have reportedly triggered such actions. There have been a whole rash of reports of Rambo imitators killing and terrorizing people in the past few years. As warned before, we must not just accept these accounts at face value. In some instances the connection seems clear, however, especially when the details of the act closely match those of the portrayal. Yet even there, the question remains whether the film affected only the form the aggression took, not its occurrence. Moreover, these cases often involve pathological mental states; hence it may be argued that if the movie had not triggered these individuals, something else would sooner or later have done so. Once again, just about anything can set off an unstable personality.

On the other hand, experiments in the laboratory and in real-life situations have given indications that ordinary persons are also influenced by portrayals of aggression. A huge number of such tests have observed depicted violence to elicit or facilitate minor aggressive actions.[1] This has been found even without producing anger or that trivializing excitement effect in the experimental subjects. One type of test has discovered that salient aspects of the original viewed violence have a special influence in this regard. For example, when the experimental "victim" has had the same name or been of the same sex (female) as the portrayed victim, higher levels of aggression have occurred in the laboratory.[2] Of course, the strong doubts raised earlier apply to these experiments as well, notably, whether the permission-bred minor aggression involved in most of them can be extrapolated beyond the laboratory to real life.

Evidence from societal statistics suggests it can, though it faces doubts of its own. In one remarkable study, for example, it was concluded that the homicide rate in the United States jumps appreciably for a few days after each widely broadcast major prizefight. More specifically, the additional victims tend to be of the same race (and sex—male) as the loser in the fight. It would seem from this that observing violence inflicted on someone can indeed trigger hostile acts, at least on the part of individuals already prone to violence. On the other hand, this result has been seriously challenged by other researchers.[3] As has been warned here repeatedly, getting firm knowledge about anything as complex as human behavior is often extremely difficult.

Something that may be much more serious than the immediate triggering of aggression is the subtle effect of long-term, large-scale exposure to presentations of violence on the population in general. It is certain that the level of aggression in a given society is largely determined by socialization; though violence is a human universal, some groups have far less of it than others. Given that fact, and given that the media are such a pervasive force in our own society, it is difficult to believe all the violence they portray does not have a significant impact. This suspicion has been reinforced by a number of long-term studies of children and adolescents. Correlations between exposure to media violence and real aggression by them have indeed been found: those who watch the most TV violence tend to be the most aggressive. Unfortunately, getting reliable data of this type is much more difficult, and the results of different investigators have been mutually inconsistent.[4] In particular, as usual, it is difficult to tell whether the viewing of aggression caused the real aggression or some common cause—notably, a previous liking for violence—produced both.

So the debate goes on. For whatever it is worth, the majority of investigators evidently believe that exposure to media aggression produces long-term and short-term tendencies toward the real thing.

SEXUALLY VIOLENT DEPICTIONS

If portrayals of violence in general are able to elicit violent behavior, one would expect that the same holds for depictions of sexual violence. In fact, the same sorts of anecdotes and experimental evidence are reported in this special case as in the general one.[5] In addition, two factors that might make portrayed violence particularly dangerous have come to light in connection with sexual explicitness. One of these is stimulus-response conditioning: if something a person finds highly desirable, such as sex, is associated unconsciously with something else, the latter will tend to be seen in the same positive light as the former. The use of honor by association to sell products, we should all be aware, has been very successful in modern advertising. In particular, then, associating the desirable thing with violence can result in the one triggering thoughts of the other, and could possibly even result in real violence. Some evidence for this sort of response, over and above the effects of disinhibition expected from exposure to violence per se, has been found in certain experiments in the form of higher aggression levels.[6] As usual, to what extent this laboratory reaction represents an increased danger in real life is not at all clear. Even so, one might suspect that a steady diet of such associations could make the connection seem very strong to susceptible persons; perhaps young people would be particularly vulnerable.

A related type of influence might be of even greater concern, that involved in the case where violence is represented as bringing about some good end. This not only associates it with something desirable but makes it appear that the violence—something which in itself is an evil—is justified by the end it achieves. The particular scenario that has been experimentally investigated in connection with sex is that of a rape in which the victim is shown as becoming sexually aroused and enjoying it. Since this type of scene is found sexually exciting by many of both sexes, it is sometimes found in pornography and romances. It is also symbolically played out in many a Hollywood and TV movie. A kiss is forced on the woman; at first she resists but then becomes aroused and passionately returns it. Once again, such portrayals are not meant to send any general message about what women or men really want. But the question here is, might that message not be received by some individuals? Or might the use of force be seen as less serious, if not completely justified, by the positive outcome.

There is some evidence, acquired from experiments on college students, for a small effect of this type.[7] After being exposed to the kind of scene just described, male subjects have been found to aggress more strongly against females in the laboratory. The effect is very short-lived, however, and it has been found to occur only immediately after exposure to violent sex films, not later on. Moreover, the seeming triviality of other laboratory results we have looked at that involve aggression counsels against putting much weight on these. The increased "aggression" is of the same kind as that occurring after exercise or watching comedy.

Nevertheless, another type of experimental result does warrant concern, one that has to do with attitudes. After viewing rape scenes with a "positive" ending, certain males are a little more apt to report a belief that women may enjoy being raped. They also show a somewhat reduced perception of the amount of trauma involved or similar attitude changes. Such results have been obtained repeatedly, in fact. Even these tests have yielded mixed results, however; some of them have been unable to replicate the others. In one of the latter, male subjects assigned *longer* prison terms to rapists afterward viewing rape scenes of the type in question. Furthermore, whether the seeming attitude changes go very deep, or would last very long, is still not at all clear. It seems unlikely that a few books or movies could have much effect on a person's thinking compared to all the other influences of a lifetime of socialization.

On the other hand, there are disturbed individuals who might expose themselves to large amounts of this type of thing, and there are persons whose tendencies already have them on the borderline of employing coercive behavior. We also know that a certain type of rapist has a difficult time distinguishing reality from fantasy in regard to sex.[8] He imagines either that the woman already wants to be forced or else that he will make her want him through his masterful manner or lovemaking skill. So complete is the self-deception in some cases that such rapists have not infrequently been caught as a result of arranging a future date with the woman: they find the police waiting instead. It would certainly be important to know whether any of these rapists have been appreciably influenced by movies or stories depicting rape (or by those forced-kiss scenes, for that matter). Anecdotal evidence of such an effect from pornography depicting "enjoyed" rape and sadomasochistic acts has recently been uncovered, in fact, in the form of statements reportedly made by sadistic rapists while in the act.[9] Given that individuals willing to use violence will grasp at any pretext they can find, whether the effect is real is uncertain, but this serious matter must continue to be studied.

So there is evidence of particular dangers posed by certain kinds of violent pornography. As usual, however, both the evidence and the effects seem to be mixed. For one thing, psychiatrists have told of cases of disturbed individuals using violent materials in order to ward off their desires for real sexual violence.[10] For another, laboratory studies indicate that repeated exposure to portrayals of sexual aggression make them less sexually arousing to the viewer, not more so. Nor are there any good correlational data from real life on this matter. In fact, at the time when large amounts of violent pornography became available in Germany, the United States, and other countries, there was no increase in the rate of reports of violent sex crimes.[11] Nevertheless, the bulk of the evidence involving violence in general and certain types of sexual violence in particular indicates that such depictions may carry a serious risk.

ARE SEXUALLY VIOLENT PORTRAYALS MORE DANGEROUS?

Should one conclude from the foregoing that portrayals of violent sex are especially dangerous—more so, that is, than violent presentations in general? Was this book perhaps wrong in earlier condemning those who campaign against sexual violence in the media while ignoring all other types of aggression? No such conclusion may be drawn. For once again, sex is only one of many factors that powerfully influence people's emotions. It is only one of many strongly desired things that can be associated with violence in the imagination, or that can be portrayed as ultimately justifying aggression. To name a few others that commonly are so portrayed, there is ambition for money or power, honor, loyalty, love, ideology—even the desire for justice and right. Moreover, it seems quite clear that the association of these things with violence has long been, and continues to be, instrumental in promoting coercive and violent actions in the world. Let us look at each of them briefly.

The last one on the list is often mentioned with concern by social scientists because the portrayal of aggression by "good guys" to achieve their ends is so common in the entertainment media. But nearly everyone sees himself or herself as a "good guy," sees her or his own ends as legitimate. Hence the effect of such portrayals could well be to elicit a lot of real (and not at all genuinely justified) physical and nonphysical aggression. That this is the case has again been suggested by the results of several laboratory experiments. As a closely related matter, the association of ideology with violence has a long history of producing violent behavior. Take religious ideology, for instance, and in particular the Bible: it carries many messages, not only of love and peace but also of hostility toward outsiders and unbelievers. Its commandments to kill witches and homosexuals and its endorsements of slavery have quite clearly been a factor in some gross evils of the past. Even today, we constantly hear stories about individuals and sects who murder, calling it God's vengeance on evil ones, and about parents who beat their children unmercifully, quoting a certain biblical passage as requiring the beating to save their children from the devil.[12] The human proclivity for blind allegiance to a grand system of beliefs makes it a very serious matter what such systems contain.

As for honor and self-esteem, we certainly know how often they are behind acts of violence. Moreover, the possibility of borderline personalities being triggered by media presentations of the violent defense of honor seems clear. To mention just one example, a man who was reportedly obsessed by the violent movie *First Blood* killed a policeman who stopped his car on the street. ("Persecuted little guy fights back against the corrupt system.") The matter of ambition seems too obvious to need comment. To end with the case of romantic love, let us merely note that it, not sexual desire, is the most plausible reason for the results of a much publicized experiment.[13] Questionnaires given to male students after they had viewed certain films indicated a slightly increased acceptance of violence against women. The two movies were not sexually explicit—hence would not generally be regarded as pornographic—but they did involve rape and/or brutality toward women. And the acts were portrayed in each case as winning the love of the woman involved.

So there are many kinds of portrayed violence that present dangers. Nor can it even be claimed that those involving sex are *more* apt to provoke antisocial acts.[14] That might or might not be true; we have no good evidence one way or the other, and such would be very difficult to get. In fact, there is a little laboratory evidence that violence without sexual explicitness has a more negative effect on attitudes than sexually explicit violence does.[15] To be concrete, the latter may well be less likely to promote rape myths than children's movies and cartoons are to promote the belief in them that violence does not really hurt anyone. It is worth noting in this same regard that many rapists are sexually aroused by *non*sexual as well as sexual violence.[16] In general, in fact, there is every reason to suppose that some of the violence stimulated by nonsexual portrayals of aggression would itself be of a sexual nature. Add to all this the fact that people are exposed to vastly greater amounts of nonerotic violence, and it is very clear where the real problem lies.

Another possible defense of special concern over sexual violence is that the welfare of women is particularly at stake in that case, and that they are more vulnerable to assault. But, for reasons such as the proportion of aggression against each sex in the media in general, it is not at all clear that the dangers to them from violent portrayals are greater. Furthermore, some of the things typically associated with violence toward males are especially powerful motivators, things like glory, comradeship, and social approval. The best-documented anecdotal case to date for violence incited by a movie involves the many self-inflicted deaths of young men imitating the Russian roulette scenes in *Deer Hunter*.[17] Most powerful of all, perhaps, even more so than the desire for sex, is the basic need to be regarded as a man. Yet what media image is constantly associated with manhood? Being brave and tough, being able to face harm and danger "like a man." The feminists and traditionalists who complain only about portrayals of violence against women plainly do not care as much about the welfare of men. Yet even these sexists ought to realize their tactics may be counter-productive. After all, empathy toward others requires being able to acknowledge one's own pain; thus men conditioned to accept violence against themselves are also apt to see it as more acceptable against women. Furthermore, there is no guarantee that condoning violence against one class of human beings will not generalize, in the minds of the violent, to include the others as well.

It would be a serious mistake, however, to become so concerned about portrayed violence that we lose sight of the really important sources of social violence. The correlations found to exist between the latter and exposure to the former are always small at best, indicating that other causes of aggression are much more significant. Those other causes are already well known: unstable or disturbed family life, physical and emotional abuse by parents (modeling, again), chronic unemployment, drug and alcohol abuse, mental illness, and so on. It would be tragic if these were ignored in favor of efforts to clean up the media, especially since the latter's influence on behavior is still uncertain.

To conclude this section on a related matter, what about the category of nonviolent but "degrading" pornography? The U.S. Attorney General's Commission on Pornography claimed it had been "demonstrated" to produce a whole raft of antisocial ills, but that is a gross falsehood. For just one thing, once again, it is not at all clear what this description includes. How can it be "determined" that A causes B when it is not even determined what "A" *is?* It is plausible that materials seen by viewers as seriously degrading would have ill effects, for anyone who comes to be less valued is more apt to be exploited and abused. The fact is, however, that there has been almost no special study of materials considered by anyone to fall in this amorphous category. To support their claim, the members of the commission were evidently appealing to two experiments already cited here, namely, the one finding decreased punitiveness toward a rapist and the one discussed at the end of the last chapter.

By their own admission, however, the latter study faces problems requiring that it be "viewed with caution." In addition to the overwhelming doubts mentioned earlier, its results for "erotica" were not significantly different, statistically speaking, from those for "degrading pornography." As for the former study, the researchers' own descriptions of the films involved—in contrast to their rhetoric about them—indicated no real degradation: the men and women were portrayed alike, with no power inequality or coercion, no pain, no humiliation, or anything similar. They did not even engage in highly unusual sexual acts, but were merely "promiscuous" and generally uninhibited. (And contrary to the researchers' claims, once again, no evidence of harmful changes in attitude was actually found.) Consequently, these movies would not appear to have differed significantly from those used by other investigators, who have not even discovered any *seemingly* harmful effects. In summary, the issue of "degradation" is in a state of total uncertainty. It must genuinely be investigated by scientists before any conclusions at all may be drawn.

12

Sexual Repressiveness and Violence

Thus far our discussion of the alleged connection between sexual explicitness and violent behavior has uncovered no adequate grounds for believing any such thing exists, over and above possible links between that
behavior and just about anything that might be portrayed in the media.
By way of contrast, however, there are some good reasons to believe
antisexual attitudes are a factor in producing sexual violence. By this point
in the book, that should not be surprising. We have found again and again
that harmful things associated with sexuality are the result, not of "permissiveness," but of antisexualism. For an analogy, consider a racist con-
templating a black or hispanic ghetto in a big U.S. city: the poverty and
the crime and the broken lives. "What a terrible thing a dark skin is," he
or she might say. "Look at all the harm it causes!" But it is discriminatory
attitudes toward race, and the behavior stemming from those attitudes, that
historically created the conditions that have produced those ghettos and
their horrors. So it has often been with sex.

Antisexual attitudes are still endemic in this culture, producing emotions
ranging from uneasiness to outright aversion toward sexuality. These feelings are inculcated particularly strongly in children and youth, where the
foundations of adult behavior are laid. While there is certainly no uni-
formity in regard to child-rearing across the population, in some cases the
methods used are extreme, such as threatening to withhold love or telling
children God will torture them in hell for sexual acts or feelings. It is only
to be expected that harm results from this. And it does, for psychologists
and psychiatrists have recorded large numbers of cases of people trau-
matized as children by such attitudes regarding sex.[1] This matter was mentioned before in regard to sexual health; now it is highly relevant to our

subject to point out the effect antisexualism seems to have had in the production of violence.

Sometimes the effect is pretty obvious. In one recent incident in Italy, a teenage boy murdered a woman for going topless on the beach. Of special interest to us, however, is the case of sexual violence. Those who commit coercive or brutal sex crimes evidently fall into various categories, with different types of motivation, but clinicians who work with them and social scientists who interview them have repeatedly reported the following fact: among a certain percentage of these persons, a background of sexual repressiveness appears to be a significant factor in producing their violent behavior. Nudity and talk of sex were especially tabooed as they were growing up, and punishments for showing interest in sex were particularly severe. For example, certain clinicians speak of a tendency for rapists to have had harsh disciplinarian mothers: "Such mothers appear to be preoccupied with sexual morality, and the most excessive repression occurred in response to any expression of erotic interest or pleasure."[2]

As an apparent result of this, researchers have noted, rapists tend to be unusually ignorant about sexuality, and so sex education is recommended as part of their therapy. This should give pause to those who think keeping young people in ignorance is the best way of avoiding problems with sex. A more surprising result is that as a group, the rapists the clinicians see are erotically inhibited. They often have strong feelings of guilt or distress toward sex; for example, they report that they are sexually aroused but also disgusted by erotic depictions. As Nicholas Groth puts it, these men have "a value system that is highly conservative and confining in regard to what is acceptable sexual activity, but uninhibiting and nonconfining in regard to what is acceptable aggressive behavior."[3] For whatever it means, this mirrors the fact that children are liberally exposed to violence and assiduously shielded from sex in our society. There is evidently another category of rapists who simply take what they want if they think they can get away with it, whose histories should tend to show a lack of moral training of any sort. Yet the existence of the former category is highly significant.

The link between the attitude that sex is unclean and sexual violence becomes more clear when we consider the question of its exact nature, of *why* the former might lead to the latter. There are several types of possible motivation here, and all would appear to be involved. To begin with, the bare fact that sex is seen as defiling makes it a natural means of punishment—a good way to degrade someone who, for whatever reasons, is regarded as deserving of harm. This would be especially true in cases where sex has been associated with physical or emotional violence by parents who severely punish their children's expressions of eroticism. (Recall the dangers of sex-violence association? In a similar vein, it has been found that many especially violent rapists were themselves sexually assaulted

sexual reprogrammers.

on =

GET RESULTS FASTER WITH

SHAPE®

SAVE 69%*

☐ **YES!** Send me one year (12 issues) of SHAPE for $12.00.** I'll save over $32.00* — **Plus, I'll receive the** *Absolution* **workout guide FREE.**†

Name _____
(Please print)

Address _____ Apt. _____

City _____ State _____ Zip _____

Fill in your e-mail address to receive related information

☐ Payment enclosed   ☐ Bill me later

Roni Ramos

when young. The cycle continues, but how did it get started?) That such a punishment motive is in fact involved in many cases of rape is universally recognized, once again. We can even see this influence at work in milder forms of aggression in our society, such as the use of sexual profanity toward another person. As one might expect, it is found in sexually permissive cultures that sexual terms are not generally used as insults. Even more revealingly, the few such insults they do use tend to involve the few sexual taboos they have, such as incest.[4]

Sex-negative feelings can promote sexual coercion in a second direct way, in cases where there is no preexisting wish to punish but only the desire for sex itself. For they suggest a ready pretext for taking sex by force, namely, that "she (or he) deserves it anyway"—that is, if she's a "bad" woman, say, one who lets herself be "picked up." If one can find an excuse to be angry at or contemptuous of an intended victim, it is easier to avoid facing the fact that what one wants to do is wrong. Such a rationale is commonly reported by rapists themselves. It is also reflected again and again in the excuses they give, such as "She was only a tramp, after all— look how she was dressed!" These men tend to have an extreme whore/ madonna view of women; thus "good" women, in their eyes, are nonsexual. It is amazing that so many people who deplore such attitudes toward women think they can be altered by teaching sexual guilt to men; in fact, the effect is precisely the opposite. This sort of influence on rapists' thinking has already been discussed in Chapter 9. It is evidently a serious one indeed.

Other ways in which antisexual attitudes might lead to violence involve the power of shame. For the message sent to impressionable children and youth is not just that sex itself is bad, but that they are evil for having sexual feelings. As discussed earlier, various sorts of psychological defense mechanisms are used to resist being devalued in this way. In some individuals, the forms these defenses take are distinctly conducive to the elicitation of violence. What is a young person apt to do if he is consistently sent the message that his feelings make him an "animal"? One response is to develop a macho toughness, an attitude of not caring, to escape the emotional pain of it. If the message is more particularly that his needs degrade those toward whom they are directed, that they mean he regards those persons as mere "objects" for his "exploitation," it would hardly be surprising if the result is a tough-mindedness toward them: "What *they* feel doesn't matter *anyway*." The best way to stop someone's attitudes from hurting you is to convince yourself that she or he does not count.

Further possible effects of this kind of shame are not far to seek. Having been labeled "bad" can produce a tendency to reject society's rules in general, "to prove how little I care what you think." Such labeling can also lead a young person to seek out companions who, being "bad" as well, will accept him, thus providing a further influence facilitating antisocial behavior. An attitude of "I might as well get the benefit of what I'm being blamed for anyway" would also not be surprising in such conditions. As psychological studies of despised minority groups have made very plain, young people are highly vulnerable to damage to their developing self-images. Furthermore, it is clear that such damage underlies a great amount of youthful rebellion and conflict with parents and society. Those who have other strong sources of self-esteem can usually compensate for harm to their feelings of personal worth. But some do not.

Let us return to an earlier parallel to try to get this important point across. Suppose the young women in this society were taught, much of the time at least, that their romantic feelings and fantasies are ugly and evil, and even degrading to those toward whom they are directed. Suppose it were said, for example, that the teen idols of the day are being "exploited" by being paraded on stage to arouse or satisfy those emotions, and that pictures and movies of them were denounced as immoral, or even legally prohibited to minors as obscene. Suppose a girl were constantly admonished that she must repress her romantic feelings, even toward the boy next door, until after marriage—at which time it would be all right to have them for her husband, provided she were suitably sensitive to his aversion to being regarded as a mere "love object." Does anyone think this would not cause psychological harm to young women? That it would not lead, in a vulnerable few, to antisocial acts? It is known that such actions are often precipitated by feelings of failure or rejection; hence there can be no doubt that sexual shame has had that effect.

Yet another possible motivation toward violence suggested by the foregoing is the wish for revenge. Human nature being what it is, a person who has been made to feel despised is apt to harbor conscious or unconscious desires to get even. Certain individuals would be particularly prone to this reaction, and some of them would be apt to answer the emotional violence with physical violence. Moreover, the use of sex in doing so would be predictable, as if to say, "You have used sex to degrade me, so I'll do the same to you!" Such a reaction could be directed at society as a whole or at a particular individual who has caused the pain (or at a surrogate for the latter—though we will ignore the specific theories about rapists and their mothers). Given that so much of the traditional sex guilt has been aimed at males by and on behalf of females, it would not be surprising if such feelings were sometimes directed at the latter in general. As Nancy Friday puts it, "How can a man not be in a rage with members of the sex who make him feel dirty and guilty?" Personal conversations in the course of research for this book yielded one story that illustrates the effect with chilling irony. A certain young man described himself as having a violent emotional reaction toward women, an angry desire to hurt them, at the sight of sexual pictures. Such a revelation would be met by cries of "We told you so!" from many. But the man himself claimed to be aware of the source of his emotions: it was a lifetime of feeling rejection and contempt from females because of his sexual desires toward them.

Given their general lack of capacity for introspection, violent individuals might well be influenced by such emotions without realizing it. The need to feel strong and manly would also prevent many from admitting they have been hurt this way, even to themselves. Nevertheless, anger over being made to feel inferior sometimes appears in rapists' own accounts of their motives; a desire to "knock her off her pedestal" or "drag her down to my level" is spoken of not infrequently. And occasionally, specific mention is made of a desire for revenge over feelings of sexual shame. One of the rapists Groth discusses at length makes this assertion. For he had grown up "in a home where any mention of sex was forbidden. His parochial school instilled in him the attitude that sex was sinful and that girls were good and boys were bad." The tendency of criminals to seek excuses for their behavior must prevent us from accepting such reports uncritically. Yet it is clear that anger is a major motive in a significant proportion of rapes. Although sexual shame is certainly not the only cause of this hostility, it is far too salient a factor to be ignored.

The universal hatred of women that the extremist feminists decry does not exist, but certain men do feel great hostility toward women. Perhaps this emotion is even reflected in some male sexual fantasies and hence in some pornography. The question is, what produces such feelings? In the thinking of these ideologues it is just an expression of natural male nastiness or else the result of men having been systematically taught to despise women. The ironic truth, however, may well be exactly the opposite, that men have been told they are morally inferior and made to feel hated themselves for attributes that are a basic part of their nature as males. It is often suggested that violent or degrading pornography represents a backlash against the women's movement, and in this there might be a small grain of truth. A familiar defense against psychological assault is to jeer at those making it and to act out the very behavior one has been accused of. So that aspect of feminism that equates male sexual feelings with sexism, and worse, is well designed to create such a backlash. As for the traditionalists who are fighting against sexual openness, they are guilty of similar blindness. In their zeal to protect women by putting them back on the pedestal, they reinforce the very conditions that create misunderstanding and hostility between the sexes.

This alienation from women has other possible consequences that are very disturbing. Some people react to being shamed and rejected by withdrawing rather than with anger and defiance. And something that is true of male pedophiles in general—the majority of whom are passive, nonviolent individuals—is that they feel threatened by women. This suggests that their sexual interests are turned toward children precisely because of anxiety over rejection and hostility from adult females. In other words, what makes children sexually preferable to such persons is that they are accepting and unthreatening. The extent to which this culture's negative attitudes toward sexuality in general, and male sexuality in particular, might play a part in this has not been adequately explored by psychologists. Nevertheless, the possibility that those attitudes are partially to blame is very real. Unfortunately, a culture that reacts to emotional deviance with vengeance rather than compassion is not likely to look in this direction for solutions to the problem.

One final way in which sex-negative socialization could lead to acts of violence involves internalized shame—that is, guilt—and the power it can have to twist a person's mind. One who is especially susceptible to this emotion can be drawn into a deepening spiral of anxiety. Each time he "falls," through sexual fantasies or sexual actions, the emotional stress becomes greater; and the chance that the latter will express itself in some sort of act harmful to himself or others increases correspondingly. (If the sexual "sin" to which he has given in includes the use of pornography, it may thus be "involved" in the causation of crime—but only in this secondary fashion.) The teenage son of a childhood friend of the author was driven to suicide by guilt, guilt produced by his religion's telling him he was sinful and unworthy if he could not stop masturbating and having sexual thoughts. The conclusion that sexual guilt is at fault in some violent sex crimes is difficult to escape; it is virtually written on the face of certain cases. In the words of psychologists Hans J. Eysenck and Glenn D. Wilson, discussing serial murderers such as the Boston Strangler and the Yorkshire Ripper, "Many of these individuals seem to have a high libido but regard sex as 'dirty' and unacceptable, and their ghastly crimes seem to be some kind of function of this conflict."

More specifically, the phenomenon of guilt projection would appear to be involved here: the individual transfers his own painful feelings of evil onto others, seeking to punish them instead. Psychiatrists often remark that serial murderers appear to be motivated by an obsession to destroy something they hate in themselves; and the case of the quiet, obedient "good boy" who suddenly commits an act of bizarre or brutal violence also lends itself to this explanation. In *Sex without Shame,* Dr. Alayne Yates tells the story of a boy named Timothy which bears all the marks of sexual guilt projection. He was unnaturally close to his mother in ways that could only have produced feelings of sexual arousal, but she also shamed him when he showed an interest in sexual materials. One night when a girl acted seductively toward him, he exploded into a rage and murdered her—sealing the act symbolically by stabbing her vagina full of knives.

Recently, one Sean P. Flanagan was put to death by the state of Nevada for a string of murders of gay men. He left behind a statement saying he hated his own homosexual desires and that the killings were motivated by that emotion. Unlike Bundy's pronouncements, this admission did not attempt to shift blame off himself, and thus rings chillingly true.

Whatever the total etiology of these attacks may be, sexual guilt certainly appears to be a crucial part of it. Serial murderers who compulsively kill people they do not know fall almost entirely into two categories: heterosexual men who kill women—especially prostitutes or other women who might seem "loose," and homosexual men who kill men—especially homosexual men. This striking fact argues that their heinous deeds have to do with sexuality rather than with gender: They are killing persons who attract them sexually. Why under heaven would anyone desire to do that? The arguments in this chapter suggest a chilling answer. As for mass murderers, that category of multiple killers who run amok publicly until they are killed or kill themselves, they usually attack members of both sexes. One exception is the recent horrifying antifeminist rampage of Marc Lepine in Montreal. Whether, as many would claim, he was simply a crazed male supremacist, or whether he was influenced by the ongoing torrent of hatred against men from extremist feminists, we will never know.

A terrible irony has emerged from the preceding paragraphs. Not only is there no good reason to believe that sexual explicitness per se leads to violence, but the antisexual attitudes that underlie the antipornography campaign are themselves a cause of violence. The message of sexual aversion that is conveyed by opposition to erotic materials (and by many other means, of course) is to blame for some, perhaps much, of the sexual aggression and hostility that plague this society. Indeed, there seems to be a vicious circle of repressiveness and violence here. Each time a particularly heinous sex crime occurs, many say, "See how dangerous sex is? This proves it has to be suppressed!"—which merely prepares the soil for more such acts. In George Washington's day, a respected medical tradition said disease was caused by "bad blood" and was cured by letting it out. To treat an illness, Washington's physicians repeatedly bled him; when instead his illness only grew worse, they frantically let even more blood out, until he finally died. Our tragically counterproductive attitudes about sex must somehow be changed; people must be educated to the evil that is being done.

Of course, violent behavior has many sources. If we are to do anything significant about all the aggression in this society, the remedy must include a lot of things, such as attacking its socioeconomic roots. It must also include simply doing a better job of teaching morality to children—real morality, that is: respect and concern for others, and equal dignity for all. If guilt is to be taught (and it probably must be), let it be only over genuine evils like aggression itself.

13

Pornography and the Law

In the course of this book, we have surveyed the major arguments that bear on the question of whether pornography is evil: whether it is intrinsically immoral or whether its use causes harm of any sort. From all that has been explored, it is clear that neither conclusion is justified. This being so, there is also no warrant for the traditional treatment of sexually explicit materials and performances, with the plausible exception of child pornography, under the law. All the rationalizations notwithstanding, the fundamental motive for criminalizing sexual materials is nothing more than feeling offense that such things should exist. (The legal term "obscene," be it remembered, refers to what is highly offensive, not to what is harmful.) Centuries of horrible religious war and persecution finally made Western societies realize that merely disliking the activities of others is not a morally acceptable reason to interfere in their lives. This understanding is sometimes called "the harm principle," the principle that only actual or probable harm or hurt by others justifies harming or hurting them. Further, the harm must be publicly verifiable, involving physical or psychological pain or disability, not the metaphysical damage to the soul that the warring religionists alleged. Unfortunately, the lesson has not yet been fully learned.

Legal punishment is itself a type of violence, one performed by the state; for it to harm anyone for something that is not likely to harm others is grossly immoral. The same holds true for using the law to coerce behavior by threatening such violence. Similarly, denying access to what one desires or needs is a type of harm; the moral rights of not only those who supply but also those who want to obtain nonharmful things are violated by such coercion. There is no more justification for antipornography laws than for "Jim Crow" laws, which harmed and coerced people for the color of their skin—and which were also rationalized, in their time, as promoting both moral values and the physical safety of society. In addition, we have seen ample evidence of the evils produced by sexual repressiveness; by fostering antisexual attitudes, such laws do yet more harm than that of restricting liberty and punishing unjustly. There is far better reason to punish those who propagate sexual aversion than those who promote sexual pleasure. Beyond all this are the other evils laws like this are known to spawn; for example, the high profits produced by black or gray markets attract criminals and lead to such vices as blackmail, exploitation of workers, and the bribing of judges and police. Laws against sexual explicitness are not only terribly unjust to individuals but terribly unwise for society as a whole.

OTHER DEFENSES OF SEXUAL CENSORSHIP

Those who want to ban pornography have often sought ways to excuse the laws without reasonable evidence of harm. One of the arguments runs like this: "We don't know it's harmful, but we also don't know it's not; since it might be, and since so much is at stake, we can't take the chance." It is true that even a low likelihood of bad consequences can justify preventing a given type of action, at least if the harm is potentially great enough. But in this case that fact is of no avail, for there is as much or more evidence against even a low probability of serious consequences than in support of such. Indeed, there is about as much reason to believe pornography prevents harm as that it causes it. So the argument can just be turned around: "We don't know it doesn't prevent harm; since it might, and since much is at stake, we must allow it." Beyond this, the principle of not punishing unjustly stands supreme—we *do* know that being fined or put in prison hurts people. Hence we are morally obligated to be very sure that what someone does is apt to have ill effects before we apply any legal sanctions.

Another argument in this same "There may be no harm, but . . . " category appeals to the concept of democracy. "If a majority of people find something offensive—whether or not they are justified in feeling that way—surely they have a moral right to keep it out of their society." Again the reasoning is fallacious. In fact, it becomes something of an embarrassment when it turns out, as it has done repeatedly of late, that the majority believe sexual explicitness per se should not be banned. As is so often the case, the laws in question are promoted and maintained by the inertia of tradition and powerful minorities, not the majority. The fundamental point here, however, is that not even a majority is morally justified in harming those who have done or threatened no harm. Indeed, there is something especially pernicious about the power of the many being used to oppress a minority or an individual. Would it be right if the majority in this society decided to imprison, say, those who practice Judaism or Christian fundamentalism? Majority rule without the legal standard of the harm principle to protect individuals is not just; it is mob rule. Those who argue for the importance of "shared values" to a society often do not seem to regard justice, much less tolerance, as being among those values.

This is why the "community standards" criterion of U.S. and Canadian obscenity law is a miscarriage of justice. A plainer admission that nothing but popular prejudice underlies the statutes could hardly be asked. For it tacitly acknowledges what was true all along, that those particular standards have no objective moral basis that can be stated but are subject solely to the arbitrary and variable forces of socialization. This criterion has not been used to carve out exceptions to other basic rights, for example, to support laws against other things many have found obscene, such as interracial marriage. That reveals pretty clearly how much it is really worth. In fact, as the latter comparison also reveals, a history of prejudice against a certain type of behavior provides an excellent reason for giving it *special* legal protection. At least this is so if it involves an important area of human life—which sexuality, like religion, certainly is. Traditional laws prohibiting nonharmful sexual behavior violate the most fundamental moral rights, those of privacy and personal dignity. Majority rule is required for enterprises that are unavoidably cooperative, such as our highly interdependent economic system. But behavior that is not intrinsically harmful, and which influences others only as they choose to emulate it, should be protected as a private matter.

An issue closely related to that of majority rule involves the aesthetic intolerance, mentioned in Chapter 3, that is central to judgments of what is "obscene." Historically, the suppression of sexual materials has involved a large element of class conflict. For the entertainment of the lower classes is typically sweaty and boisterous, their tastes unsubtle (i.e., explicit) and "unrefined," according to the ruling classes (upper or middle). In other words, "erotica" is what the latter enjoy, while "pornography" is what the former like. If the story ended there, it would be of small concern. But the law has been used to enforce these matters of taste. And the law always falls more heavily on the lower classes; it is often an instrument of class oppression. Even if such differences do not divide along class lines, however, the political oppression remains. In recent times, aesthetic standards have entered the criminal law overtly, by way of the judicial dictum that "artistic merit" can decide whether or not a sexual representation is legal. Whether a person is to be locked up in prison hinges on something as trivial and subjective as bad taste, as morally irrelevant as aesthetic judgment.

All this brings us to the question of what kinds of things should be protected by a governmental constitution or bill of rights. That is much too complex an issue in philosophy of law to deal with at length here; the more general issue of what ought to be legal or illegal is the important one for our purposes. However, since the "community standards" criterion has arisen in the context of judicial interpretation of constitutional law, one further point should be made. The main purpose for having a special system of legal rights to restrain government bodies, in a democracy, is to protect minorities and individuals from abuse of power by the majority; what is popular certainly does not need much protection. Hence appealing to that criterion to interpret the right of free expression is a clear violation of that original intent: it says some sort of majority can after all override a legal right that was meant to be above majority rule. In the process of trying to find an objective measure for the subjective notion of obscenity, what the average person finds offensive, the justices have undermined the very purpose of constitutional law.

It is sometimes claimed the only freedom of expression that should be constitutionally assured is that of political speech, narrowly construed, on the grounds that such speech has a special importance in the democratic process. This view has its value-priorities backward. Democracy (i.e., majority rule) is justified by freedom, not the other way around; exercise of power by the majority is good only because, and to the extent that, it promotes people's control over their own lives. Beyond this, the fact that the voters get to be heard only once every few years means they have little control over most of the decisions of government and its massive bureaucracy. Individual members of a majority also need protection against the vast power of the state. Finally, even granting the special importance of political expression, that category surely must be construed broadly, so as to cover not only who should be elected but how life in the nation should be lived. After all, the freedom to influence others and be influenced by others is essential to making informed decisions, in all the aspects of life that government might touch and that voting might influence.

Yet another way of defending sexual censorship takes the attitude that good evidence of harm is not necessary to justify the state in using force against its citizens. This time the claim is that the burden is on the latter to show what they want to do is *good* for society, not merely nonharmful. This is also clearly perverse since it could result in the punishment of everything from having blue eyes to religious ceremonies. Yet something like it is evidently the rationale of those who insist that only laws censoring "ideas" (intentional claims of fact, or some such thing) are bad—not those that prohibit mere "entertainment." Notice that this distinction would also deny protection to much art and literature, whose sole or primary purpose is likewise emotional or aesthetic enjoyment rather than the promotion of beliefs. Given that so many "ideas" are totally trivial or downright perverse, it is difficult to see why they should get a blanket constitutional defense while other kinds of representation and behavior get none.

Beyond this, the distinction between cognitive and noncognitive representations is by no means a sharp one in either purpose or effect. Sexual "entertainment" most certainly does convey ideas, even if that is not the primary or conscious intent. It presents a certain view about human sexuality, that sex is good for its own sake, and also contains more specific ideas about what some find good in regard to sex. It can sometimes do this, moreover, in a far more powerful way than abstract treatises could. In fact, pornography has special political significance, for the ideal of sexuality it presents is often at odds with that of mainstream thought, a distinct social alternative. As was pointed out in Chapter 7, a clear awareness of alternatives is crucial to the search for knowledge; suppressing other viewpoints cripples progress. Indeed, many of the other arguments against pornography are based precisely on *ideas* it allegedly conveys that are considered objectionable (e.g., claimed messages about women). The primary motive of most advocates of censoring pornography is the desire to live in a society where only their vision of sexuality is allowed to be promoted by what is portrayed; they do not want the sort of freedom that would permit ideas to be influenced in this way.

The fact that sexual entertainment is uniquely punishable by the law is itself a powerful influence on social beliefs. It creates or reinforces a societal stigma, an atmosphere of anxiety, around the entire subject of sex. It also encourages prosecution and threats of prosecution of presumably protected treatments of sex by legal officials willing to bend the law to their own ends. It has even affected scholarly and scientific study of sexuality in these ways. Those who have done research on that vitally important human subject can tell us how obscenity laws and the fears they spawn have hampered the acquisition of knowledge about it. For just one example among many, even in the 1970s, a history professor undertaking a study of homosexuality was considered potentially subversive by the FBI.[1] Indeed, certain views about sex are now dominant in this culture partially because alternative ones were suppressed by the law so strongly for so long. Whether or not messages are conveyed by this or that sexual portrayal, censoring them most certainly has a profound influence on "ideas" about sexuality. One way or another, freedom of thought is very much at stake here.

Beyond all this, however, the central point remains: only clear danger of genuine harm ever justifies coercion, especially coercion by the state. That is why freedom of expression has not been made the major issue here, only the harm principle. There are indeed good reasons for that liberty, given that communication is such an important part of life and that it is so basic to many other freedoms. Nevertheless, not all types of expression *should* be free. There are and ought to be laws against such things as lying under oath, libel and slander, false emergency alarms, harassing threats, and giving government secrets to the enemy in wartime. However, note well that it is in every case the serious damage that can be done that makes exceptions of these kinds of expression. Next to them the obscenity laws stand out like the proverbial thumb: the latter represent the only real case where mere gut-level dislike is allowed to compromise this right. A clearer moral inconsistency could hardly be imagined, and we must marvel again at the power of antisexualism in this society.

CENSORSHIP OF VIOLENCE AND DEGRADATION

So we have still found no justification of any sort for maintaining the laws against pornography per se. That is not necessarily the case, however, for other things in the media, notably violence. This society has long been permissive toward aggression, and the high level of violence we suffer under may be in part a consequence of that. In particular, evidence suggests that all the media aggression we are exposed to is a causal factor in real violence. Perhaps it is time we put at least some restrictions on such portrayals. Note well that some of the reasons for objecting to sexual censorship do not apply in the case of portrayed violence. Though humans have a natural capacity for violent behavior, there is not a corresponding need for it, as there is for sex. Consequently, restricting its portrayal in various ways should send no message harmful to the feelings of self-worth of normal individuals. Of course, censoring aggression in general would automatically include censoring sexual violence.

On the other hand, media violence is not a simple issue either. For one thing, the evidence for harm from it is still far from fully clear. For another, the perennial problem of "where to draw the line" is as horrendous in this case as it has traditionally been with regard to sex. Should news coverage be censored for violence? (It may be much more likely than mere fiction is to incite copycat crimes.) Or should we censor the Bible, which contains the original "snuff" story and much other violence?[2] What about portrayals of *non*physical aggression, such as deceit and emotional cruelty and character assassination? Those ever popular murder mysteries? Grand opera? All these things and others like them have reportedly triggered violent acts. Given that different kinds of portrayed aggression are not equally dangerous, there are surely some limits on how far we would want to go in this direction. Given, in addition, all the other perils posed in general by legal censorship, it might be that the best approach to the problem is to rely on educating the public to reduce the amount of aggression in the media. Alternatively, perhaps we might legally restrict the violence children are allowed to see, as many countries already do.

Whatever may be the best solution to the problem in general, one thing that would be highly objectionable is to use standards that are morally arbitrary in deciding what violence to censor. Specifically, it is wrong to single out violent depictions that involve sex for prohibition, while ignoring equally dangerous ones that do not. Such double standards violate a fundamental principle of fairness, of equal protection under the law. For they make a criminal of one person but not another, even though there is no moral difference between their actions. As the U.S. Supreme Court once ruled: "When the law lays an unequal hand on those who have committed intrinsically the same quality of offense . . . it has made as invidious a discrimination as if it had selected a particular race or nationality for oppressive treatment."[3] (Imagine there being a special set of laws against certain acts by Jews, but none against far greater amounts of the same behavior by all other groups in society.) The reason for mentioning this is that so many proposals have been made and enacted for using civil and criminal law to ban portrayals of sexual violence but not other kinds. Although the main influences that have produced this reaction have already been discussed, they are worth repeating in this context.

For one, there is the disinformation about such things as what motivates the making of such materials, who enjoys them, how common they are, and who is shown on the receiving end of the violence. Then there is the traditional prejudice against pornography in general; this is a major reason why sexual violence attracts so much attention while the steady stream of nonsexual aggression goes unnoticed. When the U.S. Attorney General's Commission on Pornography declared the production or use of violent pornography "an offense against humanity," making no distinction among the different types and no mention of any nonsexual violence, this motive was illustrated very well. The other primary reason behind the moves to ban only sexual violence is the perception that the welfare of women is particularly at stake in that case. Once again, portraying the rape of a woman is considered far more horrible than depicting the bloody murder of a man. Also once again, this is sexist and morally wrong. The possible message of a rape-scene that women can be victimized is no less evil than the traditional one that "men can take it," that their safety is less important and their lives more expendable. Serious crimes such as sexual assault on women deserve our grave concern, but not to the exclusion of that over other violent crimes against other persons.

Actually, those actively seeking to prohibit only violent pornography seem to be outnumbered by those agitating for censorship of sexual portrayals in general. Many of the latter show no concern about media violence at all, no matter how brutal or glorified it may be. On the political right, in fact, some even seem to endorse it, at least against men. (Perhaps they feel it helps keep people strong for resisting criminals and Communists.) After all of its alarms about violent pornography, the Meese Commission recommended no changes in the legal definition of obscenity, merely more vigorous enforcement of the laws. Since in the United States violence is not part of that definition, it was business as usual: just ban the sex. In fact, the U.S. government has since made no moves to censor violence, though it acted quickly to adopt and enforce strong new penalties against portrayed sex.[4] The only violence apt to be involved in the prosecutions is that committed with the guns and prisons of the government. Even so, such actions likely will influence the amount of violence viewed. In some places where sexual videotapes have recently been banned, there have been reports of an increase in rentals of violent ones; if some people cannot watch men and women making love, it seems, they will see them being shot and sliced up instead.

Let us now turn to that other special legal issue, sexual portrayals that are genuinely or allegedly degrading to someone. In an important way, the case for censoring depictions or descriptions that are genuinely debasing is stronger than that for violent ones. (Certain types of violence are themselves degrading, of course.) For though there is still considerable doubt about the effects of exposure to the latter, little such doubt remains concerning the former. At least this is true when identifiable individuals or groups are recipients of the debasement. For we know something about the harmful effects of an atmosphere of racist messages, effects on the attitudes and behavior of both the victims and others. Not the least of the evils of debasing messages is the immediate psychological pain of those being degraded: *hatred hurts*. It can be more damaging than a physical assault—it can easily lead to physical violence, in fact, to others or to oneself. (See Chapter 12 again.) Self-dignity is a fundamental human need, as vital as food and water, and to be robbed of it is devastating.

Just as with violence, however, the legal proposals standardly made on this subject in recent years are blatantly selective, since they usually mention only sexual degradation and degradation of women. As discussed shortly, one of these proposed laws was actually passed in two or three different localities. Under its provisions, portrayals of female nudity or of women inviting intercourse could be legally punishable, while those of the gang rape and murder of a male would not. (The law was struck down by the courts, not on grounds of violating equal protection of the law, but on those of threatening freedom of expression.) An ironic aspect of these proposals warrants mention. As has been stated earlier, likely the sole reason for the existence of genuinely degrading sexual materials is the way this culture traditionally degrades sex itself. That being so, a sane law— not to mention a just one—against degradation would also be applied to writings and portrayals exhibiting the original kind of degradation. A law that would punish people involved with, say, that infamous cover on *Hustler,* but not those guilty of the antimale bigotry that leads to such defensive reactions, would be as unjust as any other law that punished acts of self-defense but not the original assault.

The irony goes deeper yet, however. Some of the people most actively involved in the campaign to eradicate sexual portrayals they consider degrading to women are the most vicious in their sexism against men; they can only be described as hatemongers. One of the most extreme of these women has been very influential in government antipornography efforts. She regards any sort of vaginal penetration as equivalent to rape, and makes statements such as "Men especially love murder." She calls the killing of women "the prime sexual act for men in reality and/or in imagination." Without the knowledge that he could kill his partner with impunity, she insists, a man would not enjoy sex. In spite of all this, she managed to induce the city councils of Indianapolis and Minneapolis to pass her proposed censorship law, and she later contributed heavily to the conclusions of the Meese Commission.[5] Dozens of charges that are equally hateful (if not equally insane), in books by scores of extremist feminists, are to be found in most bookstores and libraries and are required reading in many college women's-studies programs. If anyone is to be locked up for sexually degrading anyone, it is clear where we should start.

Yet it is not clear that there *should* be laws against degrading communications, that the very real harm they can cause would not be outweighed by the harmful effects of the laws themselves. One serious difficulty is the vagueness and subjectivity of the concept of degradation. Part of the problem here is in making clear to individuals just what the law does and does not allow. The continuing scandal of the existing obscenity laws is that the terms they use, such as "patently offensive" (United States) and "undue exploitation of sex" (Canada), are hopelessly unclear. All laws are vague to some degree, but in this case the degree is extreme. Moreover, experience has shown that the community-standards test does not solve this problem; no one ever knows what the "average person's" standard will be judged to be in a given case, or whether it might continue to be so judged tomorrow. To the question, "What type of thing *is* obscene, anyway?" the usual answer has been, "You'll find out in court." Imagine what it would be like, someone has suggested, for speeding laws to be handled this way: that is, for the law to read simply "Don't drive too fast," and it would be up to the judge or jury to decide whether you have done so.

Part of what is evil about this is the "chilling effect" it has on behavior in general. Such laws can be used to prevent things that would never actually be prosecuted, or at least not convicted in court, out of concern that they just *might* be punished. Beyond that, such legal uncertainty is a terrible injustice because of the fear it can generate in people's lives. To make this point as vivid as possible, the reader should ask how safe she or he would feel living in a society where the law said, in effect, "Anyone who says or produces anything that is degrading will be put in prison." Another thing that is wrong about vague laws is the ease with which they can be manipulated. As we have seen regarding degradation in particular, many are only too happy to attach the label "degrading" to behavior they actually consider bad on other grounds. That description has been promiscuously applied to all sorts of things involving sex, from being outside a committed relationship, to being only for fun rather than affectionate, to being too enthusiastic. With equal ease, it could be charged that socialism or capitalism, atheism or religion, are degrading to some or all people. It seems clear enough why we do not have *general* laws against degradation—and clearer still why it would be so unjust to police for this offense only one special category of expression, the sexual one.

In fact, special prohibitions regarding sexual degradation are a far *greater* threat to justice than would be those directed at other sorts of degradation. The reason is that in this society, all sorts of sexual behavior that are not debasing are commonly regarded as being so. Indeed, once again, most of what those calling for such laws want banned is perfectly innocuous.[6] In a society where for one person to do something she enjoys can be seen as degrading to all other persons of the same gender, where the general level of sexual anxiety is so high that extremists can manipulate the system with false charges, and where so many people think a feeling of revulsion in their gut is all the justification they need to lock another human being in a cage, laws against "degrading" portrayals of sex can only make an already grossly unjust situation even worse. Until such time as we as a society are able to tell the difference between what is and what is not debasing with regard to sex, such laws are a grave threat to that very human dignity they would ostensibly defend.

THE PRESENT PERIL

Unjust and irrational though it is, the legal suppression of sexual materials has gotten worse at an accelerating rate in the last ten years. The main reason for this is increased activity on the part of extremist feminism and the right wing, and of certain others who share their sexual views. They have achieved great political power by getting well organized. Beyond that, as noted before, are two major reasons why they are able to wield such great influence in this special matter.

First, there is the high level of ignorance and misinformation about sexuality that characterize the general public. They can so easily be misled by further misinformation under these conditions. A case in point is the recent investigation by the Commission on Pornography appointed by the U.S. attorney general. The staff, the chairman, and a majority of the commissioners were on record in advance as strong opponents of sexual materials, while none of the others were known as proponents of erotic materials, or even as defenders of the status quo concerning obscenity laws. Their mandate was to make recommendations "concerning more effective ways in which the spread of pornography could be contained," which *assumes* it is evil and all but instructs them to declare it so. The obvious purpose of appointing the commission in the first place was not to explore the issues objectively but to indict pornography. This is borne out by the highly biased way in which their hearings were conducted, under conditions well suited to elicit gross exaggerations and outright falsehoods from the large numbers of antipornography zealots called to testify.[7]

The second reason for the strong influence of the campaign against pornography is the shame and anxiety most people in this culture already feel regarding sexuality and its portrayal. These make it easy for those with positive sexual attitudes to be intimidated; if they speak out, they'll be labeled immoral and suspected of being closet perverts of some sort. This is especially true of politicians, who are notoriously afraid of being seen as "soft on smut." (Their votes can be bought wholesale by powerful lobbies such as the tobacco industry and gun-control opponents, in spite of the millions the products at issue have maimed and killed). This fear is relieved only in the privacy of the voting booth, where majorities from conservative Utah to conservative Maine have cast their ballots against sexual censorship.[8] Even that could change, however; for if such fear continues to assure that only one side is heard, a majority will eventually be converted.

Under these influences, a wave of legal oppression has already been created, and in some places it has become a virtual witchhunt. The vagueness of the obscenity laws has been a particularly powerful weapon in this, deliberately used to coerce behavior far beyond what would be upheld in court. Since storekeepers can seldom know whether they have broken the law until a judge or jury decides, they are frightened into removing from their shelves everything even remotely sexual. Government attorneys and police chiefs, often working hand-in-glove with private censorship groups, have large amounts of taxpayers' money with which to harass and prosecute store owners and employees, and they have been doing so with a vengeance. The U.S. government's sweeping new censorship legislation is meant to promote country-wide prosecutions of the sale of sexual materials.[9] (One tactic has been the seizure of all money and property of the accused, on grounds that one item may later be judged obscene, so that he or she has no funds for a legal defense.) With all the highly conservative judges appointed to the Supreme Court and lower courts in the United States in recent years, even the incomplete constitutional protection existing previously is threatened with being swept away.

As if unjust laws were not bad enough, in many places there have been gross violations of supposedly protected legal rights. From all across the land have come reports of police harassment and brutality, blatant entrapment, intimidation of defense witnesses, and judicial misconduct.[10] After all, "bad guys" do not deserve the protection of law and order. With official attitudes of such kinds, extremists are encouraged to acts of violence of their own; there have been firebombings of adult bookstores and the like in many places while these campaigns were going on (conveniently blamed on "organized crime"). It is precisely in circumstances of high emotion, such as those sexophobia involves, that protection of rights is most needed; without a strong stand against racial prejudice by an earlier

Supreme Court, the United States today would very likely still be segregated. If silent citizens do not start speaking up, however, the sexual McCarthyism will continue.

In the course of this book, the more important moral, scientific, and legal issues in the debate over sexual explicitness have been discussed. Obviously much more could be said, and needs to; but most of the essentials are represented here. As has been noted repeatedly, pornography by itself is not the basic issue. Opposition to it is only a symptom of more general attitudes toward sexuality that are both false and harmful to us all. But sane and humane attitudes about that subject can never be cultivated as long as harmless sexual fantasies are despised by the general public and suppressed by the power of the state. Indeed, the current campaign against pornography is also harming sex education and the rights of sexual minorities; in the long run, it is a threat to the privacy, liberty, and dignity of everyone. Though much broader values are at stake, then, the specific matter of sexual explicitness is of crucial importance. It is there that those who are opposed to sexual superstition and concerned about real justice must take a stand, if this society is to escape the forces pushing it back toward the even greater cruelty and irrationality of the past.

Notes

CHAPTER 1

1. Definition used in Webster's many dictionaries: "the depiction of erotic behavior intended to cause sexual excitement." The meaning of the English word "pornography" should not be confused, as it has been by some, with that of its Greek ancestor, "writing by/about harlots." It does not have that old meaning any more than most other Greek-derived English terms do: for example, our word "gymnasium" does not mean "place of nakedness." If the ancient definition were used, there would be very little pornography, since most of what is so labeled is not writing and only a tiny amount of it is about prostitutes.

2. Notice that the black-and-white dichotomy between "pornography" and "erotica" leaves us without a value-neutral word for sexual materials whose purpose is sexual arousal. Consider how difficult it would be to talk if we had a term meaning "evil person" and one meaning "noble person" but none that just meant "person." Ideologues dislike words that are not emotionally loaded, of course, but objective discourse requires them. Notice also that even if we did consider the traditional negative connotations of the word "pornography" to be part of its actual meaning, that meaning would have to be "bad *because* sexually frank," rather than bad for some independent reason such as the absence of affection or artistic value. Though the former has arguably been some people's intended definition, it simply assumes that sexual frankness *is* bad, which begs the question under discussion here.

3. For the information on the Muria and the Tahitians, the reader is referred to Verrier Elwin's *Kingdom of the Young* and Bengt Danielsson's *Love in the South Seas*. A good history of Western erotica is the book by H. Montgomery Hyde, *A History of Pornography;* Vern Bullough's *Sexual Variance in Society and History* discusses other major civilizations.

4. See Dolf Zillmann's *Connections between Sex and Aggression*, pp. 79–81.

5. See articles on this subject in the *Archives of Sexual Behavior*, 1:2 (Daniel Masica et al.), 3:1 (Arye Lev-Ran), and 3:3 (John Money and Charles Ogunro).

6. For example, stretching the labia minora. Robert Suggs's *Marquesan Sexual Behavior* and Gladwin and Sarason's *Truk: Man in Paradise,* among other sources, have information on this. Turnbull's account is to be found in *The Forest People.*

7. From *Sexual Behavior in the Human Female.* For more recent data, see Barry Singer's review of the evidence in the *Journal of Sex Research*, 21:4, and the books by Symons and Hagen.

8. For information on cultures with sexually assertive women, consult Ford and Beach; also, for example, the books by Danielsson, Gladwin and Sarason, and Suggs.

9. Consider just one illustration of this. Among certain birds, such as phalaropes and jacanas, the male and female roles found in so many animal species are reversed. The females are larger, more aggressive, and more "promiscuous," and it is they who court the males. But the males alone tend the nest once the eggs are laid; they ultimately make the greatest investment of time and energy in the offspring. Nothing of substance in the rest of this book, be it noted, depends on the theory of natural selection of behavioral traits; the empirical data on human sexuality will stand on their own. Many people find it difficult to accept such data, however, without a plausible explanation underlying them, and in this case there is one. For the same reason, it is not necessary for us to enter into the acrimonious debate over sociobiology. Some explanations given in its name are wild speculations, often culture biased. Others, however, are quite impressive; natural selection is *not* a "just so" story, contrary to ideologues of the left and the religious right.

10. One of the studies finding this difference between males and females regarding sexual arousal is reported in Donald Mosher's "Psychological Reactions to Pornographic Films." Many find it surprising that one sex would require conditioning to experience what the other one does automatically, but such differences are not uncommon in nature. For a more striking example, in certain bird species the females are biologically programmed to recognize the males as potential mates, whereas a male is programmed to be sexually attracted to individuals of the same type as the one that raises it. In nature, of course, they are raised by their mothers, hence males mate with females of their own species; but on those occasions when these male birds are reared by humans, they are environmentally programmed to be sexually attracted to humans instead.

11. See, for example, Glenn Wilson and David Nias's *The Mystery of Love.* Perhaps things like competence and high status send a primal message about how well a male can provide, or whether he has "superior" genes; Symons discusses evolutionary explanations of that type. (This does *not* mean, of course, that successful reproduction is any part of a female's conscious *or* unconscious motivation. It is *nature's* "purpose," not hers, to ensure survival of her genes.) On the other hand, perhaps the tendency is wholly the result of cultural influences.

12. Notably, in Polynesia. Danielsson suggests this results from their method of childrearing being very different from ours. Many relatives and others act as parents to an infant, so that it never learns to invest all of its emotional needs in one person.

13. See Money and Ehrhardt again. The small sample sizes and subjective assessments necessarily involved here have made some doubt these results, but they surely carry some weight.

CHAPTER 2

1. Some even go to the Cartesian extreme of denying that biology has any appreciable influence on our psychological natures at all. Often, however, they themselves unwittingly presuppose natural emotional traits, such as the human need (found only in "social" animals) for self-respect. To take an example that is relevant to sexuality, in insisting on monogamy over promiscuity and polygamy certain people who deny claims about natural sexual needs tacitly assume jealousy as a given. In the absence of jealousy there is no more reason to have only one sex partner than to have only one friend.

2. The story is told of an ocelot in a zoo that constantly bit at its own skin, painfully shredding its beautiful coat. Eventually, it was realized that such animals have a natural need to pluck their prey; the zoo's prepared diet did not allow it to meet the need in a natural way, and in frustration it turned to an unnatural one. Human behavior is less rigidly programmed than that of any other animals, but we still have natural psychological needs. When these are not met, neuroses and psychoses can result.

3. For one of numerous sources, see Danielsson again.

4. See Bullough on this. Believing erroneously that semen cannot flow upward, Thomas

Aquinas taught that sexual intercourse in any but the "missionary position" was a serious sin. The New Testament itself does not unambiguously treat marital sex as unclean, but does present it as being inferior to celibacy. See I Corinthians 7:1–12, Galatians 5:16–17, and Matthew 19:1–12.

5. For details, consult Suggs, Gladwin and Sarason, Turnbull, Danielsson, and many others who have reported on sex-positive cultures. Warning quotes are used around the word "promiscuity" here to distinguish its scientific use from popular ones. It does not mean literally "*anyone* will do," only that there is attraction to a variety of partners.

6. Hrdy's explanation for female promiscuity among primates is that it helps to elicit protection and material aid from more than one male for herself and her offspring: getting a little support from each of many males serves much the same purpose as getting a lot from one. As for a male himself, it is to his "biological advantage" to be supportive toward a female he's had sex with, since her offspring might be his. And it is certainly to his genetic advantage to sire offspring by more than one female, since it can increase the total number of his descendants with little "investment" on his part.

7. For the sake of the philosophically trained, I should mention my view that this principle is empirical. The matter cannot be discussed here, but the following may have heuristic value: an organism incapable of experiencing pleasure or suffering would not even have a *concept* of good and bad. For example, if it had visual or auditory sensations, such as colors and tones and patterns, but got no pleasure or displeasure from any of them, it would have no concept of beauty or ugliness.

8. At least, this may be said in cases where the deliberate actions of the *other* person can be ignored, so we do not have to consider issues such as self-defense. That is not generally true, of course; but raising the much more complex case of multiple agency, which has its own equality constraint, would obscure the fundamental point being made here.

9. As is illustrated by the celebrated case of the prostitute's "pornographic" acts for porn-denouncing televangelist Jimmy Swaggart, the idea that it only takes a strong determination to crush powerful natural feelings leads to a lot of hypocrisy and tragedy. It was not "demons with long fingernails" but testosterone that produced Mr. Swaggart's visual desires.

CHAPTER 3

1. For those who have seen it, the one thing in all the world that is best described by this familiar rhetoric is artist Judy Chicago's tableful of plastic vaginas, *The Dinner Party*. Since male sexual desire is not involved, however, it is politically acceptable to many if not all feminist foes of pornography. Had it appeared in *Hustler* instead of in feminist circles, it would no doubt be cited as a paradigm of the male objectification of women. Traditionalists, of course, are scandalized by it. Of related interest is the feminist movie *Killing Us Softly*, which inveighs against the portrayal of parts of women's bodies in the media. Ignoring the parallel treatment of male body parts, and the artistic and practical reasons for it, the film draws unwarranted conclusions about its motives and its psychological impact.

2. Though it involves actual sexual behavior rather than just desire, the reader might consider a related double standard. A teenage boy whose sexual needs result in an unwanted pregnancy is standardly said to have exploited the girl. This is often true, of course, though our society refuses to acknowledge the pain of those needs as an extenuating circumstance. But suppose a girl deliberately gets pregnant, in spite of lacking both the financial resources and the emotional maturity to care for a child, in order to fulfill her need to have someone to love or to feel like a real woman. *She* is not then said to be exploiting *it*. She only gets sympathy over her inability to get love any other way—and the boy is blamed again for *that*.

3. To read about a culture where sex and sexual organs really *were* considered sacred, yet in which shame over them was unknown, see Milton Diamond's "Cross-Generational Sex in Traditional Hawaii."

4. To satisfy the reader's curiosity, let me say that the explicit scenes of hard-core pornography do not appeal to me; I find them very unaesthetic. (I also detest the taste of baked
squash and fresh onions.) But I have decent, caring friends who get great pleasure from
them, including some who use them to augment loving marital relationships. Of course, it
makes no difference to the value of the arguments in this book what my personal predilections
are. Any writer's motives must be taken into account in deciding how much to trust his or
her word; but the claim, "Your self-interest is at stake, so your position is unjustified" is a
regrettably common fallacy. From the fact that most South African foes of apartheid are
black it does not follow that their moral stance is illegitimate.

5. No attempt will be made here to survey the literature of such arguments. For an extended
treatment of traditionalist arguments against sexually explicit materials, the reader is referred
to Harry Clor's *Obscenity and Public Morality;* an extended liberal treatment of about the
same vintage is G. L. Simons's *Pornography without Prejudice.* Other sources of arguments,
notably feminist ones, will be cited as we continue.

CHAPTER 4

1. For example, T. S. Palys, *Canadian Psychology,* 27:1.

2. See Gay Talese's *Thy Neighbor's Wife* regarding Dodson; another such report comes
from stripper Deborah Sundahl in *The Advocate,* Oct. 13, 1983. Tracy's conversion was
staged for the movie *Not a Love Story,* produced for the National Film Board of Canada.

3. See Ann Snitow et al., *Powers of Desire;* Carol Cassell's *Swept Away;* and the books
by Friday and Faust. An influential piece involving members of the Feminist Anti-Censorship
Taskforce is the legal brief by Hunter and Law published in the *University of Michigan Journal
of Law Reform,* Vol. 21. Unfortunately, many feminists who oppose censorship do so admittedly for reasons of self-interest only, fearing their own works will be attacked next, rather
than because of sex-positive attitudes or concern about justice for others. And they still often
have terribly distorted views of male sexuality. See Varda Burstyn's *Women against Censorship*
for some of both stances, mostly the sex-negative one.

4. See Sheila Rothman's book, *Woman's Proper Place.*

5. Those who have not been exposed to their voluminous literature may find this difficult
to believe. John Gordon's book *The Myth of the Monstrous Male* gives numerous references
and an analysis of that literature. A good source of articles against pornography by extremist
feminists is *Take Back the Night,* edited by Laura Lederer. One especially influential extremist
is Susan Brownmiller; the claim that all men support rapists and secretly cheer them on is
the central theme of her best-selling book *Against Our Will.* The public would not stand for
it if such things were being said about women, blacks, hispanics, or any other social group
but men.

6. Compare the fantasies in Nancy Friday's *Men in Love* with those in *My Secret Garden.*
They may not be typical of men's or women's fantasies in general, but they illustrate this
point.

7. For example, see David A. Scott's *Pornography and its Effects on Family, Community
and Culture.* Be warned that the claims it makes are frequently not supported by the literature
cited in its numerous footnotes—or by any other evidence. A more accessible source of such
views may be *Pornography: A Human Tragedy,* edited by Tom Minnery.

8. See the article by lawyer-feminist Karen DeCrow in *Penthouse,* May 1985. DeCrow is
a former president of the National Organization for Women; she has both fair-minded attitudes toward men and positive attitudes toward sex.

CHAPTER 5

1. Refer to the Palys article, and to the *Journal of Communication,* Summer 1984, for
Slade's discussion. The Ohio survey found the following numbers of violent acts per hour.

G-rated: 9.2; PG-rated: 7.9; R-rated: 14.1; and X-rated: 4.6. From Joseph E. Scott's "Violence and Erotic Material—The Relationship between Adult Entertainment and Rape?"

2. See Palys again; producers of "adult" films make the same claim. Further evidence is cited in Barry Lynn's *Polluting the Censorship Debate*, p. 69.

3. Kathleen Mahoney's "Obscenity, Morals and the Law: Feminist Critique" contains a list of such definitions. Interestingly, meaning changes like these reduce a lot of antipornography slogans to empty tautologies.

4. The incidents were reported in Canadian newspapers on October 25, 1983, and in November of 1984. The videotape in question was *The Summer of '72;* others banned at the same time were not at all violent by television standards, and some were totally tongue-in-cheek humor.

5. For data on various crimes against men and women, see the annual *Criminal Victimization in the United States*.

6. *Time* magazine, Feb. 7, 1977, pp. 42–43.

7. Notably, Robert J. Stoller in *Perversion: The Erotic Form of Hatred* and elsewhere. Those who cite his totally unsupported views as evidence that pornography expresses hatred ignore his wider claims about all sexual desire. The feminists who cite them as evidence are not nearly so anxious to believe in such Freudian dogmas as penis envy and "immature" clitoral sexuality as they are to embrace this one.

8. See the books by Faust and Friday, and the *Time* article just cited; also Pelletier and Herold in the *Journal of Sex Research,* Vol. 24. Various surveys have found that as many as half of their women subjects enjoy rape fantasies. Morton Hunt's figure (*Sexual Behavior in the 1970's*) of 24 percent for women under 35 is much lower, but it applies only to masturbation fantasies.

9. The laboratory research was reported in Wendy Stock's "The Effects of Violent Pornography on Women" and is discussed on pp. 73–74 of Philip Nobile and Eric Nadler's *United States of America vs. Sex*.

10. From Hunt; also Masters and Johnson's *Homosexuality in Perspective*.

CHAPTER 6

1. From pp. 334–335 in the *Final Report* of the U.S. Attorney General's Commission on Pornography (hereafter, *AGCP*).

2. See Gloria Steinem in *Take Back the Night*, p. 39.

3. From Alan Soble's *Pornography: Marxism, Feminism and the Future of Sexuality*, p. 19. (Although its special concern is Marxism, Soble's book has a lot of information and argumentation on subjects discussed here.) The conflicting result is reported in Charles Winick's "A Content Analysis of Sexually Explicit Magazines Sold in an Adult Bookstore." The large survey by Dietz and Sears mentioned in note 4 is unhelpful in this regard, for it counted portrayals of heterosexual S&M and B&D without noting how frequently each role is occupied by each sex.

4. The first survey was reported by Dietz and Evans in the *American Journal of Psychiatry,* the second by Dietz and Sears in the *University of Michigan Journal of Law Reform.* (The authors make a fuss over the high proportion of paraphilic material in these stores, as if unaware that the reason it is concentrated in that ghetto is its social unacceptability.) The information that such magazines are only issued once is from Robin Badgley et al., *Sexual Offences against Children*.

5. Of course, the commission did not even mention the subordination of women endorsed by the Bible, much less recommend censoring such teachings. See for example I Corinthians 11:3–10 and 14:34–35 and I Timothy 2:11–15. In Paul's teaching, women at prayer are to cover their heads as a symbol of their subservience to men, but it is degrading for a man to

do so. In addition, there are many passages in the Old Testament condoning or commanding male subordination of females.

6. Quoted in Nobile and Nadler's critique of the commission, pp. 236–237. Interestingly, the other ten members voted to delete mention of all but one of them; they were convinced that most pornography is degrading but not very willing to commit themselves to examples.

7. See Dietz and Sears.

8. Consult Pelletier and Herold for these details.

9. The picture is of a young woman's legs protruding from a giant meat-grinder; the caption quotes Flynt as saying they would no longer treat women as pieces of meat.

CHAPTER 7

1. Propper's study, in Vol. 9, and that by Davis and Braucht in Vol. 8, of the *Technical Report* to the U.S. Commission on Obscenity and Pornography (*USCOP*, hereafter). As will be mentioned later, Davis and Braucht's sample was biased by its high proportion of religious people. Both studies also claimed to find a high level of sexual deviance among young persons exposed to pornography; but what they considered deviant included many things that are biologically normal for human youth, notably just having sex itself. One psychologist who appears to take the generalized-corruption theory seriously is Victor Cline; he ignores the obvious explanations listed here. See his book *Where Do You Draw the Line?*

2. James Prescott, in *Bulletin of the Atomic Scientists,* Nov. 1975. For information on the Muria and the Trobrianders, see Elwin and Malinowski; Mangaia is discussed by Donald S. Marshall in Marshall and Suggs, *Human Sexual Behavior.* Elwin is particularly eloquent in describing the moral superiority of the gentle Muria youth over traditional sex-segregated English boys; the former "would be scandalized by the Public Schools of England—the atmosphere of competition, the corporal punishment, the bullying, the petty tyranny of senior boys." He could easily have added " . . . and the coerced buggery."

3. See Lynn, pp. 51–56, for a good discussion of this matter. As for certain porn distributors having "connections" with organized crime figures, that is true of some antipornography crusaders as well. Ronald Reagan's Justice Department was caught trying to protect his friend and political supporter, Teamster boss Jackie Presser, from prosecution by the FBI for racketeering.

4. The mainstream press has not given these women the publicity they deserve, but for three examples, see Sundahl again, John A. Fall's article in the *New York Native,* p. 22, Jan. 27, 1986, and the one by Sheldon Ranz in *Shmate,* Spring 1989. The fact about "snuff" movies has been noted by the Williams Committee, which studied the pornography issue for the British government (Bernard Williams et al., *Obscenity and Film Censorship*), and by many other researchers.

5. See Judith Walkowitz in *Signs: Journal of Women in Culture and Society,* Autumn 1980. To learn about female prostitution today from the women themselves, read *A Vindication of the Rights of Whores,* edited by Gail Pheterson. The *Time* article, citing unnamed sources, is from April 5, 1976.

6. Data from a puritanical country in which pornography has long been suppressed reveal the usual striking difference between male and female capacities to be sexually aroused by the sight of an attractive person: Rainer Warczok, "Correlates of Sexual Orientation in the German Democratic Republic."

7. One researcher interviewed a sample of date rapists, expecting to learn their fathers had taught them to go out and "score"; instead he found their sexual feelings had merely been depreciated less than others' had. Unfortunately, he does not report trying to discover whether they received less instruction about right and wrong behavior in general. See Eugene Kanin's "Date Rapists" in the *Archives of Sexual Behavior.*

8. Though her anecdotes involving coerced sadomasochism are not to be dismissed lightly,

Diana Russell's much cited statistics on this are flawed by ideological bias. She asked no questions to verify that the sexual activities suggested to her respondents had indeed come from pornography, rather than its merely being a convenient scapegoat; nor did she try to determine whether men have learned better ways to pleasure a woman from that source; and her numbers do not distinguish *intrinsically* unpleasant acts from those found aversive due to cultural conditioning. See her article on research in *Take Back the Night*. For a criticism of her biased research methods, see Paul Okami's paper in *Pedophilia: Biosocial Dimensions*.

9. From Harold Nawy, *Journal of Social Issues*, 29:3. A good brief discussion of the use of pornography by couples is in Dr. Zilbergeld's essay, pp. 348–350, in Nobile and Nadler.

10. It is difficult to tell, since so many cultures were influenced by the major civilizations before anthropologists studied them. But see Ford and Beach for a cross-cultural survey. Pre-Christian Europe's attitudes are described in John Money's *Love and Love Sickness*, and other ancient civilizations are discussed by Vern Bullough.

11. Note Danielsson and Elwin on this matter; also Ronald and Sarah Berndt, *Sexual Behavior in Western Arnhem Land*. Among Turnbull's Mbuti, for example, the frequent "infidelities" of both partners cause no concern unless they are flagrant. Among the Polynesians, with their low regard for private ownership, anyone unwilling to share a spouse's sexuality with others would have been an antisocial outcast.

12. From the study by Patricia Schiller, Vol. 9 of the *USCOP Technical Report*.

13. From the Alan Guttmacher Institute's *Teenage Pregnancy in Developed Countries*. For one of the studies that have found a strong and substantial correlation between sexual guilt and failure by teenagers to use contraceptives, see Strassberg and Mahoney in the *Journal of Sex Research*, Nov. 1988.

CHAPTER 8

1. Discussed by Eysenck and Wilson in their book *The Psychology of Sex*.

2. For one source among many, see Money and Ehrhardt.

3. This experiment is described in Zillmann and Bryant's "Shifting Preferences in Pornography Consumption," *Communication Research*, Oct. 1986. Regarding the claim that mild violence might be needed to enhance the excitement of regular partners, see Zillmann's *Connections between Sex and Aggression*, p. 198. Their other relevant research result is the finding that prior massive exposure to "common" erotica resulted in reduced levels of excitement when viewing it but not when seeing the "uncommon" type, at least temporarily. But that "excitement" was not sexual arousal; it was measured by heart rate and blood pressure readings and was likely nothing but mild anxiety. Moreover, excitement from seeing the "uncommon" materials will also drop after large exposures, as they also admit.

4. Reported by Condron and Nutter in the *Journal of Sex and Marital Therapy*, 1988.

5. This fact was mentioned by the Williams Committee and is pretty well universally acknowledged by clinicians.

6. See Prescott; also Welch and Kartub, *Journal of Sex Research*, 14:4.

7. From Ismond Rosen's chapter in his anthology, *Sexual Deviation*.

8. From *Sex and Repression in Savage Society;* see also Elwin.

9. The books by Malinowski, Berndt and Berndt, Danielsson, and Elwin are good sources of information on this matter; see also Floyd Martinson in Benjamin Wolman's *Handbook of Human Sexuality,* and Chapter 10 of Milton Diamond and Arno Karlen's *Sexual Decisions*.

10. From anthropologist Melvin Konner's *The Tangled Wing*.

11. Paul Gebhard et al., *Sex Offenders: An Analysis of Types*.

12. From Berl Kutchinsky's article in *Comparative Social Research*, 1985.

13. This was admitted by the Attorney General's Commission on Pornography in its *Final Report*. Yet it went on to recommend a vast new machinery of draconian federal laws and policies to deal with the nonexistent problem, and the U.S. Congress quickly complied. In

fact, about the only child-porn being offered for sale in the United States today is from the U.S. government, in its entrapment attempts. See Lawrence Stanley in *Playboy,* September 1988.

14. After years of dismissing reports of child sex abuse as too horrible to be true, in the 1980s this society swung to the opposite extreme of considering them too horrid to be false. A few of the more heartbreaking stories about the hell that many innocent parents *and* their children have since been put through are chronicled in Paul and Shirley Eberle's *The Politics of Child Abuse.* In a much more insidious way, vast psychological harm is being done by those programs that tell children, "Don't let anyone touch you there." Since *they* want to touch each other sexually, the message of self-hatred is being planted more fearfully than ever. We can expect the next generation to exhibit more sexual dysfunction and perversion than we have yet seen.

CHAPTER 9

1. See Freda Adler, *Sisters in Crime.*

2. Consult Zillmann and Bryant in the *Journal of Communication,* Fall 1982, and Christensen's critique in the Winter 1986 issue.

3. A little over five years, on average. For the Canadian data, see the *Toronto Star,* Nov. 24, 1982, p. A6. The U.S. data can be found in *Prison Admissions and Releases* (1983).

4. For instance, see Donald Marshall in Marshall and Suggs.

5. This survey is reported by Luis T. Garcia in the *Journal of Sex Research,* Aug. 1986.

6. More thorough discussions of the rape-sentence test, and other experiments on effects of pornography not mentioned here, are to be found in Donnerstein et al., and in Christensen's article in *Philosophy of the Social Sciences.*

7. Leonard and Taylor, *Motivation and Emotion,* 7:3, 1983.

8. These people evidently assume, and some have said it explicitly, that it is biologically natural for men to feel hostile toward promiscuous women and to be inclined toward raping them as a result. (See the article by Shepher and Reisman in *Ethology and Sociobiology,* 1985.) The evidence from human cultures and other primates, and biological theory as well, indicate otherwise. There may indeed be such natural tendencies, born of jealousy, toward one's own wayward mate, but not toward other females. Aside from the fact that there is no need to rape a promiscuous female in order to get sex, having feelings of hostility toward her would evidently be biologically maladaptive; look again at footnote 6 in Chapter 2.

9. The articles by Hindelang and Davis and by Cohen et al. in Chappell et al. are good sources of information about rapists.

10. Refer to Barry Singer's brief but comprehensive remarks. The most extensive study of the issue to date, Dolf Zillmann's *Connections between Sex and Aggression,* argues at length that no special link of this type exists in humans. The *general* sort of excitement connection it claims has already been mentioned here and will be discussed further in the next section. Regarding rates of rape in permissive cultures, see Prescott again. The claim of rapeless societies has been made about the sexually uninhibited pygmies and Yapese. Such things are obviously difficult to verify, however, and small groups have much greater control over their members' antisocial tendencies than do large societies like ours.

CHAPTER 10

1. The Williams Report cites cases in which an alleged stimulus to violence, seeing a particular movie, had not really occurred.

2. Among other places, the Haigh story is told in an article by Earl Finbar Murphy in the *Wayne Law Review,* Vol. 10. For the Doss account, read Richard Deming's *Women: The New Criminals.*

3. From the paper by Thornberry and Silverman, in Vol. 9 of the *Technical Report, USCOP.*

4. William Marshall, in an unpublished report to the Federal Department of Justice (Canada), 1983. An expanded account was later published in the *Journal of Sex Research,* 25:2.

5. C. Eugene Walker, Vol. 8, *USCOP Technical Report.*

6. For instance, this is discussed in the Williams Report. Another example of many such claims is in Carter et al., *Report to NIMH* (1985), cited in the *AGCP Final Report,* p. 961. Money's remarks are from testimony at a U.S. government hearing, cited in Lynn, p. 34. Goldstein and Kant's work is reported in their *Pornography and Sexual Deviance.*

7. In Vol. 8 of the *Technical Report, USCOP.* The studies by Goldstein et al., Cook and Fosen, and Walker all found greater prior exposure to sexual materials in at least one major control group than among their sex offenders; the one by Johnson et al. was not suitable for a quantitative conclusion; and the one by Davis and Braucht found more such exposure among sex criminals.

8. Abel et al., "The Effects of Erotica on Paraphiliacs' Behavior." The paper was criticized in the Meese Report, but this writer has been unable to obtain a rebuttal from its authors.

9. See the summaries of the studies by William Marshall and Mary Koss in the *Final Report* of *AGCP,* pp. 950, 961. The recent study by Condron and Nutter again found no greater exposure to pornography among sex offenders and deviants than among other men.

10. From Eugene Kanin in *Psychological Reports,* 52:1.

11. Larry Baron and Murray Straus, in Malamuth and Donnerstein's *Pornography and Sexual Aggression.* Their later work is cited in the *AGCP's Final Report* and is reported in "Four Theories of Rape: A Macrosociological Analysis." Though measuring several related variables, they did not directly test the possibility that the proportion of all young men in the total population of each state was the reason for the rape-pornography correlation.

12. The adult bookstore result is from Joseph Scott's paper.

13. Baron and Straus, "Four Theories of Rape."

14. Reported by Richard Ben-Veniste, and by Berl Kutchinsky, in Vol. 8 of the *Technical Report, USCOP.* See also the latter's article in *Diseases of the Nervous System,* March 1976, Vol. 37.

15. There is so much misinformation on these studies among nonprofessionals, and so much shallow treatment of them even by some professionals, that the concerned reader is urged to consult Kutchinsky's own writings to get a clear picture of the data. For instance, it is often claimed that the rate of sex crimes dropped only because certain acts were decriminalized at the same time. That does *not* apply to the statistics presented here. For his own reply to Bachy's claim that his statistics were wrong, see Kutchinsky's 1985 article. See also the discussion in the Williams Report.

16. John Court, in the *International Journal of Criminology and Penology,* Vol. 5; also in Malamuth and Donnerstein. The following information concerns his three more recent claims in the latter. The Australian data conflict with others from the same country, as he himself notes, though I have been unable to get more information on either set. His remarks about New Zealand are vague, and the ones regarding the availability of sexual materials are entirely speculative. The only precise claim involves a large drop in the rate of reported rape following 1974. "It is possible," he writes, "that the decline arose due to the introduction of the Auckland Task Force, established to take a tough line with crime." It is indeed possible, but not for the reason Court insinuates. He clearly wants the reader to believe the task force cracked down on pornography; but from his own cited source, it is equally clear it did nothing of the sort. It was a kind of SWAT team to deal with nighttime violence on the streets: "The concept was one of highly-trained men using superior skills and mobility to quell—rapidly and firmly—any uprisings before they erupted into full-scale brawls" (Gideon Tait, *Never Back Down,* p. 174). As for the Hawaiian case, it is the figment of someone's imagination.

There was a drop in the rate of rape in the two years in question, but as a review of local newspaper articles for the same period reveals, there was no crackdown on pornography; in fact, there was a glut of it, as well as live sex acts on stage. (See, for example, the *Honolulu Star-Bulletin,* Nov. 6, 1975, p. E1.) It was in earlier and later years, when rape rates were higher, that there was some legal action against sexual materials.

17. Both sets of data can be found in the *Sourcebook of Criminal Justice Statistics—1986* (edited by Jamieson and Flanagan), pp. 180 and 243.

18. See Zillmann for an excellent discussion.

19. For example, consult Donnerstein et al. Their book is the best easily accessible source of information on all the experiments discussed in the preceding paragraphs.

20. The details of this study are to be found in James Check's "The Effects of Violent and Non-Violent Pornography"; note especially pp. 32 and 71. Opposing results are reported in Malamuth and Ceniti, *Aggressive Behavior,* Vol. 12.

CHAPTER 11

1. For a survey of this data, see *Television and Behavior,* edited by David Pearl et al. for the National Institute of Mental Health, 1982.

2. See Donnerstein in Malamuth and Donnerstein.

3. See the article by Phillips and Hensley in the *Journal of Communication,* Summer 1984, and that by Baron and Reiss, together with Phillips and Bollen's reply, in the *American Sociological Review,* June 1985.

4. Compare the study by Milavsky et al. with the review by Huesman in Pearl et al.

5. A famous court case involving a bottle rape is described, among other places, in the Donnerstein et al. book.

6. Reported in many places; for example, Donnerstein's article in Malamuth and Donnerstein.

7. In the essay by Malamuth in Malamuth and Donnerstein. See also the account in Donnerstein et al.

8. For example, Gebhard et al.

9. Mimi Silbert and Ayala Pines in *Sex Roles,* 10:11/12.

10. The article by Robert Stoller in Frank Beach's *Human Sexuality in Four Perspectives* contains an interesting case study.

11. From Kutchinsky in *Comparative Social Research.*

12. The passage about beating children is Proverbs 23:13–14. The statements on homosexual acts and witches are found in Leviticus 20:13 and Exodus 22:18. (During the Inquisition, hundreds of thousands of women were put to death as witches, convicted of things like having sex with devils.) Those about slavery include Deuteronomy 20:10ff. and Leviticus 25:44–46.

13. Described by Malamuth, though he ignores the possibility that the *love*-violence link in *Getaway* and *Swept Away* was to blame for the results. The latter, by the way, is a woman's fantasy of domination, produced by moviemaker Lina Wertmuller.

14. This was admitted by the Attorney General's Commission on Pornography; see p. 328 in their *Final Report.*

15. The evidence for greater ill effects from portrayed violence that is not sexually explicit is reported on p. 111 of Donnerstein et al.

16. For example, see Quinsey et al. in the *Journal of Consulting and Clinical Psychology,* Vol. 52, pp. 651–657.

17. Wayne Wilson and Randy Hunter in *Psychological Reports,* 53:1.

CHAPTER 12

1. Anecdotes like those to be told in this section are found scattered throughout the clinical literature. For a general discussion of the effects on later adult life, see William Kroger's article in the *Journal of Sex Research,* 5:3.

2. From Cohen et al.

3. In his book *Men Who Rape*. The tendency of rapists to have had a highly conservative rearing regarding sex has been noted by many investigators. For another example, see Thorne and Haupt, *Journal of Clinical Psychology*, Vol. 22, 1966.

4. This phenomenon was noted by Suggs in his *Marquesan Sexual Behavior*. Other good data on it are found in the books by Malinowski and Elwin.

CHAPTER 13

1. See Vern Bullough's article in the *Journal of Sex Research*, November 1985. For more such information, read Wardell Pomeroy's book, *Dr. Kinsey and the Institute for Sex Research*.

2. *Judges* 19:25–30. As for sex in general, the Bible contains many stories which, if they appeared anywhere else, would be called obscene by advocates of censorship.

3. Skinner *v*. Oklahoma *ex rel*. Williamson, 316 U.S. 535 (1942).

4. The Child Protection and Obscenity Enforcement Act of 1988. Comprehensive discussions of the history of censorship laws and court cases are to be found in the reports of all the obscenity commissions; an especially enlightening treatment is Walter Kendrick's *The Secret Museum*.

5. See Andrea Dworkin's books *Our Blood, Pornography: Men Possessing Women*, and *Intercourse*, along with articles in *Take Back the Night*. Her influence on the Meese Report is chronicled by Nobile and Nadler. Scenes cited as degrading under Dworkin and MacKinnon's proposed ordinance are listed by Donnerstein et al.

6. A case in point is Canada's Bill C-54, allowed to expire only after much protest by artists, librarians, and academics, under which a person could have gone to prison for five years for things like recommending the use of a dildo. Most of the other acts whose portrayal or encouragement were punishable under the bill were also not genuinely degrading to anyone.

7. See Lynn, pp. 7–18; *The Washington Post*, Oct. 15, 1985; *Forum*, March 1986; *The Los Angeles Times*, May 1, 1986; and very many more. The most comprehensive account of the hearings is the book by Nobile and Nadler. Though certainly polemical, it has been described to me by Judith Becker, one of the two liberal members on the commission, as factually very accurate. It is true that the earlier President's Commission on Obscenity and Pornography had a liberal bias; but I would argue that it was basically intellectually honest, unlike this commission.

8. Refer to Milton Diamond and James E. Dannemiller, "Pornography and Community Standards."

9. In Canada, as of this writing, the number of prosecutions does not appear to have increased, but the ongoing situation is repressive enough. An excellent homosexual magazine, *The Body Politic*, was evidently driven out of existence there by obscenity-law prosecutions; even without winning in court, legal harassment bankrupts and demoralizes.

10. *Inter alia*, see Professor Thomas Tedford in *Penthouse*, April 1986; also "An open letter to the citizens of Ft. Wayne," by the Rev. Ted McIlvenna, 1982. I have personally talked with a number of people who reported these frightening and illegal tactics were used on them.

Bibliography

Alan Guttmacher Institute. 1986. *Teenage Pregnancy in Developed Countries*. New York.

Abel, Gene, Mittelman, M.S., and Becker, Judith. 1985. "The Effects of Erotica on Paraphiliacs' Behavior." Unpublished paper cited in AGCP *Final Report*, pp. 969–970.

Adler, Freda. 1975. *Sisters in Crime: The Rise of the New Female Criminal*. New York: McGraw-Hill.

Attorney General's Commission on Pornography. 1986. *Final Report*. U.S. Department of Justice, Washington, D.C. (Cited as AGCP *Final Report* elsewhere in this bibliography.)

Badgley, Robin, et al. 1984: *Sexual Offences against Children*. Ottawa: Canadian Government Publishing Centre.

Barbach, Lonnie. 1975. *For Yourself: The Fulfillment of Female Sexuality*. Garden City, NY: Doubleday.

Baron, James N., and Reiss, Peter C. 1985. "Same Time, Next Year: Aggregate Analysis of the Mass Media and Violent Behavior," *American Sociological Review*, 50, pp. 347–363.

Baron, Larry, and Straus, Murray. 1984. "Sexual Stratification, Pornography, and Rape in the United States." In Malamuth and Donnerstein.

––. 1986. "Four Theories of Rape: A Macrosociological Analysis." *Social Problems*, 34:5, pp. 467–489.

Ben-Veniste, Richard. 1970. "Pornography and Sex Crime—the Danish Experience." In Vol. 8, USCOP *Technical Report*.

Berndt, Ronald M., and Berndt, Sarah H. 1951. *Sexual Behavior in Western Arnhem Land*. New York: Viking Fund Publications in Anthropology.

Brownmiller, Susan. 1975. *Against Our Will: Men, Women and Rape*. New York: Simon and Schuster.

Bullough, Vern. 1976. *Sexual Variance in Society and History*. New York: Wiley.

––. 1985. "Problems of Research on a Delicate Topic: A Personal View." *Journal of Sex Research*, 21:4, November, pp. 375–386.

Bullough, Vern, and Bullough, Bonnie. 1977. *Sin, Sickness and Sanity*. New York: Garland.

Bureau of Justice Statistics. 1986. *Prison Admissions and Releases, 1983*. Washington, D.C.: U.S. Department of Justice.

Burstyn, Varda (ed.). 1985. *Women against Censorship*. Vancouver: Douglas and McIntyre.

Carter, D.L., et al. 1985. "Use of Pornography in the Criminal and Developmental Histories of Sexual Offenders." Report to the National Institute of Mental Health. Cited in AGCP *Final Report,* p. 961.

Cassell, Carol. 1984. *Swept Away: Why Women Fear Their Own Sexuality.* New York: Simon and Schuster.

Chappell, Duncan, Geis, Robley, and Geis, Gilbert (eds.). 1977. *Forcible Rape: The Crime, the Victim, and the Offender.* New York: Columbia University Press.

Check, James V.P. 1985. "The Effects of Violent and Non-Violent Pornography." Unpublished submission to the Department of Justice for Canada.

Christensen, F. M. 1986. "Sexual Callousness Re-Examined." *Journal of Communication,* 36:1, Winter, pp. 174–184.

—. 1990. "Cultural and Ideological Bias in Pornography Research." Forthcoming in *Philosophy of the Social Sciences.*

Cline, Victor. 1974. "Another View: Pornography Effects, the State of the Art." In Victor Cline (ed.), *Where Do You Draw the Line?* Provo, Utah: Brigham Young University Press.

Clor, Harry. 1967. *Obscenity and Public Morality.* Chicago: University of Chicago Press.

Cohen, Murray L., et al. 1971. "The Psychology of Rapists." In Chappell et al., pp. 291–314.

Condron, Mary Kearns, and Nutter, David E. 1988. "A Preliminary Examination of the Pornography Experience of Sex Offenders, Paraphiliacs, Sexual Dysfunction Patients, and Controls Based on Meese Commission Recommendations." *Journal of Sex and Marital Therapy,* 14:4, Winter, pp. 285–298.

Cook, Robert F., and Fosen, Robert H. 1970. "Pornography and the Sex Offender: Patterns of Exposure." USCOP *Technical Report,* Vol. 8.

Court, John. 1977. "Pornography and Sex-Crimes: A Re-evaluation in Light of Recent Trends Around the World." *International Journal of Criminology and Penology,* 5, pp. 129–157.

—. 1984. "Sex and Violence: A Ripple Effect." In Malamuth and Donnerstein.

Danielsson, Bengt. 1956. *Love in the South Seas.* London: G. Allen and Unwin.

Davis, Keith E., and Braucht, George N. 1970. "Exposure to Pornography, Character, and Sexual Deviance: A Retrospective Survey." In USCOP *Technical Report,* Vol. 8.

DeCrow, Karen. 1986. "Strange Bedfellows." *Penthouse,* May, pp. 96–97.

Deming, Richard. 1977. *Women: The New Criminals.* New York: Thomas Nelson.

Diamond, Milton. In press. "Cross-Generational Sex in Traditional Hawaii." In J.R. Feierman (ed.). *Pedophilia: Biosocial Dimensions.* New York: Aldine Publishers.

Diamond, Milton, and Dannemiller, James E. 1989. "Pornography and Community Standards." *Archives of Sexual Behavior,* 18:6, December, pp. 475–495.

Diamond, Milton, and Karlen, Arno. 1980. *Sexual Decisions.* Boston: Little, Brown.

Dietz, Park, and Evans, Barbara. 1982. "Pornographic Imagery and the Prevalence of Paraphilia." *American Journal of Psychiatry,* 139:11, November, pp. 1493–1495.

Dietz, Park, and Sears, Alan E. 1987–1988. "Pornography and Obscenity Sold in 'Adult Bookstores': A Survey of 5132 Books, Magazines and Films in Four American Cities." *University of Michigan Journal of Law Reform,* 21:1 and 2, Fall-Winter, pp. 7–46.

Donnerstein, Edward. 1984. "Pornography: Its Effect on Violence against Women." In Malamuth and Donnerstein.

Donnerstein, Edward, Linz, Daniel, and Penrod, Steven. 1987. *The Question of Pornography.* New York: The Free Press.

Dworkin, Andrea. 1976. *Our Blood: Prophesies and Discourses on Sexual Politics.* New York: Harper and Row.

—. 1981. *Pornography: Men Possessing Women.* New York: Perigee.

—. 1987. *Intercourse.* New York: The Free Press.

Eberle, Paul, and Eberle, Shirley. 1986. *The Politics of Child Abuse*. Secaucus, NJ: Lyle Stuart.

Elwin, Verrier. 1968. *Kingdom of the Young*. London: Oxford University Press.

Eysenck, Hans J., and Wilson, Glenn D. 1979. *The Psychology of Sex*. London: J.M. Dent.

Fall, John A. 1986. "Redefining Porn." *New York Native*, January 27, p. 22.

Farrell, Warren. 1986. *Why Men Are the Way They Are*. New York: McGraw-Hill.

Faust, Beatrice. 1980. *Women, Sex and Pornography*. New York: Macmillan.

Ford, Clellan, and Beach, Frank. 1951. *Patterns of Sexual Behavior*. New York: Harper and Row.

Fraser, Paul, et al. 1985. *Pornography and Prostitution in Canada*. Ottawa: Canadian Government Publishing Centre.

Friday, Nancy. 1973. *My Secret Garden*. New York: Trident.

—. 1980. *Men in Love*. New York: Delacorte.

Garcia, Luis T. 1986. "Exposure to Pornography and Attitudes about Women and Rape: A Correlational Study." *Journal of Sex Research*, 22:3, August, pp. 378–385.

Gebhard, Paul, et al. 1965. *Sex Offenders: An Analysis of Types*. New York: Harper and Row.

Gladwin, Thomas, and Sarason, Seymour B. 1953. *Truk: Man in Paradise*. New York: Wenner-Gren Foundation for Anthropological Research.

Goldstein, Michael J., et al. 1970. "Exposure to Pornography and Sexual Behavior in Deviant and Normal Groups." USCOP *Technical Report*, Vol. 8.

Goldstein, Michael J., and Kant, Harold S. 1973. *Pornography and Sexual Deviance*. Berkeley: University of California Press.

Gordon, John. 1982. *The Myth of the Monstrous Male—and Other Feminist Fables*. New York: Playboy Press.

Gosselin, Chris, and Wilson, Glenn. 1980. *Sexual Variations*. New York: Simon and Schuster.

Groth, Nicholas A. 1979. *Men Who Rape: The Psychology of the Offender*. New York: Plenum.

Hagen, Richard. 1979. *The Bio-Sexual Factor*. Garden City, NY: Doubleday.

Hindelang, Michael J., and Davis, Bruce L. 1977. "Forcible Rape in the United States: A Statistical Profile." In Chappell et al.

Hrdy, Sarah Blaffer. 1981. *The Woman That Never Evolved*. Cambridge, Mass.: Harvard University Press.

Huesman, L. 1982. "Television Violence and Aggressive Behavior." In Pearl et al.

Hunt, Morton. 1974. *Sexual Behavior in the 1970's*. Chicago: Playboy Press.

Hunter, Nan D. and Law, Sylvia A. 1987–88. "Brief Amici Curiae of Feminist Anti-Censorship Taskforce, et al., in American Booksellers Association v. Hudnut," *University of Michigan Law Reform Journal*, 21:1–2, Fall and Winter, pp. 69–136.

Hyde, H. Montgomery. 1965. *A History of Pornography*. New York: Farrar, Straus and Giroux.

Jamieson, Katherine M. and Flanagan, Timothy J. (eds.). 1987. *Sourcebook of Criminal Justice Statistics*-1986. U.S. Department of Justice, Bureau of Justice Statistics, Washington, D.C.

Johnson, Weldon T., Kupperstein, Lenore R., and Peters, Joseph J. 1970. "Sex Offenders' Experience with Erotica." USCOP *Technical Report*, Vol. 8.

Kanin, Eugene. 1983. "Rape as a Function of Relative Sexual Frustration." *Psychological Reports*, 52:1, February, pp. 133–134.

—. 1985. "Date Rapists—Differential Sexual Socialization and Relative Deprivation." *Archives of Sexual Behavior*, 14:3, pp. 219–231.

Kendrick, Walter. 1987. *The Secret Museum*. New York: Viking.

Kinsey, Alfred, et al. 1953. *Sexual Behavior in the Human Female*. Philadelphia: Saunders.

Kirkland, Gelsey, and Lawrence, Greg. 1986. *Dancing on My Grave*. New York: Doubleday.

Konner, Melvin. 1982. *The Tangled Wing.* New York: Holt, Rinehart and Winston.

Koss, Mary P. 1985. "Nonstranger Sexual Aggression: A Discriminant Analysis of the Psychological Characteristics of Undetected Offenders." *Sex Roles,* 12:9/10, pp. 981–992.

Kraus, J. 1979. "Trends in Violent Crime and Public Concern." *Australian Journal of Social Issues,* 14:3, pp. 175–190.

Kroger, William. 1969. "Comprehensive Approach to Ecclesiogenic Neuroses." *Journal of Sex Research,* 5:1, February, pp. 2–11.

Kutchinsky, Berl. 1970. "Towards an Explanation of the Decrease in Registered Sex Crimes in Copenhagen." In USCOP *Technical Report,* Vol. 8.

—. 1976. "Deviance and Criminality: The Case of a Voyeur in a Peeper's Paradise." *Diseases of the Nervous System,* 37, March, pp. 145–151.

—. 1985. "Pornography and Its Effects in Denmark and the United States: A Rejoinder and Beyond." *Comparative Social Research: An Annual.* Vol. 8. Greenwich, Ct.: JAI Press.

Lederer, Laura (ed.). 1982. *Take Back the Night: Women on Pornography.* New York: William Morrow.

Leonard, Kenneth E., and Taylor, Stuart P. 1983. "Exposure to Pornography, Permissive and Non-Permissive Cues, and Male Aggression Toward Females." *Motivation and Emotion,* 7:3, pp. 291–299.

Lev-Ran, Arye. 1974. "Sexuality and Educational Level of Women with the Late-Treated Adrenogenital Syndrome." *Archives of Sexual Behavior,* 3:1, January, pp. 27–32.

Liebowitz, Michael. 1983. *The Chemistry of Love.* Boston: Little, Brown.

Lynn, Barry. 1986. *Polluting the Censorship Debate.* Washington, D.C.: American Civil Liberties Union.

Mahoney, Kathleen. 1984. "Obscenity, Morals and the Law: Feminist Critique." Paper presented to Canadian Institute for the Administration of Justice conference.

Malamuth, Neil. 1984. "Aggression against Women: Cultural and Individual Causes." In Malamuth and Donnerstein.

Malamuth, Neil, and Ceniti, Joseph. 1986. "Repeated Exposure to Violent and Non-Violent Pornography." *Aggressive Behavior,* 12, pp. 129–137.

Malamuth, Neil, and Donnerstein, Edward (eds.). 1984. *Pornography and Sexual Aggression.* New York: Academic Press.

Malinowski, Bronislaw. 1927. *Sex and Repression in Savage Society.* London: Kegan Paul.

—. 1929. *The Sexual Life of Savages in North-Western Melanesia.* New York: Halcyon House.

Marshall, Donald S. 1971. "Sexual Behavior on Mangaia." In Donald Marshall and Robert Suggs (eds.). *Human Sexual Behavior—Variations in the Ethnographic Spectrum.* New York: Basic Books.

Marshall, William. 1984. "The Use of Pornography by Rapists and Child Molesters." Unpublished report to the Department of Justice for Canada.

—. 1985. "Use of Pornography by Sexual Offenders." Unpublished paper cited in AGCP *Final Report,* p. 961. Revised version, "The Use of Sexually Explicit Stimuli by Rapists, Child Molesters and Non-Offenders," published in *Journal of Sex Research,* 25:2, May 1988.

Martinson, Floyd. 1980. "Childhood Sexuality." In Benjamin Wolman (ed.), *Handbook of Human Sexuality.* Englewood Cliffs, N.J.: Prentice-Hall.

Masica, Daniel, Money, John, and Ehrhardt, Anke. 1971. "Fetal Feminization and Female Gender Identity in the Testicular Feminizing Syndrome of Androgen Insensitivity." *Archives of Sexual Behavior,* 1:2, pp. 131–142.

Masters, William, and Johnson, Virginia. 1966. *Human Sexual Response.* Boston: Little, Brown.

—. 1970. *Human Sexual Inadequacy.* Boston: Little, Brown.

—. 1979. *Homosexuality in Perspective.* Boston: Little, Brown.

McIlvenna, Ted. 1982. "An Open Letter to the Citizens of Ft. Wayne." Unpublished manuscript obtained from the Institute for Advanced Study of Human Sexuality, San Francisco.
McIlvenna, Ted, and Haroian, Loretta. 1985. "Testimony before the Attorney General's Commission on Pornography." Unpublished manuscript submitted to AGCP.
Milavsky, J.R., et al. 1982. *Television and Aggression: The Results of a Panel Study*. In Pearl et al.
Minnery, Tom. 1986. *Pornography: A Human Tragedy*. Wheaton, IL: Christianity Today.
Money, John. 1980. *Love and Love Sickness*. Baltimore: Johns Hopkins University Press.
—. 1986. *Lovemaps*. New York: Irvington.
Money, John, and Ehrhardt, Anke. 1972. *Man and Woman, Boy and Girl*. Baltimore: Johns Hopkins University Press.
Money, John, and Ogunro, Charles. 1974. "Behavioral Sexology: Ten Cases of Genetic Male Intersexuality with Impaired Prenatal and Pubertal Androgenization." *Archives of Sexual Behavior*, 3:3, May, pp. 181–205.
Mosher, Donald. 1970. "Psychological Reactions to Pornographic Films." USCOP *Technical Report*, Vol. 8.
Murphy, Earl Finbar. 1963–64. "The Value of Pornography." *Wayne Law Review*, 10, pp. 655–680.
National Criminal Justice Information and Statistics. 1979. *Criminal Victimization in the United States*. Washington, D.C.: U.S. Department of Justice.
Nawy, Harold. 1973. "In the Pursuit of Happiness? Consumers of Erotica in San Francisco." *Journal of Social Issues*, 29:3, pp. 147–161.
Nobile, Philip, and Nadler, Eric. 1986. *United States of America vs. Sex: How the Meese Commission Lied about Pornography*. New York: Minotaur.
Okami, Paul. In press. "Sociopolitical Biases in the Contemporary Scientific Literature on Adult Human Sexual Behavior with Children and Adolescents." In J.R. Feierman (ed.), *Pedophilia: Biosocial Dimensions*. Aldine Publishers: New York.
Palys, T.S. 1986. "Testing the Common Wisdom: The Social Content of Video Pornography." *Canadian Psychology*, 27:1, January, pp. 22–35.
Pearl, David, Bouthilet, L., and Lazar, J. (eds.). 1982. *Television and Behavior: Ten Years of Scientific Progress and Implications for the 80's*. Rockville, Maryland: National Institute of Mental Health.
Pelletier, Lisa A., and Herold, Edward S. 1988. "The Relationship of Age, Sex Guilt, and Sexual Experience with Female Sexual Fantasies." *Journal of Sex Research*, 24 (Special-Issue Volume), pp. 250–256.
Pheterson, Gail (ed.). 1989. *A Vindication of the Rights of Whores*. Seattle: The Seal Press.
Phillips, David P., and Bollen, Kenneth A. 1985. "Same Time, Last Year: Selective Data Dredging for Negative Findings." *American Sociological Review*, 50, pp. 369–371.
Phillips, David P., and Hensley, John E. 1984. "When Violence Is Rewarded or Punished: The Impact of Mass Media Stories on Homicide." *Journal of Communication*, 34:3, Summer, pp. 101–116.
Pomeroy, Wardell. 1972. *Dr. Kinsey and the Institute for Sex Research*. New York: Harper & Row.
Prescott, James. 1975. "Body Pleasure and the Origins of Violence." *Bulletin of the Atomic Scientists*, November, pp. 10–20.
Propper, Martin M. 1970. "Exposure to Sexually Oriented Materials among Young Male Prison Offenders." USCOP *Technical Report*, Vol. 9.
Quinsey, V.L., Chaplin, T.C., and Upfold, D. 1984. "Sexual Arousal to Nonsexual Violence and Sadomasochistic Themes among Rapists and Non-Sexual Offenders." *Journal of Consulting and Clinical Psychology*, 52, pp. 651–657.
Ranz, Sheldon. 1989. "Interview: Nina Hartley." *Shmate: A Journal of Progressive Jewish Thought*, Spring, pp. 15–29.

Rosen, Ismond. 1979. "Exhibitionism, Scopophilia and Voyeurism." In Ismond Rosen (ed.). *The Pathology and Treatment of Sexual Deviation.* New York: Oxford University Press.

Rothman, Sheila. 1978. *Woman's Proper Place.* New York: Basic Books.

Russell, Diana. 1980. "Pornography and Violence: What Does the New Research Say?" In Lederer.

Samois collective. 1981. *Coming to Power.* Palo Alto, Calif.: Up Press.

Schiller, Patricia. 1970. "Effects of Mass Media on the Sexual Behavior of Adolescent Females." USCOP *Technical Report,* Vol. 9.

Scott, David A. 1985. "Pornography and Its Effects on Family, Community and Culture." *Family Policy Insights,* 4:2, March, entire issue. Published by the Free Congress Research and Education Foundation, Inc., Washington, D.C.

Scott, Joseph E. 1985. "Violence and Erotic Material—The Relationship between Adult Entertainment and Rape?" Paper presented to the annual meeting of the American Association for the Advancement of Science, May, Los Angeles.

Shepher, J., and Reisman, J. 1985. "Pornography—A Sociobiological Attempt at Understanding." *Ethology and Sociobiology,* 6:2, pp. 103–114.

Silbert, Mimi, and Pines, Ayala. 1984. "Pornography and Sexual Abuse of Women." *Sex Roles,* 10:11/12, pp. 857–868.

Simons, G. L. 1972: *Pornography without Prejudice,* London: Abelard-Schuman.

Singer, Barry. 1985. "A Comparison of Evolutionary and Environmental Theories of Erotic Response." *Journal of Sex Research,* 21:4, November, pp. 345–374.

Slade, Joseph W. 1984. "Violence in the Hard-Core Pornographic Film: A Historical Survey." *Journal of Communication,* 34:3, Summer, pp. 148–163.

Snitow, Ann, Stansell, Christine, and Thompson, Sharon (eds.). 1983. *Powers of Desire: The Politics of Sexuality.* New York: Monthly Review Press.

Soble, Alan. 1986. *Pornography: Marxism, Feminism and the Future of Sexuality.* New Haven: Yale University Press.

Stanley, Lawrence A. 1988. "The Child-Pornography Myth." *Playboy,* September.

Steinem, Glória. 1982. "Erotica and Pornography: A Clear and Present Difference," in Lederer.

Stock, Wendy. 1983. "The Effects of Violent Pornography on Women." Paper presented to a meeting of the American Psychological Association in Anaheim, California. Cited in AGCP *Final Report.*

Stoller, Robert J. 1975. *Perversion: The Erotic Form of Hatred.* Pantheon Books: New York.

——. 1977. "Sexual Deviations." In Frank Beach (ed.). *Human Sexuality in Four Perspectives.* Baltimore: Johns Hopkins University Press.

Strassberg, Donald L., and Mahoney, John M. 1988. "Correlates of the Contraceptive Behavior of Adolescents/Young Adults." *Journal of Sex Research,* 25:4, November, pp. 531–536.

Suggs, Robert. 1966. *Marquesan Sexual Behavior.* New York: Harcourt, Brace and World.

Sundahl, Deborah. 1983. "Stripping for a Living." *The Advocate,* Oct. 13, p. 41*ff.*

Symons, Donald. 1979. *The Evolution of Human Sexuality.* New York: Oxford University Press.

Tait, Gideon (with John Berry). 1978. *Never Back Down.* Christchurch, N. Z.: Whitecoulls.

Talese, Gay. 1980. *Thy Neighbor's Wife.* Garden City, N.Y.: Doubleday.

Tedford, Thomas. 1986. "North Carolina's War on Sex," *Penthouse,* April, pp. 94–95.

Thornberry, Terrence P., and Silverman, Robert A. 1970. "Exposure to Pornography and Juvenile Delinquency." In USCOP *Technical Report,* Vol. 9.

Thorne, F.C., and Haupt, T.D. 1966. "The Objective Measurement of Sex Attitudes and Behavior." *Journal of Clinical Psychology,* 22, pp. 395–403.

Turnbull, Colin. 1961. *The Forest People.* London: Chatto and Windus.

—. 1965. *Wayward Servants*. Garden City, N.Y.: The Natural History Press.

U.S. Commission on Obscenity and Pornography. 1970. *Technical Report*. U.S. Government Printing Office: Washington, D.C. (Cited as USCOP *Technical Report* elsewhere in this bibliography.)

Walker, C. Eugene. 1970. "Erotic Stimuli and the Aggressive Sexual Offender." USCOP *Technical Report,* Vol. 8.

Walkowitz, Judith. 1980. "Prostitution and Victorian Society: Women, Class and the State." *Signs: Journal of Women in Culture and Society,* 6, pp. 124–135.

Warczok, Rainer. 1988. "Correlates of Sexual Orientation in the German Democratic Republic." *Archives of Sexual Behavior,* 17:2, April, pp. 179–188.

Weinberg, Thomas, and Kamel, Levi. 1983. *S&M: Studies in Sadomasochism*. Buffalo, N.Y.: Prometheus.

Welch, M.R., and Kartub, Pamela. 1978. "Socio-Cultural Correlates of Incidence of Impotence: A Cross-Cultural Study." *Journal of Sex Research,* 14:4, November, pp. 218–230.

Williams, Bernard, et al. 1979. *Obscenity and Film Censorship*. Cambridge: Cambridge University Press.

Wilson, Glenn. 1982. *The Coolidge Effect*. New York: William Morrow and Company.

Wilson, Glenn, and Nias, David. 1976. *The Mystery of Love*. New York: Quadrangle.

Wilson, Wayne, and Hunter, Randy. 1983. "Movie-Inspired Violence." *Psychological Report,* 53:1, pp. 435–441.

Winick, Charles. 1985. "A Content Analysis of Sexually Explicit Magazines Sold in an Adult Bookstore." *Journal of Sex Research,* 21:2.

Yates, Alayne. 1978. *Sex without Shame*. New York: Morrow.

Zillmann, Dolf. 1984. *Connections between Sex and Aggression*. Hillsdale, N.J.: Lawrence Erlbaum.

Zillmann, Dolf, and Bryant, Jennings. 1982. "Pornography, Sexual Callousness, and the Trivialization of Rape." *Journal of Communication,* 32:4, Autumn, pp. 10–21.

—. 1985. "Shifting Preferences in Pornography Consumption." Paper submitted to AGCP; later published in *Communication Research,* 13:4, October 1986, pp. 560–578.

—. Forthcoming. *Pornography: Recent Research, Interpretations, and Policy Considerations*. Hillsdale, N.J.: Erlbaum.

Index

188

ABOUT THE AUTHOR

F. M. CHRISTENSEN received his undergraduate and some graduate training in science, then took his M.A. and Ph.D. degrees in History and Philosophy of Science, at Indiana University—the latter in 1971. Since that time he has taught in the Department of Philosophy of the University of Alberta. Professor Christensen has published various articles in professional journals on philosophy of science, and two involving the methodology and ethics of pornography research. He helped to found, and continues to work in, an organization meant to promote full equality between the sexes.